THE BOARD BOOK

THE BOARD

BOOK

Making Your Corporate Board
a Strategic Force in Your
Company's Success

Susan F. Shultz

Special discounts on bulk quantities of LULU Press books are available. For details, contact LULU Press at www.lulu.com.

Library of Congress Cataloging-in-Publication Data

Shultz, Susan F.
    The Board Book: Making Your Corporate Board a Strategic Force in Your Company's Success / Susan F. Shultz

Includes bibliographical references and index.
 ISBN: 978-0-557-00327-3
1. Directors of corporation – United States   2. Strategic planning – United States 3. Corporate Governance
4. Boards of Directors   I.   II. Title.
HD2745.S475 2000
658.4'22 – dc21   00-026633

Printing number

10 9 8 7 6 5 4 3 2 1

To all those who get it and who care; to those who understand the importance of strategic governance to the future of corporate America and the success of our global economy; to all those who are actively engaged in making a difference with integrity, vision, and common sense.

Contents

Acknowledgments

My heartfelt thanks to Anne Zaphirio and Ed Tuton, without whom we wouldn't have made it; to Tom Detorrice, who brainstormed and cared; to Patsy Lowry, Mark Edwards, Susan Slesinger, Doug Young, and Bob Kile, who encouraged me in different ways; to Tom Lanin, who gave me a day; Cindy Marquis, who helped with the graphs; to Lyn Adler, Susie Cohill, Robin Curle, Richard Goldberg, Shiela Wellington, Steve Yastrow, Frank Christensen, Tom Ringer, Sharon Boyiajan, Kathleen Lucier, and Chuck Krause for sharing their contacts; and to Jerry Brisco, who helped me with research.

I am especially grateful to the scores of extraordinary people who gave so generously of their wisdom and their time and who inspired my faith in the potentials of corporate America. All quotations not specifically referenced in the endnotes come from my personal interviews. A complete list of the persons interviewed and their credentials appears in Appendix 10.

Feel free to contact us at ssaexecsearch.com or theboardbook.com.

Introduction

In December of 1995, I was in the passenger seat of a Lexus on my way to a dinner party. We turned left in front of a car that slammed into me at 65 mph. Six surgeons with just the right specialties came together to save my life. If even one of those six surgeons had been absent, I would not be here today. I might have lived, but I wouldn't have recovered and flourished. The fact that there were six surgeons with the exact and complementary skills and the synergy that came from focusing together on the strategic goal—saving my life—was what mattered.

You may have heard the saying that being a director is like flying an airplane—boredom punctuated by sheer terror. I was in the hospital for many months, and all I and my board of surgeons focused on was my survival. Boards are like that. Most of us have companies and investments that run pretty well. But, what if something catastrophic happens? Where would we turn? Could we be better? Must we have a catastrophe before we reach out? Is the challenge of the new millenium catastrophic enough?

I want to challenge you. You all have some stake in successful companies or you wouldn't be reading this book. You each are using your talents. If you had six people, each with experience that was precisely targeted to your strategic needs, and if those people were focused on making your company the best it can be, would it be different? In what way?

I have worked with boards quite a few years, but I got to thinking about those six surgeons and how their coming together at that critical moment is the way boards should work. Obviously this is an extreme. At least, I hope so. You don't have to have a car accident to appreciate how important it is to focus on the critical things and to take advantage of the best talent available. So this is my challenge to you. Think about those six surgeons as a wake-up call. Use your board to your advantage. Make your corporate board a strategic force in your company's success. Great boards do mean great companies.

I have a retained executive search business and, since the early 1980s, much of our practice has been recruiting, structuring, strengthening, and benchmarking boards of directors. I have been struck by the value of good boards and horrified by the wasted opportunity of those companies that could—but don't—profit from their boards. So I decided to write a practical, hands-on board book to document some examples of best and worst boards, a how-to-book to persuade more CEOs to recruit and use strategic boards. I hope to reach more directors and potential directors to underscore the power of good boards. And, I will add my voice to the others to raise the awareness of the importance of governance to all constituencies—CEOs, directors, shareholders, employees, customers, and communities. My premise is simple—great boards mean great companies.

Part I

The Case
for
Strategic Boards

Chapter 1

◆────────

The Board Basics

The message is simple. Boards of directors are increasingly recognized as a critical success factor for companies, public and private, large and small. Boards of directors deliver a powerful, competitive advantage to companies of all sizes, especially those that do not have the in-house resources of larger Fortune 500s. Today, when a crisis unfolds, we ask "Where was the board?"

WHY DO BOARDS MATTER?

What has propelled boards onto center stage? It's the change, the technology, the information glut, the rampant globalism. The fact is that now, like it or not, boards are everybody's business. No longer do we have the luxury of unilateral mistakes, sleepy companies and isolationism. In today's world, mistakes are increasingly fatal. Companies that don't compete and grow, fail. Why not be the best you can be? Why not leverage one of the most powerful resources available today?

The order of power has shifted to economic force, diffusing traditional policy making. Power is moving to the creators of wealth, the money machines—our corporations. America's great competitive advantage is that our economy, more than any other, fosters creation of wealth. We are succeeding, because our economy enables innovation and empowers the individual who owns the ideas and because we impose the fewest encumbrances on the realization of those ideas.

Corporations are becoming multinational and a major source change—the drivers of our future. Slowly, they are wresting power from public institutions, because centralized power is failing to keep

3

up. Government no longer controls information. And, business is spilling across borders. With this power shift, as government regulation is eroded, the role of corporations in our society is increasingly pivotal—and powerful. Thus, the governance of our companies is crucial—and rightfully spotlighted. And, because this phenomenon of diffused power has no boundaries, corporate governance, based on the free enterprise U.S. model, is going global. This mega-transformation poses critical challenges to autocratic countries. Where free enterprise flourishes, so does wealth creation. And that is the measure of the future.

The subject of boards has been elevated to a cacophony. Directorships are so in, they are like trading cards. Directors boast about revenues, technologies and compensation packages. They crave a board seat on the hot-com companies. Still, as they evolve, boards and the role of directors are awash in misconception, cronyism, inertia, and missed opportunities.

Those who manage boards and those who sit on them often do a disservice to the process, to their role, and, most critically, to their potentials. And those affected by boards—the shareholders, the employees, and the communities—underestimate the value, complexity, and power of a strategic board. As the value of good governance becomes apparent, there is danger in reducing governance to a formula, to a set of superficial lists. Because, it always depends on the people. The quality of the directors is what matters.

This is a simple book about a powerful subject. *The Board Book* will explain why a board is so valuable and show the best ways to recruit and structure strategic boards, dispel some of the common myths, and explain how to avoid the ten most common mistakes in creating and using strategic boards

The Board Book is for anyone who wants to affect a company's success, and for everyone who wants to assess a company's strategic prospects. In addition to officers and directors, *The Board Book* is equally relevant to all constituencies who want to benchmark companies—employees, shareholders, and customers—everyone with a stake in corporate America. In a world of fierce competition, the boardroom secrets in this book offer critical insights into the magic of corporate success. Avoiding the ten mistakes that underlie the strategic board continuum provides the roadmap.

There is a remarkable number of CEOs who fail to proactively recruit and use strategic boards. There is an even larger number of directors who seem to forget they are in the boardroom to protect shareholders' interests. The board is the shareholder's link to their company. Just as our Congress represents us at the Federal level, so boards look after our investments—and thus our financial security. Over half of America's adult population owns stock in a publicly traded company. Pension funds, representing many investors, are amassing huge portfolios and demanding access and influence. So, governance affects real people in real time. Considering the amount of money in the stock market, the subject of corporate governance is no longer a matter of dalliance or intellectual curiosity. Great boards mean great companies. Great companies mean a healthy America.

WHAT IS A BOARD?

The duty of a statutory board is to protect and represent the interests of the shareholders. It is the ultimate legal authority within the corporation. Essentially, the role of the board is to address the big issues. The board can't run the company. A board's responsibilities derive from law, custom, tradition and current practice. And, those responsibilities are mushrooming as boards are evolving in response to the explosive demands of the marketplace.

To quote from the American Bar Association's Model Business Corporation Act, "All corporate powers shall be exercised by or under the authority of, and the business and affairs of the corporation managed under the direction of, its board of directors, subject to any limitation set forth in the articles of incorporation."[1] In other words, authority resides in the board of directors as the representative of the stockholders. The board delegates authority to management to implement the company's mission.

Shareholders delegate their decision control rights to agents [directors] as a more efficient way to ratify and monitor management's decisions than having every shareholder assemble to do that. It's like representative democracy versus the town hall. The power of the board to manage an enterprise is effectively absolute. Once board members are selected to run the business, the shareholders have no authority to force the board to take any particular action upon demand. Thus, shareholder authority over the board is limited to electing the directors and removing them from office.[2] So, shareholders have a right to expect excellence—and, at the least, fair and thoughtful representation.

By specific statute in most states, board approval is required for the following actions:

- Amendments to the corporation's bylaws.
- Issuance of shares by the corporation.
- Declaration of dividends or repurchase of the corporation's shares.
- Recommendations to the shareholders of plans to amend the

articles of incorporation, dissolve the corporation or merge, consolidate or sell substantially all the assets of the corporation.[3]

Further duties include:

- Ensuring legal and ethical conduct.
- Selecting, evaluating, compensating, and where necessary, replacing the CEO and other senior executives.
- Approving corporate strategy.
- Providing general oversight of the business.
- Evaluating board processes and performance, including selecting and compensating directors.
- CEO succession planning.
- Evaluating major investments.
- Advising management on significant issues facing the corporation.

FMC Corporation defines the responsibilities in practical terms: "The fundamental roles of the Board of Directors are (1) to ensure continuity of leadership; (2) to ensure that a sound strategy for the success of the enterprise is in place to carry out that strategy. The Board will represent the shareholders best by supporting a strong Chief Executive Officer and top management team, who in turn provide leadership throughout the Company. The Board will provide accountability, objectivity, perspective, judgement and in some cases, specific industry or technical knowledge or experience."[4]

Within these parameters rest some large issues. How does the board juggle long and short-term interests of the shareholders? What is the proper balance of power among owners, directors, managers and stakeholders? And, once determined, how does the board maintain and foster that balance? "The measure of the board is not simply whether it fulfills its 'legal' requirements but, more importantly, what is the boards' attitude and how does it put into practice its awareness and understanding of its responsibilities."[5] (See Chapter 12 for a discussion of the legal aspects of board membership.)

Compaq director Kenneth Roman, in an interview in *Directors & Boards*, says a board can basically do three things: "Number one is to select the chief executive. Number two is to endorse the chief executive's strategy—not write it, but endorse it. This is not the business plan. It's the direction of the company. And, third is to assure that the chief executive can put together a team to execute the plan that we have approved and deliver the plan in terms of financial results and in all other respects. That is all that you can do."[6]

Says Herbert Baum, Chairman and CEO of Quaker State Corporation, "I don't think boards initiate very much, nor do they kill very much. How they guide the CEO through major business decisions is how they really add value."

"I see an effective board as an incredible brain trust of backgrounds, experience, perceptions intellect, and specific skills. When we put it all together, we have this enormous asset and resource to the company. If it's anyway restricted," observes Betsy Sanders, a Wal-Mart director, "it becomes a pro forma kind of exercise."

As Henry Wendt puts it, "A board should focus entirely on the future success of the enterprise. It should reflect, in its construction, the nature of the company that is to be. In other words, the desired future of the company should be represented by the board today. The board," he continues, "should pull the company toward its vision. The terrain that is ahead of the company is as much the responsibility of the full board as anything I can think of. . . . Most managers are scared of tomorrow. Defining tomorrow in a strategic sense and the requirements for success . . . is where the board can be most helpful"[7]

STATUTORY VS. ADVISORY BOARDS

As more companies embrace strategic boards as a critical competitive force, many are turning to advisory boards instead of statutory boards. The decision depends on the needs and attributes of the individual organization. Quite often, in small and growth businesses, an advisory board will evolve into the statutory board. Statutory boards are mandated by state law. Advisory boards are voluntary.

Statutory: Working for the Company

- Fiduciary responsibility.
- Responsibility for management succession.
- Evaluate performance of CEOs and key executives.
- Hire and fire CEO.
- Review and approve major corporate objectives, policies, budgets, and strategies.

Advisory: Working for the Owners/CEO

- Good way for wary CEOs to test drive a board.
- Don't get ensnared in minutia of audits, compliance and regulatory matters.
- Minimal liability.

- Serve at pleasure of the owner/CEO. Instead of the directors having the power to fire the CEO, the CEO can fire the directors.

Regardless of whether the board is statutory or advisory, if the CEO or founder is not willing to be accountable, its value is negligible. The owner or CEO always has the final vote.

"A CEO has a lot more flexibility in dealing with an advisory board," says industrial psychologist, Bill Amberg. "He can do whatever he wants. He wants to disband it, he disbands it." Amberg describes one company, whose members were on the board because of the perks and prestige and were therefore "reluctant to take on the CEO." When the CEO made a questionable acquisition, they went along instead of challenging it. Their allegiance was clearly to the CEO and not the organization. (See also the detailed comparison of statutory vs. advisory boards in Appendix 1.)

Industry boards are a type of advisory board and provide a means by which to enlist the counsel of potentially conflicted directors, to gain the input and support of customers, suppliers, and other business related directors. The focus is informational and frequently strategic, but does not include any oversight duties. (See Chapter 8 for a discussion of International Advisory Boards.)

The board is there to ensure that management is working in the best interest of the corporation and the shareholders—by working to enhance corporate economic value. How can this be left to default? How can so many CEO's and directors ignore this imperative?

THE STRATEGIC BOARD CONTINUUM

The Strategic Board Continuum (SBC) helps evaluate boards of directors according to ten strategic elements. Companies who make all or most of the ten most critical mistakes in corporate governance are at the low end of the strategic board continuum and are characterized by weak, passive boards. The great boards are at the high end of the scale and avoid those mistakes. Great boards mean great companies.

Ultimately, boards are everyone's business. Not just shareholders, but employees, customers, suppliers, and communities. All of us should know where companies we have an interest in fall on the continuum. The impact of corporate life reverberates through every aspect of our economy, and the way those companies are governed should matter to everyone.

So, here is a board benchmark, the Strategic Board Continuum, to help you determine your board's value. No list is magic. Scoring a

10 on the Strategic Board Continuum is not synonymous with good governance. But it is an indicator and a platform. The mission of this book is to raise the awareness of the value of strategic boards and to encourage all companies to recruit and use boards as a critical success factor. Therefore, the distinction between boards that are passive and reactive—three points or less on our continuum—and strategic boards platformed on ten key ingredients is vital.

Of course, what drives the value of any board is the quality of the directors and their willingness and ability to assume the tremendous obligations inherent in board membership. No set of systems, no

The Strategic Board Continuum Ladder

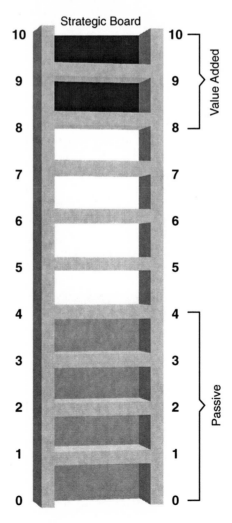

checklist can ever ensure good governance. Only good people can. The magic comes when outstanding directors combine with best practices.

Here is a list of the ten most critical mistakes:

1. Failure to recruit strategically.
2. Too many insiders.
3. Too many paid consultants.
4. Too much family.
5. Too many cronies.
6. Getting the money wrong.
7. Fear of diversity.
8. Information block.
9. Passive directors.
10. Failed leadership.

These ten mistakes are the symptoms of a toxic, captive board. If your board exhibits these weaknesses, look to see where else there is weakness in your company. How was the board recruited? How is the board used? What is the attitude of management toward corporate governance? Why are they indifferent to one of the most powerful tools available to management today? These ten mistakes are the indicators of a failed board—and perhaps a failing company.

Look at your company's board and answer the following ten questions. Give your board a point for each yes answer. If your company scores a 9 or 10, the fundamentals—the platform for a great board—are in place. A 10 means your company is positioned to leverage this powerful resource to the maximum; it means the foundation is there for success. *Anything less than 8 is reason for investigation. Anything less than 5 is cause for alarm. Anything less than 3 cries out for action.*

Is your board recruited strategically? See Chapter 2.   _____

Does your board have no more than two insiders? See
    Chapter 3.   _____

Do you have no paid consultants and no more than two venture
    capitalists on your board? See Chapter 4.   _____

Are family members outnumbered at least 3 to 1 on your
    board? See Chapter 5.   _____

Do you have no conflicted directors? See Chapter 6.   _____

Is compensation fair and performance based? See Chapter 7.   _____

Is your board diverse? See Chapter 8.   _____

Is there open and effective information flow? See Chapter 9.   _____

Are your directors proactive, strategic, and independent? See
   Chapter 10.   _____
Does the CEO empower the board? See Chapter 11.   _____

Total Score: _____

WHO NEEDS A BOARD?

Every company incorporated for business in the individual states is
required by law to have a governing board of directors—a statutory
board. Some states only require a single director. Others mandate a
minimum of three directors. All publicly traded companies are required to have a governing board of directors by the stock exchanges
on which they are listed. Public companies can legally have as few as
three members, the minimum required for audit committees by the
Securities and Exchange Commission. Corporations are required to
hold an annual board meeting. State statutes prescribe requirements
for corporations, which generally follow Section 8.01(b) of the American Bar Association's revised Model Business Corporation Act.

Small and Private Companies

The importance of strategic boards for Fortune 500s is increasingly recognized. Less valued are the boards of midsized and small, private,
services, closely held, and/or pre-IPO companies. Yet, every company
regardless of size or complexion can recruit board members precisely
to meet critical needs. Strategic boards vibrate through an organization. Every director can make a difference. All companies can make
their corporate board a strategic force for success.

   Small and private companies are best positioned to leverage a strategic board, because they lack the resources, the resilience, and the

The Strategic Board Continuum

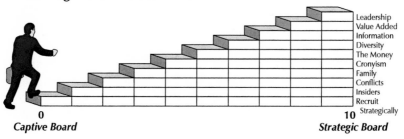

	Leadership
	Value Added
	Information
	Diversity
	The Money
	Cronyism
	Family
	Conflicts
	Insiders
	Recruit

0   10 Strategically
Captive Board   **Strategic Board**

scope of the Fortune 500s, and because of their fragility. Strategic small company boards tend to be more helpful and action oriented; more hands on, more mentoring, more informal, more likely to help build strategic relationships than the more formal Fortune 500 boards. Mistakes can be fatal in our new millennium, especially to growth companies in competitive spaces. We know that ninety-five of every hundred start-ups fail. Why not pull in every possible resource to help lock in success?

General Electric's CEO Jack Welsh talks about the difference in working in a big company versus a small company and "the numbing feeling you can have in the parking lot. But there's also an advantage to being huge," he says. "Last year, we made 108 acquisitions for $21 billion. We know that 20 percent or 30 percent or them will blow up in our face. A small company can only make one or two bets, or they go out of business. But we can afford to make lots more mistakes, and in fact we have to throw more things at the wall. The big companies that get into trouble are those that try to manage their size instead of experimenting with it."[8]

Fueled by technology and the tremendous infusion of available money which has been amassed in the last ten years of prosperity, competition among start-ups and small business is exploding. Venture capitalists, angels, investment bankers, and pension funds all have a mandate to invest—and invest well. And, as their funds swell, the pressure ratchets up. As a result, start-ups, especially technology companies, are now typically confronted by four or five well-funded companies in their space. Thus, the importance of independent directors escalates—to help compete and avert the fatal mistakes that resound beyond the founding entrepreneurs.

Yet, most small businesses have perfunctory boards. They exist because of the legal requirements, and meetings too often consist of a few minutes on the phone to approve minutes and meet the legal requirements. In a survey of Management Action Program clients designed by SSAExecutive Search, the results were dismal. About half of the companies surveyed are family owned, over 90 percent are private, and the majority has fewer than 100 employees. Of these smaller companies, 80 percent had zero outside directors, 75 percent had no women on their board, and over 90 percent had no ethnic minorities. In fact, half of the companies admitted that they didn't use their boards at all.

According to Patrick McGurn, director of corporate programs for Institutional Shareholder Services, the most influential shareholder consortium, most governance problems occur at smaller companies, such as violation of auditing standards, too many family and conflicted directors, and controlling insiders. "That's where the problems with independence are now," says McGurn. "Serious meltdowns violate fundamental dictums."

The best private companies are managed as if they were public companies. Their CEOs understand that boards add value by giving a company a long-term perspective and helping to manage growth intelligently. The core changes driving corporate growth today are the real catalysts to strategic boards, Customers are more educated and powerful than ever before and commoditization is accelerating. Strategist Doug Young, Managing Director of Wilcap, LLC, talks about "inflection points," that are going to make or break a company. "You have to change radically. If you are wrong, your value goes to zero." If you are right, "your value quintuples."

If logic and demonstrations of success are not impetus enough, realize that activists are now looking beyond Fortune 500s. Look at the New York Society of Security Analysts' recent decision to target $100 million National Presto. The Society, made up of stock analysts and money managers, used National Presto as an example of how investors may be able to benefit from shareholder advocacy relative to small companies. The pressures for reform are escalating dramatically, both internally and externally, and it's impossible to imagine that non-Fortune 500s will be insulated much longer. Nor should they be. The smaller the company, the more valuable a synergistic board can be.

SERVICE BUSINESSES

For some reason, many executives and professionals in the service business believe boards are for others. It's ironic. Very often these "do as I say, not as I do" firms are led by the very professionals who counsel their clients to recruit strategic boards. Is there no competition for law firms, consultancies, media, real estate, design or accounting firms? Is their future static? It's a disconnect in an arena where intangibles are the product, and differentiation is achieved through strategic acumen.

Typically, professional services firms have internal boards of directors, allegedly to avoid any client conflict of interest. Since their competitive advantage is no longer the information they dispense, competitive professional services are, by necessity, redefining themselves. Would not great independent boards, strategically recruited, empower them for the future?

According to Daniel Doheny, Partner in Charge, KPMG is an example of a Big Five accounting firm that debated creating an outside board, consulted Ira Millstein and other corporate governance experts, and decided against it. When their consulting group goes public in the near future, the issue will come up again, because an independent board will be legally required for that entity.

ADVANTAGES OF A STRATEGIC BOARD

The advantages of having a strategic board are compelling. A well-recruited board:

1. *Allows a company to gain valuable expertise available in no other way.* Whatever your key needs, you can attract board members with the precise background to enhance your strategic plan. A carefully recruited board exposes your company to opportunities and ideas not otherwise available.

Recently, Craig Weatherup, Chairman and CEO of the Pepsi Bottling Group, had the opportunity to form a board when the company went public with one of the largest initial public offerings (IPO) ever. "Instantaneously, you do see you are getting tremendous expertise and that multiplies your own. There is no denying the fact that, if you have eight or nine really smart people who are very, very experienced and have some diverse perspectives and background, you will get tremendously valuable input."

2. *Enables strategic relationships and provides access.* In addition to industry and corporate expertise, directors make powerful introductions—not only to money, but also to markets, to customers, to resources. A board helps fast-forward your company in a very real way. Maryland-based Ruppert Landscaping recruited an advisory board in Atlanta to guide the company's entry into Atlanta some years ago. One of the four outside directors was marketing guru, Al Nucifora, who writes a column for the *Business Journal.* Nucifora introduced the company to the Atlanta Committee on the Olympic Games (ACOG) as opening bids were being let for landscaping services for the Olympics. Ruppert Landscaping secured a significant amount of the ACOG business and went on to build a successful division in Atlanta with more than 120 employees.

Intellitecs is a spin-off of Standard Textile, a private, multimillion dollar textile company that was formed to commercialize stress incontinency products, such as Compose. Attorney Michael Burke, Managing Director of Keating, Muething, & Klekamp, became a director and suggested adding the retired chairman of a drug company, who "had a career full of relationships." The director knew buyers who helped design the packaging and early strategies and introduced the company to Walgreen's. Compose now sits on over 30,000 drugstore shelves. Through other contacts provided by the board, Intellitecs raised $28 million in private financing. "Probably, the company would never have gotten off the ground without having been introduced to board members able to help them ramp up so quickly," says Burke.

A call to a prospective strategic partner by an unknown manager will usually go unanswered. But, says Robin Curle, cofounder of Evolutionary Technology Inc. (ETI), "if one of your directors picks up a phone, out of courtesy, they will see the company." In ETI's case, director John Jarvey arranged an introduction to his college alumnus, Ray Land at Oracle, which proved to be tremendously valuable.

3. *Facilitates financing.* A strategic board sets your company apart and validates it to the financial community. Bankers and venture capitalists demand a strong board of directors. A weak board is a checkmark for failure. Bankers require accountability for the use of their funds. And, the board provides that. When ProLink CEO Doug Lecker was preparing for a $15 million private financing round, he e-mailed his newly recruited strategic board. Within three days, he had names and introductions to some eighteen major financing sources. In addition, two board members with strong finance experience helped position the message and the materials for success.

Before Pacific Aircraft, a small model collector airplane company, went out for bank financing to fund inventory and a new product line, founder Ed Tuton e-mailed his proposal to his informal advisory board. Board member Steve Draizin, chairman of Rad Energy Corporation, responded: "My reaction as a banker is that some of what you are thinking is overly ambitious. Put in caveats that new product introduction will be dependent on reaching profit objectives or that the new products do not require any capital investments, or that outside capital will help fund these new projects. The banker wants to finance your inventory, not new product development. On the financials, if possible, throw in a couple of graphs. Otherwise spectacular job." Where else can you get advice like that?

At Intellectual Development Systems, Chairman and former Secretary of Labor Bill Brock said, "our first two board members not only contributed strategically, but helped us raise early money." A third younger member with his own venture capital firm brought "tremendous enthusiasm and intellect" and opened doors at a different level. "It gave us a surge of capital which exceeded our offering goal by about 50 percent."

4. *Serves as a think tank for big issues and strategic thinking.* A strategic board will focus on critical success factors, those areas which must go well to produce high performance and ensure success. According to Terry Lee, Chairman of Bell Sports Corporation, "I like to use a board for strategic issues and opportunities to stimulate me to make

better decisions. If you care and are the type of person who likes to be stimulated like that, you'll put together a group of thoughtful, entrepreneurial people pretty confident with their decisions."

Mired in day-to-day operations, CEOs often fail to focus on strategic options. Doug Young talks about "tactics in search of a strategy," an all too common failing in companies of all sizes. In the case of Whitman Corp., where Herbert Baum serves as a director, "the board played a big role in helping management spin-off Midas and Hussman. The board worked very hard to make sure the deal was priced right and that the right people were in place to run the companies." At Quaker, management presented two major acquisitions to the board, recommending the weaker company because of the business synergies. The board persuaded Quaker to change its priorities. "Now to me," says Baum, "that is a great example of an intelligent board looking at a business and saying you should always opt for the stronger company. It was very useful." It's difficult to sustain an investment in the future. Most companies are usually backfilling—reacting. A board helps anticipate the unexpected.

5. *Establishes accountability.* A strategic board provides a forum within which the CEO can measure herself against corporate goals, against the strategic plan. The existence of a board moves the focus away from the individual and encourages the development of a corporate sense of purpose and continuity, especially important in closely held and family businesses.

As David W. Johnson, the recently retired CEO of Campbell Soup Co., who made Campbell's synonymous with strategic governance, said, "Good corporate governance is increasingly recognized as simply a synonym for high accountability. It means running a business for the owners—rather than, for example, simply to perpetuate the management."[9]

Further, a board can temper the inclinations of a freewheeling CEO. In worst-case scenarios, boards can provide checks and balances against abuses of power, self-dealing, spending excesses, self-promoting, and favoritism.

6. *Supports and bolsters management.* Validates good decisions. A board is there to help the CEO succeed as well as to provide policy input. It is not adversarial, as so many wary CEOs fear. As Ken Olson, a director on several boards, points out, a board can be a CEOs best friend as a cheerleader, a helper, a counselor, advisor and listener.[10]

When Bell Sports CEO Terry Lee was making a critical decision about whether to sell the Bell brand in multitrade channels or keep it in specialty channels, he called a director, Leo Kiley, President of Coors. "I want to spend some time talking through our thinking on this issue," Lee explained. Kiley invited Lee to his home in Denver for the night. "We were up until 2 A.M. with one of the highest quality meetings on an important subject like this that you could ever have," says Lee.

"He talked about his experience at Wilson and Spaulding in mass channels. He enhanced my thinking about how much more effective we would be by attacking more price points and helped sort us out. If you have directors whom you have that much confidence in and who are willing to give you that quality of time" it's invaluable, Lee says. Lee describes another director, former chair Phil Matthews. "At 11 P.M. or 6 A.M., he's available. We can talk in shorthand. He will drop anything to work on a tough problem with you. Both of these people are so successful in their own right," Lee observes, "that the last thing they are worried about is impressing me as a board member. They are there to enhance the quality of decision making."

When America West CEO Bill Franke joined the Beringer Wine board, he helped guide the company through the IPO process. Not only can directors mentor management, but their staffs can help mentor their counterparts. When Shirley Richard went on the board of Universal Technical Institute, she and her staff from Arizona Public Service met with the director of marketing and included the sales and marketing people in sessions that her company hosted with renowned business leaders.

Further, as the CEO of Neurex, Paul Goddard says, "if you are judicious about it, you can borrow missing expertise from the marketplace, by recruiting directors who have a key skill you need."[11] According to Admiral Bobby Inman, Dell's CEO Michael Dell has extraordinary talent "in marketing and an ability to understand technology and where the consumer is and where the consumer is going." When money was scarce, Dell's inclination was to invest in sales.

According to Inman, the board played a "critical role" in providing guidance on how to organize and run a big company, manage people, and integrate financial controls. And the board persuaded Dell to invest in internal staff to bolster auditing as the company grew. The impressive thing about Dell's relationship with his board is that, "Michael never made the same mistake twice. When we brought up an issue (as directors), we got his attention. He learned it and stayed with it."

7. *Relieves isolation.* A CEO gains a bank of peers who share her commitment to the success of the business. Further, the board can help a workaholic CEO balance her life relative to the company and gain some perspective. Investment banker Jock Holliman says, as a director "I talk to the CEO once or twice a week, and we often get together for

a beer after work. I found that the biggest contribution that I could make is to be his friend and to be a good listener. The CEO's job is the loneliest job in the world—period—bar none."[12]

8. *Attracts the best employees.* Before accepting the CFO position at ProLink, George Duck wanted to meet the directors. Enlightened employees at all levels look at a company's board before accepting a position. If the board is strategic, it validates the company's commitment to success.

9. *Facilitates cross-fertilization and exposure to new ideas.* A well-recruited board will spawn new thinking and new ideas. Michael Burke says "The only way (to govern) is to open the windows to have fresh air and light. Those people who sit around the table today breathing each other's carbon dioxide have no fresh air to create the inspiration for new thoughts. It's the worst thing you can do."

Procter & Gamble Chairman John Pepper, a Motorola director, came to Motorola for several days of seminars to talk about brand management as practiced at P & G. Another Motorola director, Nicholas Negroponte, head of the MIT media laboratory who started *Wired Magazine*, talks "bits and bytes and bandwidths," says former Motorola CEO Gary Tooker. "He is constantly moving and knows people from around the world. He is attuned also from a consumer perspective. He helps us think about what devices we are going to have in the future with the capability and ergonomics to appeal to the broad population."

CEO Craig Weatherup relishes the "different perspectives" of the Pepsi Bottling Company board members because their "questions are provoking to me." As Harvey MacKay, author and CEO of MacKay Envelope Corporation, says, "even if you are running a two person lemonade stand, you must think global—because of technology and because we are one of some 210 countries in the world. Any CEO should want unfiltered feedback," Mackay says. "You have to know what's going on in the world. You can't just be an entrepreneur. You can't be sitting in smaller communities especially, and not reach out. Unless your antenna is up," MacKay insists, "unless your mindset is to look at the whole world," you can't compete.

10. *Balances stockholder interests.* A board maximizes market value and validates your company to your constituencies. In Fortune 500s as well as in closely held and family owned companies, a board tempers the demands of single-issue shareholders. The board provides consistency of focus and purpose to a company's broad constituencies and underlines the commitment to the company's success—diminishing the spotlight on a single individual.

A strategic board underlines your seriousness of purpose and your potentials for success to shareholders, employees, clients, suppliers, customers, and the community. Your board speaks volumes about you, your character, your judgment, your company—and your future. The caliber of your board defines your company's image in the marketplace, including the capital markets.

11. *Helps to avoid mistakes.* As Doug Lecker, CEO of ProLink, the golf technology company said to prospective directors when we recruited his board, "I have spent the last five years learning from my own mistakes. Now I want to learn from yours." Sears' CEO Arthur Martinez says, "If there is one thing I've learned, there are no new problems—just new circumstances."[13] Having a diverse board whose members have solved those problems from varying angles is invaluable.

Phil Matthews, Chairman of Wolverine World Wide, Inc., sat on the board of a company whose CEO came to the board "really excited" about a potential acquisition in South America. The board thought the price was too high and that it was a very high-risk acquisition. Responding to the board's concerns, the CEO let negotiations trail off, and after nine months, discussions ended. Eighteen months later, says Matthews, "we were really glad." The South American company was worth about half of what it was when the CEO proposed the acquisition to the board.

12. *Proactively manages change.* "When a company does a 180 degree turn, here is where directors make a world of difference," says director and investor relations advisor, Carl Hagberg. A company may field a new product with huge potential or, on the downside, face a marketing crisis, the call of a loan, the death of the founder, a product failure, or a takeover attempt. "When those events happen," says Hagberg, "when it is not business as usual, that's when the board comes into play."

"All businesses go through a period where they need to change their approach," says director David McLaughlin, CEO of Troy Biosciences, Inc. "Think of the great companies that have failed because the world changed around them."

In the midst of tremendous growth, Sun Orchard, manufacturer of premium citrus juice products, recruited an advisory board to provide strategic direction for expansion of the business. Instead, soon after the board was in place, a contamination scare shut down Sun Orchard's orange juice production. The board played a valuable role addressing the crisis and folding the lessons learned into strategic planning. The board also helped to assess an acquisition in Florida and assisted throughout in separating the personal aspects from the business side.

It is ironic that the board's first year of existence was the toughest year for the company, which, in addition to the recall, faced the highest fruit costs in ten years and the lowest quality. "Our mettle was definitely tested," sighs CEO Marc Isaacs. What impresses Isaacs the most? "How the group meshed and are more interested in strategic issues than operations—and how they are interested in what's best for the company as well as for me personally. We are a stronger company today."

When Square Industries, the parking garage company with share price at about $4, was deliberating future alternatives, it was board member and former investment banker Steve Bansak who helped guide the company through the investment banking process that resulted in a sale at $32 a share.

As companies transition through the stages of growth, a strategic board of directors can be critical to success. Henry Wendt, chairman of Global Health Care Partners, a unit of Donaldson Lufkin & Jenrette, reminds us that "The transition from a venture capital-backed emerging company into a publicly owned company is fraught with extreme hazards. Many of the good things that happen to companies and almost all of the bad things really emanate from the boardroom. The composition and nature of the board are crucial determinants in a company's long term success."[14]

13. *Provides extraordinary value for minimal expense.* If you recruit strategically and use your board well, your board is the best investment you will ever make. A board boosts your power and reach. One idea or a single introduction pays back the investment in multiples. This is the group with responsibility for your entire company, your management, your resources and the allocation of those resources. Yet, all too often a board is assembled randomly. As director Michael Burke puts it, "you get more horsepower for your engine than you could otherwise afford." In effect, you are able to rent that horsepower. Every director serves as a multiplier. A strategic board is a signpost of success. A board, says Universal Technical Institute CEO Bob Hartman, "is more than the sum of its parts, greater than the sum of individuals."

WHAT IS STOPPING CEOs?

If boards are a strategic force in a company's success, why doesn't every company take advantage of this tool? Here are the key reasons:

1. *Perceived threat to independence.* Even the strongest CEO may fear a loss of control. No one wants to be second guessed or have meddling directors interfere in his business. No one really wants to be supervised, least of all, CEOs and founders. Too often CEOs create a board

because they have to, not because they want to. As Terry Lee said, "A lot has to do with the CEOs' attitude. They may see it as a necessary evil."

When SSA began the process, many employees at Universal Technical Institute (UTI) initially resisted the idea of a board, worrying about the influence of "outside" people. "What if they don't understand our business? Will we have to do what they say?" But, as UTI CEO Bob Hartman, who formed an advisory board, explains, "We have the responsibility to take the advice of our directors or not. It is our responsibility to decide what we use and what we don't use. If we make a bad decision, it's our fault, not theirs."

2. *Focus on tactics.* Mired in the day-to-day operations, focused on growing and competing, it is easier and more immediately rewarding to react to urgent demands of the marketplace, than the long term.

3. *Makes extra work.* The time required to support a board can be intimidating. Establishing and maintaining relationships is a substantial time commitment. Creating an optimum climate for strategic governance, creating agendas, preparing backgrounders, keeping directors informed, engaging directors in the strategic issues, responding to director suggestions, validating the governance process internally and externally—all require attention, commitment, and time. As Bob Hartman says, "We have a high powered group. I want to make sure they are challenged, have a meaningful experience, and are getting something out of it."

4. *Resistance to change.* It's more comfortable to do what you've always done. The danger zone for companies is when they become successful. They look around and say "whatever we have done must be right. Let's keep on doing it. It becomes ingrained that their way is the best way," says Carl Hagberg. "Unless you have high level, experienced outsiders who see their real mission to ask those hard questions" business goes on as usual. Because, more often than not, employees do not get rewarded for asking the hard questions. Instead, they are told, "you are not a team player." And, so it goes. When the crisis comes, as it always does, there is no one to ask the questions and help steer the course.

5. *Ego.* What is really stopping CEOs? Robert Lear, corporate governance consultant and director, says it's arrogance. "The arrogant CEO wants his friends on his board. The board is a nuisance. He sees it as a waste of time and just wants a rubber stamp." A good CEO, on the other hand, "says I want the most wonderful balance of experience and talent on my board" that I can possibly have.

6. *Insecurity.* The fear of the unknown, which often translates into

the fear of being fired, is a powerful deterrent. Maybe this is the real reason CEOs resist. They question whether they have the ability to do what needs to be done.

Often, in lieu of using a board, a CEO will talk to advisors and trusted friends, one on one. According to Michael Burke, "the pin-wheel effect is counterproductive. People generally have a course of conduct they want to follow and one-on-one conversations usually re-inforce that. If you invest in your board, get people in a room together, expose yourself to them, make yourself vulnerable, "you'll get the right answer," he says.

A board can "operate in harmony with collective voices. Without collaboration, all you have is a solo. You can buy a soloist to sing any way you want him to sing." Burke says. It is the synergy that makes a board work. The outcomes of the dialogue of a blend of bright minds all focused on your issues. It is those six surgeons at work in concert. "If you tell me you can go into a room of smart people and not get your opinion changed, you're not being honest," Burke insists.

Maybe CEOs don't want their opinions changed. If CEOs really want independent, strategic boards, wouldn't there be more of them? Perhaps, the chilling answer is all too obvious. Obviously, many com-panies—like Disney and Coca-Cola, for example—are quite successful and will continue to be so without a strong board.

Many CEO's are comfortable just getting along. They cherish the prerogative to make all their own decisions, or to not make those deci-sions. But that is the issue. A CEO or founder will probably never know the opportunity cost of making the wrong decision, a slow deci-sion, or no decision. They probably will never know what their loss of productivity is. They will never know what could have been.

"Is there a serious commitment to boards in American corporate practice?" asks Robert Monks, chairman of Lens Investment Manage-ment. "It is not possible to draw the conclusion that so many compe-tent people over a long period of time have so seriously failed in putting together effective boards. I, very rarely, found boards that I was on that were even vaguely prepared to be serious. The only con-clusion is that people don't want effective boards."

"I can tell you that at least some of our problems were created because we didn't have a strong board," John Whiteman, CEO of fam-ily-owned Empire Southwest, confides. "A lot of privately owned com-panies don't have a strong board for a whole host of reasons. First, the directors are invited to be on the board because they like the chairman and the chairman likes them. Secondly, you patronize the chairman and you don't ask the tough questions. Thirdly, most privately held companies were started by entrepreneurial, high enterprising kinds of individuals. The founder doesn't like to get permission from the board. That's perpendicular to his mindset. He doesn't like the board to control him. So he goes out, and understandably so, he acts. He doesn't even aim and fire. He fires. And then he runs on down the road. And lastly, the board doesn't have any real authority. If you don't give your board authority," Whiteman continues, "if you don't have a strong board, you're in trouble already and you don't even know it."[15]

It takes courage to ask for help, as well as self-confidence, a global view, and a depth of vision. As Doug Foshee, CEO of Nuevo Energy, says "I don't think it [governance] works unless you believe it. The fundamental issue is education. People fear what they don't know. We, at Nuevo, believe it. And that's what makes it easy to evangelize."

There are two schools, says Harvey Mackay. "One is the very enlightened leaders who are not afraid of a board. They don't know everything, and they are not afraid to have smarter people on their board. More people want to protect their own turf—because of ego and lack of confidence. They are not strong leaders, and they don't want anybody looking over their shoulders."

What Changes the CEO's Mind?

What triggers the decision to move to a strategic board? Change. Competitive pressure. Internet time that compresses one year into ninety days or less. The speed of change where you compete against yourself instead of your peers. Globalism. And, often, crisis. Business plan projections are unmet. A new round of funding is needed. A key member of management is leaving. The management team is failing. Or a new, high financed competitor surfaces. The company is going public. Or is on the block. At some point, you realize you can learn faster—and easier—through others. If you are smart, you learn this early.

When a company is healthy, management and directors are inclined to think they have all kinds of time to make decisions. As a company slips, the next stages accelerate toward the crisis stage where only 13 percent of companies emerge whole.[16] By this time, it's almost always too late for a board to save the company. Yet, it is often at this point, when a board is recruited as a final stopgap measure. By that time, it is usually a turnaround situation, with a totally separate set of imperatives.

"Business is blocking and tackling," observes Michael Burke. "People get up early to produce at the lowest possible price. I don't know anybody selling products for more money than eight years ago, and most are selling their products for substantially less," adds Burke, who sits on nine boards in the Cincinnati area. "It's tough stuff. If someone is not keeping an eye on the horizon, it's dangerous. You need the guy with instant replay who can see your play in conjunction with others. You need someone to say, 'I've tried that play on the third down before, and it doesn't work.' Lots of entrepreneurs who are potential board members are frustrated coaches." That's why they are so valuable.

Bob Hartman, CEO of Universal Technical Institute, decided to form a board after the founder retired and left a "void of critical thinking. We were stagnating, treading water" at a time when about 40 percent of his industry had gone out of business. The board brings "critical thinking, different perspectives on options, perspectives, development of the management staff, and the opportunity to see how we ought to be thinking and what we should be thinking about. We think more globally. It's brought great growth to our organization."

The dramatic untold stories are the hundreds of companies, public and private, that have avoided crises, because of the advice and counsel of strategic boards of directors. As Ken Derr, CEO of Chevron, says, "there's nothing more important to a company's fortunes than a strong board."[17]

Ultimately, if we don't govern ourselves, the government will do it for us. So, who needs a board anyway? You do.

NOTES

1. American Bar Association, Revised Model Business Corporation Act, Section 8.01(b).
2. Charles M. Elson, Charlestown Boot & Show Co. v. Dunsmore, "Courts and Boards, the Top 10 Cases," *Directors & Boards*, September 1997.
3. Michael P. Dooley, *A Practical Guide for Corporate Directors*, National Association of Corporate Directors (1996), 12–13.
4. FMC Corporation, *Statement of Governance Principles, Policies and Procedures.* See Appendix 5 for full document.
5. Blue Ribbon Committee on Improving the Effectiveness of Corporate Audit Committees, 1999.
6. Kenneth Roman, interviewed by James Kristie, "The Workings of a Model Board," *Directors & Boards*, Summer 1998.
7. Henry Wendt, quoted in "Leveraging Your Board to Gain an Edge," *Directors & Boards*, Winter 1999.
8. Carol Hymowitz and Matt Murray, "Raises and Praise or Out the Door," *The Wall Street Journal*, 21 June 1999.
9. "Globalizing Your Board," *Directors & Boards*, Winter 1996.
10. Kenneth Olson, "Boards of Directors for Young and Growing Companies" (speech at YEO University, San Diego, August 27, 1999).

11. John Dean and Roger Kenny, "Leveraging Your Board to Gain an Edge," *Directors & Boards*, Winter 1999.
12. John M. "Jock" Holliman III, Snell & Wilmer, Arthur Andersen Board Roundtable, November 1998.
13. Arthur C. Martinez, Directors' College (speech at University of Chicago, November 1998).
14. Henry Wendt, quoted in "Leveraging Your Board to Gain an Edge," *Directors & Boards*, Winter 1999.
15. John O. Whiteman, Snell & Wilmer, Arthur Andersen Board Roundtable, November 1998.
16. William T. Scherer, Scherer Associates, Mission Viejo, Calif.
17. Ken Derr, "The Chevron Way to a Strong Board," *Directors & Boards*, Fall 1998.

Chapter 2

◆

Strategic Recruiting

✦ The First Mistake: Failure to Recruit
Strategically ✦

Recruiting directors proactively is the first step on the Strategic Board Continuum. Recruiting well requires a plan and a commitment to the process.

WHY RECRUIT STRATEGICALLY?

Good governance means good people. We all know it. If you get the people right, little else in this book matters. Because good governance will follow. A board's power is a function of its directors and how they are chosen. Former Coca-Cola and Chase Manhattan director Charles Duncan says, "Be very careful in recruitment. All other things are dependent on the right individuals. Do your due diligence. You can have any kind of processes and controls," but without the right people, it doesn't matter.

When should you create a strategic board? Before you need it. Now. Even the smallest companies are turning to engaged, informed and committed advisors for strategic direction. There is no reason not to do so.

WHO SELECTS THE BOARD?

Who appoints board members? What role does the existing board play in the selection? Is the process independent? Until very recently, CEOs dominated the process of director selection. The nominating committee, which the CEO typically chaired, and then the full board, rubberstamped his recommendations.

Still, although the selection process is allegedly democratic, with directors elected by stockholders, in reality stockholders have minimal input, if any, into the process. Generally, there is only one candidate nominated for each position, and shareholders simply vote yes or no. Further, because board meetings are closed, shareholders can't see the process.

Today, the CEOs' lock on the process is beginning to give way. As Roy Herberger, President of Thunderbird, The American Graduate School of International Management, says, "It's not simply interlocking directorships or the CEO building consensus by overbalancing the board in certain areas." Walter Auch, former PaineWebber and Chicago Board Options Exchange CEO, sits on eleven boards. He remembers "when nominations had to do with how well you knew the CEO or other directors, with little regard for what you brought to board meetings that would be beneficial to the company." Critics worry that boards are still too cozy with management and place blame on the process by which directors are selected. Boards often are little more than cheering sections who favor whatever management wants to do. It's still a matter of "dancing with the one who brought you. It's a self perpetuating thing," says Nell Minnow, principal in the Lens Fund.

As good governance gains favor, the process is moving to strategic recruiting. As the Blue Ribbon Committee on Improving the Effectiveness of Corporate Audit Committees underlines, "Board membership is no longer just a reward for 'making it' in corporate America. Now, the great majority of companies, 74 percent, have nominating committees made up of independent directors who guide, if not lead, the process. As a rule, as a further lever to independence, CEOs no longer sit on the nominating committee, and, at Fortune 500 companies, the nominating committee is made up of four independent directors.[1]"

More importantly, independent directors are beginning to partner with the CEO in their boards' nomination process. This includes determining what the needs are, overseeing the process and extending the offer to serve.

Craig Weatherup, CEO of the Pepsi Bottling Group, had an opportunity to form a new board recently. "It has become far more dynamic and important and a more difficult process than it may have been ten years ago," he observes. "It's far more complex and I think more valuable than when a group of homogenous CEOs and ex-CEOs gathered around the board table. Governance was important but not horribly topical, and boards were not nearly as engaged in the business enterprise."

According to Doug Yearley, former CEO of Phelps Dodge, a student of governance, "next to selecting your CEO, you have to have members with strategic vision." Gary Tooker, former CEO of Motorola says that you need to "get board members with different mindsets and perspectives to challenge your thinking."

Bethlehem Steel is one of many companies which relies on a director matrix matching existing skills of directors with the needs of the company, focusing on geography, knowledge, experience and diversity. Bethlehem is constantly considering candidates and always has a number of potential directors who fit their needs in mind. "I'm sure," says Curtis "Hank" Barnette, chairman and CEO of Bethlehem Steel, "they may not even know they are candidates."

As Bell Sports chairman Terry Lee says, "a board is almost a euphemism about whom you surround yourself with. . . . Generally you surround yourself with people whom you have the most respect for. People with integrity. How much do I respect their advice? How valuable is it to me? How does it make me think through the issues. How does it assist me in making my decisions?"

If you are forming a new board, advisory or statutory, you are only limited by your imagination and your attitude.

NINE STEPS TO STRATEGIC RECRUITING

Recruiting can be the responsibility of the full board, the board governance committee, or, if it is a new board, a collaboration of management with perhaps an objective outsider. In all cases, the process should include management's thinking. There are nine steps involved in strategic recruiting.

1. Create a board charter.
2. Create a needs matrix.
3. Define the board structure.
4. Develop a measurable profile for each director slot.
5. Know and specify why directors will want to serve.
6. Recruit proactively to each profile.
7. Interview and reference potential directors in the context of your board.
8. Provide comprehensive orientation.
9. Recruit in a continuum.

CREATE A BOARD CHARTER

Your board charter or corporate governance guidelines (see sample guidelines in Appendixes 3 and 4) define the role and mission of the board. It can be a simple single-page document or more complex. The charter is a critical first step in the recruiting process, because it specifies the purpose for the existing board, management, and prospective board members. Many CEOs just want a sounding board, which is fine, as long as the directors come on board with a clear understanding of their charter. Agree on your mission, purpose, and specific needs. And then recruit to those objectives.

The critical focus at this juncture is to clarify the role of the board. Where will the board fit in the strategic board continuum? Who will be in control? Will it be a captive board functioning in response to the requirements of the CEO—scored a "one" on our continuum? Or will it be a strategic board with broad governing responsibilities, scored a "ten"? What exactly will constitute success?

In a closely held company, the core question is how the owner as opposed to the shareholders defines success. Is the company going to be sold? Is the objective to preserve the company for future family generations? Is a high priority development of management and exposure to new thinking? Do you want to create an exit strategy? Do you want to grow the company? The charter aligns the board's purpose and outcomes with your strategic goals.

When Phil Matthews, chairman of Wolverine Worldwide, was recruited by a small, private company run by a couple of brothers, he asked that they get down on a piece of paper what their expectations were for the board. What kind of accountability will they hold themselves to? Large companies have guidelines for term limits and independence. But, in smaller and closely held companies, the guidelines "have more do with how the owners perceive it. How much do they want to put on the table? If you don't get that out front, if the board doesn't operate with a charter, it can be fuzzy," says Matthews. It can range from "I really want consultants to meet with and have lunch with" to "I want them to operate as if I am a public company, even though I'm not." At that point, high on the continuum, he says, you look at such things as "whether the company's plans have enough stretch, and performance appraisals."

Your charter can create a carefully restricted advisory board, which works for the owners or a statutory board, which works for the corporation.

CREATE A NEEDS MATRIX

As search consultants Robert Kile and Michael Loscavio ask, if you don't know what you are looking for, how do you find it? And, how do you know when you have found it? Once your charter is in place, create a matrix to define your critical governance needs.

First, *list your critical needs*. Detail your criteria. Think through your strategic plan and what your company will look like in the future. Prioritize your critical issues, the two or three things that keep you awake at night, the critical must haves. What expertise do you need to get there—i.e., technology, Latin American connections, merchandising, government access, internet distribution, recruiting, biotechnology, science, marketing, R & D, strategic alliances, mergers and acquisitions, IPO experience.

Then, consider the competencies, knowledge, skills and attributes that are most valuable, such as operating experience, teamwork, human resources, change management, strategic planning, diversity, corporate leadership, board experience, corporate governance expertise.

For example, Gary Tooker describes the importance of diversity to the Motorola board. Motorola targeted the consumer business and recruited John Pepper, chairman of the board at Procter & Gamble, who "comes at the world with a different perspective." He has helped with issues of brand awareness. As Motorola moves more to data and Internet issues, Nicholas Negroponte, head of the MIT media laboratory who started *Wired Magazine*, "brings terrific perspective." With Anne Jones, former Federal Communications Commissioner, understanding of "process and politics is important. And, we went out and found a key Asian business leader, Ronnie Chan." In contrast, in 1996, Coca-Cola's thirteen-person board lacked a single outside director with experience in consumer marketing.

Secondly, *define the current board members* in the context of your needs matrix (see page 32). Make a simple chart and fill in the spaces. Catalogue the qualities and experience of your existing board members and then recruit to fill in the blanks. Where are the weak spots? How could you supplement your existing board? By using such an index, your needs will be visually apparent, and you will have a document to share with the full board and key management as you recruit proactively for new directors.

The needs matrix is especially valuable in the board evaluation process to gauge the contribution of existing members and should be updated on an ongoing basis, at the least, annually. Every evaluation should be in the context of the needs matrix. This is an evolving, living document that drives the entire board recruitment process.

Being proactive allows you to be specific—and very particular. Finance, marketing and technology and a "world view" are the most often named criteria for new board members.

When recruiting for a board, as Thomas Horton, chairman of the National Association of Corporate Directors and former American

Management Association CEO, says. "Begin with criteria, not names."[2] Remember that specificity should never preclude scope. The two are not mutually exclusive.

The sample on page 32 illustrates what a partial matrix would look like. Existing and prospective directors can be assigned a number in order to protect their confidentiality.

DEFINE BOARD STRUCTURE

The third step in strategic recruiting is clarifying the basic structure of the board.

Size

The smaller the board, the greater the director involvement. Eleven members is considered optimum for complex, large companies, seven to nine for midsize companies, and as few as three to five members for very small companies. Financial services companies have the largest boards, but the days of the twenty-five-person board are gone. Five years ago, boards were typically fifteen to eighteen members. Today, the average is eleven, with two insiders and nine outside directors.[3] General Electric has a board of fifteen, Microsoft has seven, and Yahoo has five.

The trend is to smaller boards resulting in more participative and engaged boards. Two things happen with larger boards: With more than ten members or so, there simply is not enough air time for all directors to be heard. Two, because a large board is cumbersome, deliberation and decision making tends to get pushed down to the committee level, with the result that the full board evolves into an increasingly passive forum. As a result, much board time is consumed by committee reports.

As Clayton Yeutter points out, most boards are working hard not to get too big. "We were below ten board members at Texas Instruments, and we functioned better than ever before. There was more rapport, a greater reflection of personal chemistry." The challenge becomes, how do you get everyone on that you want? With a relatively small population of ten, "each selection must be carefully done."

Meeting Frequency

The average number of board meetings is eight. General Electric had eight meetings in 1998, and Microsoft had six. Many boards of

Board Needs Matrix[*]

Rank in each area from one to five with five high.
One is minimal. Five is outstanding.

Expertise:	Directors							Prospects					Total
	1	2	3	4	5	6	7	1	2	3	4	5	
Operations Leadership	__	__	__	__	__	__	__	__	__	__	__	__	__
Strategic Planning	__	__	__	__	__	__	__	__	__	__	__	__	__
Organizational Development	__	__	__	__	__	__	__	__	__	__	__	__	__
Human Resources	__	__	__	__	__	__	__	__	__	__	__	__	__
Finance	__	__	__	__	__	__	__	__	__	__	__	__	__
Mergers and Acquisitions	__	__	__	__	__	__	__	__	__	__	__	__	__
Corporate Governance Expertise	__	__	__	__	__	__	__	__	__	__	__	__	__
Technology	__	__	__	__	__	__	__	__	__	__	__	__	__
E-Commerce	__	__	__	__	__	__	__	__	__	__	__	__	__
International	__	__	__	__	__	__	__	__	__	__	__	__	__
Legal	__	__	__	__	__	__	__	__	__	__	__	__	__
Marketing	__	__	__	__	__	__	__	__	__	__	__	__	__
Federal Government	__	__	__	__	__	__	__	__	__	__	__	__	__
Health Care	__	__	__	__	__	__	__	__	__	__	__	__	__

Qualities:

Team Player	__	__	__	__	__	__	__	__	__	__	__	__	__
Leadership	__	__	__	__	__	__	__	__	__	__	__	__	__
Visionary	__	__	__	__	__	__	__	__	__	__	__	__	__

Length of board service: ____

Committees/board officer positions: ____

Number of for-profit boards: ____

Number of nonprofit boards: ____

Date of end of term, if applicable: ____

Attendance percentage: ____

Geographic location: _____

Total number of:

Age: ____ Under 35	Ethnic ____ Asian	Gender: ____ Female
____ 36-50	____ African-American	____ Male
____ 51-65	____ Caucasian	
____ Over 65	____ Hispanic	
	____ Other	

[*]Support this matrix with resumes of individuals together with a key sheet with names and numbers. This document can be circulated to the board and managers while preserving confidentiality.

smaller companies and advisory boards meet quarterly. International advisory boards usually meet once or twice a year.

Time has assumed a high place in governance. According to Korn/Ferry, outside directors spend an average of 157 hours on board-related matters each year, a full month for each board on which they serve. And, it is not unusual for travel time to exceed meeting time. So, the trend is to fewer, more substantive meetings, punctuated by two-day retreats, which are more productive and a far better use of directors' time. Governance expert John Olson believes that most meetings are too short. "A lot of boards meet for two or three hours once every third month and gloss over the issues that require more study in depth. Some CEOs will tell you that's as long as board members will stick around." But that is changing.

Motorola used to have ten board meetings a year. Gary Tooker reduced the number to six, with committee meetings grouped around the full board meetings. "Having a two-hour meeting where you rattle through the reports is not as useful," Tooker points out. "And, with fewer meetings, the ratio of travel to business time is better." Tooker also shortened the committee reports at the full board meetings to allow more time for strategic dialogue.

At Edison International, CEO John Bryson somewhat lengthened the duration of meetings, but reduced their frequency from twelve meetings four years ago to eight meetings as of 1999. More time is also spent in committee meetings "to allow real dialogue" both at the meetings and at board meetings.

When CEO Craig Weatherup of Pepsi Bottling created a board for the new $8 billion company, he scheduled five meetings a year, one of which is a two-day strategic retreat. Of course, a major event can trigger a spate of meetings. Robert Lear served on a board that met thirteen times in a single month.

Committees

Fewer committees are the trend, with less time taken at the full board for committee reports. Many boards are reducing the number of their committees to three—audit, compensation, and nominating/governance. Committee charters are likely to be prescribed in writing, and committees meet between two and five times a year.

The three most common committees are audit (100 percent of public company boards have audit committees), compensation (99 percent), and nominating, or governance (74 percent).

Smaller, more active boards seem to obviate the need for executive committees, and the percentage of boards with executive committees has shrunk from 81 percent 25 years ago to 60 percent. A striking indicator of the importance of governance is the sharp rise in the number of nominating or governance committees since 1973 when fewer than 3 percent of companies had such committees. The next most common committees are stock options, board organization, finance, and succession planning.[4] More risk management and shareholder relations committees are being formed.

A key ingredient of strategic governance is independent committees. At S&P 500 boards, 97 percent of human resources/compensation committees are made up exclusively of independent directors, and in audit committees, 92 percent of members are independent directors. But, independence is by no means assured. At nominating/corporate governance committees, only two thirds of the directors were independent.[5] How can the board be independent if its governing committee is not?

Compensation

- *Large companies.* In 1998, the average annual compensation at public companies, exclusive of stock, was $38,216. This figure includes an annual fee of $23,638 and a per-meeting fee of $1357. Average committee fees, paid by 98 percent of the companies, were $1058.[6] Most Fortune 500s (78 percent) are compensating their directors either entirely or partially in stock. Further, as risk and responsibility escalate, pay is increasing.

- *Small and midsize companies.* At small to midsize companies, the annual retainers averaged $10,000 and board meeting fees averaged $1000 and $500 for committee meetings.[7] Expenses are covered. Increasingly, compensation is entirely or partially in stock. Some private companies match with phantom stock. Stock awards range upward from $1/4$ percent with a specified number of shares, with about 5 percent of available stock reserved for all the board members. That percentage can go up to 10 percent. Many companies are paying expenses and stock, period. This is typical for high technology companies. With the 80 percent failure rate for new IPOs, there will probably be some rethinking on this trend for start-ups. But fees can surge to six figures and beyond.

- *Tiny companies.* Small gifts, typically related to the business, plus expenses. Perhaps a meeting fee of $250 to $500 per meeting. Try to build in an upside tied to growth. Include a meal. (See Chapter 7 for a full discussion of compensation.)

Term Limits

Specify the number and timing of vacancies anticipated. Fewer than 10 percent of companies have term limits, and the average time served under those limits is sixteen years.[8] (See Chapter 10 for a discussion of term limits.)

Age Limits

As the number of board seats per director shrinks, as diversity begins to take hold, and technology gains a seat at the table, board members are getting younger. About 80 percent of boards have age limits, with a great variance among industries. For instance, only 47 percent of the entertainment industry have age limits. The average prescribed retirement age is 71. Ten years ago, only about 20 percent of boards had age limits.[9]

Develop a Profile for Each Open Board Position

It is perfectly logical to build a board that will optimize your director matrix. Just as you create a profile for key management positions, do the same for your director positions. Develop position specifications around your key needs—a statement of director qualifications—and then recruit to those specifications.

Look at the director needs matrix and see where the holes are. Then think through the balance you want to achieve on your board. Some items to consider as you draw up your criteria:

Composition

CEOs are the most in demand. At Fortune 500s, CEOs/COOs and retired executives of other companies accounted for 82 percent of director seats in 1998. Investors make up 72 percent; government officials, 53 percent; academics, 49 percent; and commercial bankers, 20 percent. The greatest demand is for CEOs of industrial companies, and 54 percent of those CEOs serve on one outside board and more than 30 percent serve on two other boards. CEOs of larger companies serve on more outside boards, because they have the resources to do so. Nearly 43 percent of CEOs of S&P 500 companies serve on two or more other boards, compared to 19 percent for CEOs of MidCap firms and 8 percent of SmallCap company CEOs.[10]

SpencerStuart looked at new directors of large companies and found that almost 40 percent were drawn from less traditional sources, probably driven by a shortage of CEOs who are cutting down on outside board memberships. The new director pools are the following:

16 percent	women
12 percent	academic/not for profit executives
6 percent	consultants
5 percent	lawyers[11]

Technology companies are evolving their boards somewhat differently. Current or retired CEOs make up over half of the directors at technology companies over $1 billion, but fewer than one-third at companies with revenues under $500 million. At companies larger than $500 million, fewer than 7 percent of the directors are venture capitalists. At smaller companies, they make up almost 20 percent of the directors. Interestingly, almost one fourth of smaller high technology companies have directors who only serve on that single board.[12] Technology companies also tend to recruit younger directors, because of their facility with technology and torrential change. CEOs, typically in their 50s or 60s, honed their leadership skills before the introduction of most of today's technologies. It is difficult to internalize nanosecond change, when traditional business models move so much more slowly.

Companies need boards that are up to the challenges of the Internet Age. Investments in technology are exploding, and directors need to know what it means to the success of their company. No one, no company, is immune to the convergence that is driven by technology. Publishing, education, law firms, real estate, accounting firms, insurance companies, retail, travel, and manufacturing are all being upended. In financial services firms alone, technology now consumes from 20 percent to 40 percent of total annual operating budgets.[13] Yet, several years ago, there was not a single director at AT&T with high technology experience—what *Business Week*'s John Byrne called "a shocking omission for a global telecommunications giant."[14] Companies desperately need directors with the vision to apply technology to how we use products and services.

Look beyond CEOs. Just because someone has been successful in driving a company does not mean she is effective in the boardroom. It is not easy for a decisive, action-oriented CEO or entrepreneur to metamorphose into a collaborative team member, to sit quietly, to be a good listener, a good advisor, and a consensus builder. CEOs are mired in the business of a single company, so their perspective is limited in that sense.

According to Korn/Ferry's annual board study, 39 percent of respondents find it more difficult to recruit CEOs to their boards than in past years. The most competitive industry seems to be the healthcare industry where 64 percent of the companies say it's hard to recruit CEOs. This is forcing companies to recruit more women and minorities as well as younger and less experienced directors.[15] "It's a horrible mistake to have all CEOs," claims Betsy Sanders. If sitting CEO's are doing their job and are serving their own boards, they can serve one or maybe two other boards.

"Whenever I see a board list filled with company presidents on it, I know the board doesn't do anything," says director Gary Driggs. "In all honesty, how much time do they have to devote to the company? Do you think those people really do those things?" asks Driggs, a former CEO himself. "How can they head up six drives, sit on five boards, and twice a year participate in two day-long retreats for each of their boards?"

One concern is that a board made up primarily of CEOs and former CEOs is likely to do a poor job of hiring the next CEO, the most important responsibility of the board, because they tend to clone themselves. CEOs often choose CEOs who are comfortable with "old school" approaches to management,[16] the very approaches that need to be discarded for the future.

"I think having all active CEOs on your board is a mistake," says Gary Tooker, former CEO of Motorola. "It doesn't give as much diversity as you think it does." For example, Tooker says, "most CEOs I know would move CEO salaries higher than a mix of people would. I think it's good to have CFOs on your board. And, if you had all CEOs, you'd miss out on a Walter Massey," says Tooker, speaking of the stellar Motorola director who is President of Morehouse College and an MIT scientist.

Governance expert Robert Lear believes a preponderance of CEOs can blunt the objectivity of a board. But, if every director is "an active CEO, you run the risk of them all turning up at the Bohemian Grove and Augusta to play golf. . . . There are too many opportunities for them to see each other socially and develop buddy relationships. . . . It keeps you from being quite as intense. You don't want to embarrass a colleague by asking tough questions."

"When I read that the ideal director is a CEO, who is kidding whom? Is my experience so out of sync?" asks Robert Monks, Lens chairman. "It's not a question of competence. It's a question of time, of commitment, of balance."

Another issue is current versus retired CEOs. Phil Matthews observes that "there are a lot of people who work real hard and when they stop working, they lose touch with what's going on in business." A balance of consultants and professionals who have broad perspectives and insight is the key.

Include some directors with prior board experience. Some directors, but not all. Some, because of their ability to mentor new board members and the governance knowledge they bring. Not all, because there is an abundance of outstanding individuals who have not yet served. Perhaps, their corporation prohibited employees from accepting outside directorships. Perhaps she is a minority or a woman who is not visible at the country club, the men's grill, or the golf course. Perhaps this is a star who has been focused on her business or has not yet had the right board offer.

It's a vicious cycle—current directors are in demand. They are vetted. They are safe. They become hot property. The temptation is to recycle these proven directors—but they may or may not be the best for your company. Just because someone serves on a board does not mean that individual is a good board member.

Avoid a majority of investors. Companies can overload their boards with investors, thus sharply limiting their ability to recruit proactively to their strategic needs. Fast growth companies are especially vulnerable, because board seats are a quid pro quo for investments. Ideally, recruit a strong, core board before going out for significant funding. (See Chapter 4 for a discussion of investors as directors.)

Ensure diversity. How can you compete if your board does not reflect your constituencies? The most successful companies not only have active boards, they have diversified boards. (See Chapter 8 for a full discussion of diversity.)

A board charter, the needs matrix, the board structure outline, and a measurable profile for each director slot are the first four steps of your strategic recruiting process and help ensure success. The profile synthesizes information gathered from the prior three steps. Here follows a sample director profile.

SAMPLE DIRECTOR PROFILE

Subject: Director Search/Health Care

We are seeking a board member(s) for a $400 million, fast growth safety, health, security, privatization and outsourcing company. Essentially, we are looking for the best strategic thinker(s) in the health care/managed care business we can find.

THE COMPANY: Based in the Southwest, our client is the nation's only integrated fire and ambulance operator. The company is a leading health and safety company, providing "911" and general ambulance services, fire protection and other safety and health related services to municipal, residential, commercial and industrial customers in more than 450 communities throughout the United States. Employees now number 9000; revenue growth is averaging 45 percent annually, and growth of earnings has averaged 22.7 percent. The company provides broad regional transportation networks to meet the needs of managed care. The company responds rapidly to the evolving health care environment and relies heavily on its board to provide guidance in taking strategic advantage of the changing marketplace.

The Director:
1. Depth of experience in health care, including managed care and/ or EMS.
2. Success in growing a midsize to large organization.
3. Senior level management expertise, preferably a current CEO.
4. Marketing emphasis, particularly in consumer services to government and health care related institutions.
5. Strategic thinker, change agent.
6. Knowledge and experience in relevant functional (industrial, institutional, government) and geographic markets.
7. International expertise.
8. Entrepreneurial skills.
9. Prior board service.
10. Women and minority candidates are desirable.

The successful director(s) will be located in the Sunbelt, the Southeast, the Midwest, or the East Coast. She or he will be conversant with the changing structure and composition of the health care market and with how services are sold into that market.

The Board:
Currently eight outside members of national stature. Quarterly meetings: February, May, August, and November. The first Thursday and Friday of the month, except August which is the last Thursday and Friday of the month. Compensation: Meeting and annual fees total approximately $30,000. Also, annual equity awards.

After you develop the director profile, circulate it to your key decision makers for any amendments or corrections. Then circulate the revised profile to your other board members and broadly throughout your constituencies.

KNOW WHY DIRECTORS WILL SERVE

As you create a strategic board, before you talk to a prospective director, be prepared with three reasons that particular individual will want to join your board. If your board is well positioned and if directors are approached in the right way, you can attract superlative directors. CEOs are consistently astonished at the caliber of individual they are able to attract to their boards using this proactive approach.

Steven Whisler, President and new CEO at Phelps Dodge, which fields a powerful board, despite a challenging industry, summarizes well. "You can't let the quality dip. Quality attracts quality." To attract quality, directors shouldn't have any worry about legal irregularities. There should be outstanding outside advisors. Make sure directors don't get blindsided. Diversity is important with directors representing different businesses and industries. And, says Whisler, "You've got to get something out of your board service that you can bring back to your organization. There are a thousand examples—how to deal with a certain problem, personnel issues, a new technology."

The following factors attract good directors:

- Quality of management—ethics of the company.
- Independence of the board.
- Prospect of serving with respected peers.
- Opportunity to learn—both personal learning and take-back learning.
- Opportunity to make a difference, to make an impact on the future direction of an organization in a measurable way.
- Validation—using what you know.
- The way a director is approached is one of the key factors in her decision whether to serve.
- Compensation—but often only as a measure. If it is the first thing a prospective director wants to know, beware.
- Opportunity to network.
- Prestigious, powerful position, ego gratification.
- Entrepreneurial spirit, to be part of something being created.
- Personal challenge.

Good people serve in order to make a difference. When considering an offer to sit on a board, Betsy Sanders thinks about "what do I have to offer. It has to go beyond diversifying the board. I am proud to represent women, but token has never been my favorite job description. Rather, I think about how is this going to fit in with my life goals? What will I learn? Will this be fun? I have to feel I can make a contribution and that it means something," says Sanders, whose directorships include Wal-Mart and Wolverine.

"Does the company have a sense of serving their constituency, and are they passionate about it? What is the absolute bottom line of the company? How will they move forward? What is taking care of the customer? If we share these concerns, then we can have a strategic fit. One thing I grow from is the caliber of people I serve with," says Sanders.

Sanders has served on the Wal-Mart board for eight years. "First,

I love retail, and I can take an enormous amount of experience (from Nordstrom) and relate it. One of the great pleasures is getting to work with people at the top of their form. If everybody sitting around the boardroom were merely billionaire friends of Sam's, I'd have left. But the directors had their jackets off and sleeves rolled up and sweat on their brows. Wal-Mart is always changing and growing. We have to set new standards for our customers all the time."

Former Secretary of Labor Bill Brock admits that "I'm not big on corporate boards. They consume so much time." But, not long ago, a very entrepreneurial CEO, who created On Assignment, a career temporary agency, persuaded Brock to meet him during a two-hour layover in Denver. Twice Senator Brock postponed his departure. And, he joined the board of On Assignment. Why was Brock persuaded?

"The CEO is out of the box. He cares a lot about people. He thinks about the first, second and third level impact. He is an unusual executive who tests new ideas. What about this market and that market. It (joining the board) surprised me," laughs Brock. "I never know when I am going to say yes."

He also said yes to a start-up called Up and Up in the medical services field. "Founder Tom Blair has an incredible knack for seeing an area of need and everybody says, 'gosh, why didn't I think of that?' It is just fun to be on a board with a guy like that," Brock says.

Brock also was persuaded to join the board of a new company called Blackboard that uses an intranet to connect everybody on campuses in a "really special and unique, totally user friendly way. I'm motivated only to serve on boards that have an air of excitement, that are terrifically entrepreneurial," the Senator says. "They have to want a good board to make it happen. I don't have a very good feeling about many boards that become sort of self-serving and self-perpetuating. I don't believe enough executives draw out the talents of the board members. A lot of board chairmen try to create a board that is a reflection of themselves, which might make for a fun cocktail conversation," but little else.

The *learning and exposure* are tremendous draws. At Pinnacle West, the Arizona energy company, Roy Herberger says he is dealing with the huge issues of nuclear power, deregulation, accounting, and stranded costs. At MicroAge, "I'm sitting right there on the edge of the technology curve." As president of the American School of International Management, Herberger benefits directly from the intellectual transfer of knowledge and thereby helps sate an almost infinite appetite on the part of students and faculty for what he brings back to his university.

Make no mistake. Compensation is a key criterion for many board members. As director and former investment banker Steve Bansak says, "I am looking for a significant option play. And, I want to use my experience in finance and as an investment banker. I want to be able to really get to know an industry." When Bansak asks "why do it unless you get equity," he speaks for a lot of potential directors in today's equity driven marketplace.

Doug Yearley serves on three outside boards, in addition to Phelps Dodge, and encouraged his senior management to sit on at least one outside board. "The learnings are extremely important. I rarely go to a board meeting where I don't bring something back to Phelps Dodge," Yearley says. "I'll see a really bright benefits package and dump it on our HR guys desk and say what do you think. I can walk up to a specialist in South Africa or Thailand and say 'what is your thinking,' and get insights on political leaders. The networking is invaluable, as are the strategic thinking and the insights into investment strategies," he says.

"I've been at board meetings, where I couldn't wait to get home to implement an idea," says George Aucott, former CEO of Firestone. "You look for your weaknesses. You listen to the way the finance guy is presenting. It's well done, organized, and it makes sense. And you think, 'what's wrong with our guy?' I've never gone into a plant where I didn't come out with at least one idea." Charles Perrin joined the Campbell Soup board when he was CEO of Avon, because it's an "outstanding board, and I thought I could take a lot of lessons learned. They work at it pretty hard."

Is There a Shortage of Directors?

Statistics will tell you that there is a shortage of directors. And, there is a shortage as long as you insist on limiting board memberships to CEOs, former CEOs, and current directors of Fortune 500 public companies. In fact, nearly three quarters of Fortune 500 directors turned down offers to sit on another board last year. And, 70 percent of directors for advanced technology companies refused offers. About two thirds cite time limitations, and 14 percent say the company lacked enough prestige or size.[17]

Some companies, such as General Electric, do not permit senior operating executives to serve on any outside board. Others, like Johnson and Johnson, for example, restrict senior executives to one board outside their own. Yet, one half of CEOs age 41 to 45 do not serve on an outside board,[18] an exciting pool of potential directors to balance the broader-based board members.

Often, the safe syndrome of recycling visible, vetted candidates is what nets turndowns. "You can't make it worth people's time except for the emotional experience," says attorney John Olson. "That's why friendships between managers and directors are so prevalent." Harry Kraemer, CEO of Baxter, turned down directorships because of time, until his chairman strongly urged him to accept one or two. Kraemer is now an outspoken convert, because of the strategic thinking he takes back to Baxter.

For the first few years as CEO of Bethlehem Steel, Curtis Barnette routinely declined any other board positions. Recently, at the suggestion of his board, he went back to the CEO who first invited him and accepted. "There are any number of things I've brought back," he says, including types of reports to the board that Bethlehem Steel was not providing and sources or resources they were unaware of. "I wouldn't do it differently," he counsels. "When you become CEO, you need to focus for two or three years. After that, it is enormously helpful."

Other common reasons people refuse to serve are concerns about liability, board independence, and not being able to make a difference. One Fortune 500 CEO resigned from a board because he had doubts about the capabilities of the CEO. "The board has to have a high degree of confidence in the CEO. No board member has the time or desire to manage or micromanage situations if the comfort level is not there."

Small businesses are led by a rich panoply of talent. Consultants who head their own businesses offer an invaluable multicompany perspective. Globalists have just begun to be tapped. The reservoir of potential value is nearly limitless, if you recruit board members strategically.

Good companies will never have a shortage of outstanding director candidates. According to Motorola's former CEO, Gary Tooker, "three board members were not interested in serving on boards until asked by Motorola. In all cases, they were enticed by what they could learn as much as they were by what they could contribute."

E. W. Scripps, a company with strategic governance, innovative leadership, and a host of fascinating issues ranging from convergence to succession, has assembled a highly strategic board. In the process, however, a couple of entrepreneurs turned down offers. "Entrepreneurial individuals want to invest their time and money in the start-ups, the dot-coms of the world where they can be much more engaged," says CEO William Burleigh. "Also, we have a geographical problem. The West Coast has a lot of talent, and people don't want to spend three days four times a year tied up with an outside company. We are trying to make our company a lot more entrepreneurial," Burleigh says, "and not ossify in a bureaucracy."

Once you have described your charter, outlined your board needs matrix, detailed the board structure, and developed director profiles, think through your compelling advantages and decide what will attract the best directors to your board. Then you can begin recruiting with the assurance that your recruiting platform is in place. You know the what, where, why and how. Now it is simply a matter of *whom* to recruit.

RECRUIT PROACTIVELY

Who will do what? Who is responsible? What is the timeline? Who will do the research? Plan to talk to at least three qualified candidates for each director position. Ideally, that means reaching out to a minimum of twenty potentially qualified individuals for each director. Where will the best people be found? Will you use an objective outsider to help, such as an executive search firm?

Develop a Recruiting Strategy

Identify people who have successfully dealt with your critical issues. Instead of randomly responding to suggestions of friends, directors and acquaintances, the position profiles should ensure that you proactively approach only those individuals precisely targeted to your needs.

This is a place many recruiting plans go wrong. It is so much easier to just ask around and then make your choice from the people whom you happen to know about. It is awkward to turn down referrals from people important to you. A recruiting strategy is more work—in many ways. A recruiting strategy, however, is just that—a strategy. It forces strategic alignment. It is the difference between recruiting average, perhaps, even good—and great—people. And great boards equal great companies.

Get input from your management and current directors and your broader constituencies. With the profile in hand, talk to CEOs, directors, customers, suppliers, creditors, investors, service providers, and analysts.

Home Depot wanted a retailer on the West Coast, because of Home Depot's expansion into that area. Before discussing any names, "we first come up with how we want that board member to look," explains chairman Bernard Marcus. Marcus and other directors spent a long time with the leading candidate, Bill Devila, the former chairman of Von's Supermarkets. "All of us said the same thing. 'This takes work.' We really tried to talk him out of it. He accepted, and he's doing a fabulous job." So Home Depot knew what they wanted before naming names; they interviewed; they clarified expectations; they followed through.

Craig Weatherup described the approach he took to recruit a board for the newly public, $8 billion Pepsi Bottling Group. The "number one thing was who was on the board. I wanted a very, very broad board, a diverse board. I was really interested in different points of view on the compass, perspectives." He targeted retail, high technology, e-commerce, finance, packaged goods, telecommunications, academia "for another point of view," and an entrepreneur or two, "a very important subject for me."

Before bringing in a search firm, Weatherup spent about two months "constantly thinking" about prospects, and assembling about twenty-five possibilities. "I only wanted people who were keenly interested," he adds. "I didn't want somebody to do me a favor. It was very time consuming even before I got to the point of having dinner with people. But I think it was invaluable. We have really talented people committed to serving on our board."

"People are incredibly discerning," Weatherup says. "Unless they appreciate the company itself, the philosophy of how you are shaping the board, unless they appreciate you, they are not going to do it." There were two things that made the difference in attracting the best possible directors, Weatherup believes. First was The Pepsi Bottling Group itself, dealing with dynamic, high profile brands in an international operating company with 38,000 employees, a "big, small" company. "The business model was somewhat atypical." Second, Weatherup says, "people responded to the notion of very progressive governance. I talked about a board that would function on a very engaged basis, a smaller board with fewer committees. I described it to them."

Why has Weatherup embraced such a progressive model? "I want a board that is going to challenge me and contribute to the future of the company. And I certainly want our board members to find the experience valuable."

View each opportunity for director selection as just that—an opportunity. Use it to review the strategic capacity of your board relative to helping you achieve your goals. Franchise Finance Corporation of America (FFCA) is a NYSE-traded, finance company whose fast-food clients included every major fast-food company except McDonald's. We recruited the former EVP and General Counsel of McDonald's, who brings extraordinary breadth and access to that board.

At NCR, CEO Lars Nyberg intensively studied governance. At the end of 1996, NCR was spun off of ATT, and Nyberg had "to find a complete board in one go." Nyberg is the only inside director and says that "we intellectually agreed to have an extremely independent board."

When Rockwell Semiconductor Systems spun out of Rockwell International at the end of 1998, it recruited a new board. CEO Dwight Decker sought directors in the semiconductor business. Competitors, customers and suppliers have a built-in conflict. So Decker recruited customers of his customers, such as the CEO of Ingram Micro, distributor of computer products, and the strategic technology officer at Air-Touch, the wireless communications company. Decker then recruited a marketing executive from a completely different industry, consumer goods, to cross-pollinate Rockwell's thinking. Finally, Decker recruited an Asian director.[19]

The board of E. W. Scripps is involved in transition and sits at the epicenter of a huge bundle of strategic change issues. As CEO William Burleigh points out, the company is replete with some 125 years of media history, "amid regular predictions that the sky is falling on newspapers and television. There has been a century of change," remarks Burleigh, "but it has never been as fast and accelerating as it is today." Overlaid on the compelling business issues is the transition of family control into the fourth generation and the impending succession of a new CEO. Trusts benefiting members of the Scripps family own about 60 percent of the company and control more than 90 percent of the voting shares.

The company has begun recruiting outsiders whose experience parallels those of the family such as attorney Julie Wrigley, who was engaged in a family transition. And Burleigh is seeking a director with expertise in convergence. "How is information delivered to the consuming public, the digital age, the telephone, modems—we want someone who visions the future of communicating. Some of us understand our core business," Burleigh says, "but none of us understand adequately what the future holds." They are looking at academics, physicists, entrepreneurs. "I'm a believer in liberal arts," Burleigh adds. "Someone trained in liberal arts can grasp a lot of technical stuff. We are looking for the best minds, for someone whose perspective is not too narrow."

"We are pursuing a lot of leads," Burleigh says. "We are probably more picky than we have been in the past. It's tougher to find the right kind of board people. It's a much different climate," Burleigh observes. "The good old board club doesn't seem to be operating in the way it once did. We are producing better boards," he believes. "They are more involved, more engaged, with a much different complexion. You want diversity."

Recruiting Tips

- *Recruit to your future.* As a company evolves through different stages of growth, so do its needs and challenges. Recruit one or two directors who are there ahead of you, who have had success managing through those growth stages, and who know the issues.

■ *Avoid the groupies.* The days of the free lunch and the golf outing are over. Instead, there is huge responsibility—and, hard work. Directors are increasingly accountable to all the corporate constituencies, including the activists. Strategic directors are not there for the glory of it. To the groupies, on the other hand, board seats are belt notches to brag about at the country club or the Bohemian Grove. The groupies are there for their ego and the prestige. So, when you need them, they are unlikely to be there for you and your shareholders.

Some CEOs want marquis names. They recruit them for the glamour of it or for Wall Street—to get a bump in their stock or to attract financing. They may want the director's or the spouse's Rolodex. As long as expectations are clarified, as long as CEO, board, and management are on the same page, this is okay. Just don't expect the board to perform strategically if they were recruited for their star value.

If you set up a board to take you to a higher level, you have to accept change, conflict and challenge.

■ *Supplement management.* Why not recruit strength to balance your weakness? Studies show that CEO's feel they are weakest in the area of finance. So, a strategic CFO could be a valuable board member. Often technology companies need marketing expertise. Manufacturing and services companies need a technology perspective. Every company needs strategic thinkers and people who can bring depth when it comes time to evaluate management.

Doug Lecker, CEO of ProLink, turned to a board for all the right reasons: "To surround myself with good people and believe in them, to delegate and trust in other people." At Intellectual Development Systems, an education diagnostic company, chairman Bill Brock said "I am not sure we would have survived without the directors. We certainly would not be where we are without the active participation of the board. They have brought a discipline we desperately needed, without which we were not going to survive."

"Our business is equal parts unique program and emotion," Brock explains. "We really do well and do good at the same time. The board members we have are so good and so strong," Brock adds. "They never lose sight of the financial rigor. But they are also believers, which means they are active in the larger sense. Our first two board members not only contributed but helped us raise early money. A third younger member with his own VC firm brought "tremendous enthusiasm and intellect" and opened doors at a different level. "It gave us a surge of capital to exceed our offering goal by about 50 percent."

A privately held $10 million family company whose children grew up in the business without a college education sought a board to help position the company for growth. Director attorney Michael Burke says there has been a dramatic impact on the company by a board of what he calls "$1 million dollar people, people on the firing line with applied knowledge in the real clinic of life."

- *Think multifaceted.* Be sure a director brings more. A director must be able to vision the whole and lock in to where the company is going. A director must not lapse into the cardinal sin of micromanaging, of crossing that line between policy and operations, strategy and tactics. Avoid the temptation to recruit only to narrow expertise.

It is virtually impossible for a single person or even a small number of people to understand all the issues that come before a board, to bring all the skills necessary. The board must be a composite of individuals who each satisfy more than one need, who fill in more than one box in your board matrix. Recruit for the whole, not the parts. Complexity demands a diverse group of members whose backgrounds complement one another.

Regardless of any particular strength or expertise, each director represents shareholders in all facets of governance, not just their narrow skill set. Every director will vote on the audit committee report. Every director has input into succession issues. Every director evaluates the CEO and the management team. Every director is accountable for the ethics of the company. Every director is accountable—and liable. Referring to the Wolverine board, Betsy Sanders says that fellow director "Phil [Matthews] is a whole lot smarter than I am about finances, but I can't leave it up to Phil."

Roy Herberger cites an example from a small company, which recently went public, whose board included several new directors. They each knew the industry well, Herberger said, and when the discussion "got into their span of reference, that expertise was their contribution, and they made it over and over again without learning or asking questions. They could not track the logic of what the CEO was trying to do."

David Tappan, former chairman of Fluor Corporation, worries that academics have the same difficulty. "I find college presidents on boards know very little about business. The thing they can contribute on is advice on training and other education issues and recruiting from universities. Some of the good ones are on so many boards, they don't have time to be a good director. There is a lot of pressure," he says, "by nonprofits and universities to get their presidents and business deans on a board. If you do it, nine times out of ten, you are usually doing it as a favor. They haven't been in the trenches and too often, they panic at crisis situations in business." As far as politicians go, "sometimes they can contribute something," Tappan concedes. "But, often, their whole world is politics and only partially relevant. All they want to talk about is the next election and who will do what to whom. They are very nice, very bright, but they know what they know. Often, it has little relevance."

- *Don't count on lists.* Lists are, by definition, limiting and exclusive. Lists are reactive. They restrict your outreach. Usually, they are formed with an agenda in mind, an agenda that probably does not coincide with yours. Power, prestige, IOU's, currying favor, and business development are examples. Even if the motivation for developing a list is the best, it is not a list that has been developed with your board matrix in mind. It is not a list that is responsive to your very specific and targeted needs.

- *Cast a broad net.* Look beyond your circle. Directors outside your network are positioned to add immediate value by virtue of their ability to serve as a multiplier. Take advantage of the opportunity to talk with outstanding people whom you would otherwise never know. Even if they don't join your board, for whatever reason, you can learn from them. Pose your critical issues through what if scenarios.

Bob Hartman, CEO of Universal Technical Institute (UTI), interviewed a key principal of a prestigious worldwide Chicago advertising agency for a seat on his advisory board. Hartman happened to be negotiating a contract for Robert Unser to serve as a company spokesperson for the automotive training program at UTI. Although the advertising executive did not become a board member, he did help save UTI several thousand dollars in their negotiations with Robert Unser.

- *Go for the best.* The only person who won't serve is the one you don't ask. Remember, people serve for any number of reasons. (See Chapter 1). George Aucott, former CEO of Firestone, accepted a director slot on the UTI board. At a smaller company, he could impact an entire business in a way that he could not in a Fortune 500 company. UTI CEO Bob Hartman says, "The people on our board are of a much higher quality than I thought we could attract. I was really overwhelmed at the quality of people out there willing to serve."

Privately held retailer J. Crew recently was able to attract five powerful board members: Charlotte Beers, former chair of Ogilvy & Mather; John Burden III, former chair of Federated Department Stores; Michael Ovitz, former chair of Creative Artists Agency; Brian Swette, former chief marketing officer of PepsiCo; and Gregory Brenneman, COO of Continental Airlines. Swett said he joined the board because "smaller companies really value their directors' input."

In 1998, Internet start-up eBay garnered Howard Schultz, CEO of Starbucks, and Scott Cook, chair of Intuit. And, Green Tree Nutrition attracted Perk Perkins, CEO of catalogue retailer Orvis; John Sculley, former CEO of Apple Computer; and Scott Blu, CEO of BuyComp. com, the fastest growing computer reseller in history.

▪ *Look for people who will elevate the caliber of the board.* Thomas Horton, chairman of the National Association of Corporate Directors, recommends finding a director "a few notches better" than the directors already in place. "When you get that person on board, people" he says, "comport themselves differently." They improve by example. So don't settle. Just keep at it. "First class people hire first class people," Michael Burke insists. "Second class people hire third class people."

▪ *Cross-fertilize.* The value of different perspectives gained from different industries, viewpoints, positions, and environments is incalculable. Yet, the all too common approach is to recruit people from your industry. Doug Foshee, the CEO of Nuevo Energy, contends that "the perfect board is one where each board member brings to the party a unique set of skills and experience which together help create a competitive advantage for that company in that industry. I see some companies too focused on attracting only board members with similar experience in the same industry as that company. This approach can lead to corporate myopia and an inability to respond to the pace of change in industry in general. Computing advances, electronic commerce, the relative health of foreign economies and American foreign policy, to name a few, affect our performance, but have nothing to do with drilling a well."[20]

As Betsy Sanders, Wal-Mart director, says, "I like sharing board responsibility with someone who understands Wall Street, someone who came from a major accounting firm, someone involved in the public company experience to understand what shareholders care about. I love to have an entrepreneur with his guts in the business," she says. "That's the strength of a varied board."

▪ *Don't underestimate the soft qualities.* Don't underestimate the importance of fit—elusive, slippery, hard to measure, and subjective—but all important. In fact, it is most important, because these soft qualities define the culture of the board. The following intangibles determine just how effective your board will be:

- ▪ *Integrity.* Strength of character. Will the new director make decisions for the right reasons? Or will he be co-opted by false allegiances or potential gain?
- ▪ *Business sense.* Does the potential board member bring enough business acumen to approach problems from a broad knowledge and experiential base?
- ▪ *Thinking strategically.* How does she approach problem solving? Does she leap to judgment and then retract or modify her opinion? Does she wait to see what everyone else says? Is there any

original thinking? Does she substantiate her opinions? And, is she indeed willing to change her opinion?

- *Good nature.* Is the director easy when she is on the off side of a debate, instead of taking it personally? Do others seek her company?
- *Focus.* Does he get quickly to the essence of an issue, instead of straying off on tangents?
- *Sound judgment.* Common sense. Is he realistic and logical?
- *Scope.* Does he contribute in the context of the whole, rather than the parts? And, does she have the breadth of perspective and experience to add value at that level?
- *Curiosity.* Open to new ideas. If she is not interested in learning about your business and the space you are in, lack of imagination and resistance to change can't be far behind.
- *Listening.* If a potential director monopolizes time setting forth his credentials and trumpeting his successes, rather than listening, how will he gain the insights necessary to govern?
- *Courage.* Does she have the courage to question, to speak up, to advocate for the shareholders when it is easier not to do so. As Steve McConnell, principal of Solano Ventures, says, "you need people with a spine. A lot of people want to be polite and diplomatic on boards." Today collegiality is not enough. You have to say what you feel when someone crosses the line.
- *Life perspective.* Humility. Sense of self. In today's strategic boardroom, there is no time for egotistical displays and consuming self-aggrandizement.
- *Ability to evaluate people.* When you realize that the single most important responsibility of a director is to insure that the best people are managing in the interests of the shareholders, the urgency of this criterion becomes obvious. Yet this aptitude is often underrated and diminished. So instead of focusing on this all-important ability, CEOs tend to focus on skill sets and recruit directors because of their ability to do things.
- *Commitment to the CEO and the company.* Does the director just want to be on a board? Or does she want to make a contribution to the company and the shareholders? Does she understand the way to do that is to insure that the CEO has all the support and resources possible?
- *Being not too hungry*—whether it is hunger to sate the ego, to fill the time, or to earn the money. As Mike Burke says, "Anybody

who needs that check can't be in the room." The best directors are willing to step down.

"Whenever I take a directorship, especially at a public company, I try to take the position that I represent all the others who are not at the table. Sometimes directors do things in their own best interest," says Steve McConnell. "You almost have to be a little detached. Beware of people who think being a director is the sum of their existence."

"It's the responsibility of the CEOs to go out and get board members to challenge them as opposed to buddies they can lead around by the nose" says Gary Tooker, former CEO of Motorola. "Best are board members who are independent and vocal, but collegial. They need to be able to disagree without being disagreeable."

Avoiding the Good Old Boy Syndrome

So, where do you find the best directors for your company? As we all know, the overwhelming majority of directors are networked onto a board, usually by the CEO. "People do it the easy way out," says Michael Burke. "They go to the guys they play golf with." Beyond friends, the source of most board members is existing board members, company executives, fellow CEOs, community peers, and professional service providers, investors, bankers, attorneys, CPAs, consultants and venture capitalists. Burke, in Cincinnati, becomes a confidant of entrepreneurs often at early stages in their companies' growth, and he sits on the board of nine companies, all companies he represents or owns a piece of. "I keep a list in my drawer of people I recruit for boards." Many others do the same. As anyone who has sought a board member knows, there is an intricate underground web of networks all too ready to help. As long as you follow the nine strategic recruiting steps, these networks can be valuable. But, they should be used as a supplement to the process, not as a substitute.

It's interesting to look at Betsy Sanders' experience. She got to know the CEO of The National Bank of Southern California through her position at Nordstrom, and he recruited her to his board. She was recruited to the Carl Karcher Enterprises board because Carl liked how she operated as chair of the local United Way. In addition, Sanders was a "good old boy" in so far as she, like Carl, was a strong Catholic. Sanders was recruited for the H. F. Ahmanson Company board because she was moving up to become the first nonwhite, nonmale chair of the Chamber of Commerce, and she had enormous visibility—and success. Sam Walton was looking for a woman on his board and learned about Sanders because of her work at Nordstrom.

She interviewed and was offered a seat on the board, but Nordstrom's policy did not allow her to accept the position. So Walton instead chose a female attorney from Little Rock—Hillary Rodham. When Sanders left Nordstrom, Sam re-courted her for the Wal-Mart board.

As Phil Matthews says, "when you know what you need, go out and find someone with that background."

Interview and Reference Potential Board Members

Even seasoned directors should be interviewed in the context of your board. They need to understand your charter and what is expected of them. How will directors be measured? What do you hope to gain from their membership? Is yours a captive board beholden to the CEO or a strategic board in partnership with management—or somewhere in between? Where is your board on the strategic board continuum? Who else will they serve on the board with and how will they complement the mix and the culture?

Visit the candidates on their home turf—at their business and their home as well. Meet their families. It's a unique opportunity to see their culture and their leadership skills in action, to see whom they surround themselves with and where their priorities lie.

Questions to Ask Prospective Board Members

- Why do you want to serve?
- What is your opinion of our company? (Does she have some knowledge of how you compete, how you market, who the competition is, who your customers are, what your employee profile is, how you use your board and what your critical issues are?)
- How will you contribute? Examples.
- What are your specific areas of expertise? How will those add value to the board?
- What is your financial acumen? Each director does not need to be an accountant. She must, however, have the ability to monitor and steward resources.
- How many other boards do you sit on? For profit and not for profit. What role do you play on those boards?
- What is your view of the role of a board and corporate governance?
- Do boards add value? How?

- What are the downsides?
- How do you use your board? (If applicable.)
- What is your most rewarding experience on a board?
- How specifically have you added value? Examples.
- What is your most difficult experience as a director?
- Are you willing to commit to the level of participation and support that we need?
- What committees would you like to sit on? Why?
- Do you prefer to be compensated in stock or cash? (Nell Minow says if directors don't think that your company is the best investment they could possibly make, they should not be on the board. This includes being willing to buy stock in a turnaround situation. If they don't have enough confidence in the company to buy stock, how can they add value as a board member?)
- Are your goals and values compatible with those of our organization? Describe.
- What are your concerns?

Here are some tips for interviewing board prospects:

- Discuss the criteria in the profile and ask directors to describe their strengths and weaknesses in that context.

- Ask experiential questions based on challenges and issues before your board. What conclusions do they draw from your financial statements? How would they approach some of your key issues? You will learn a lot about the potential director—and a lot about your company.

- Invite prospective directors to your facililty. Are they truly interested in your company? In your business? What kind of questions do they ask? How insightful are they? Have they done their homework?

Referencing

Reference, reference, reference. Remember that an interview is a highly artificial situation. The most impressive credentials can mask a huge ego, a gadfly, or a disruptive personality. Everyone you recruit for your board will have a track record of success. Find out how she performed on other boards, whether nonprofit or for profit.

Referencing seems to occur in inverse proportion to the importance of the position. For some reason, out of politeness and respect, in some cases awe, people are reluctant to ask the hard questions and reference at the board level. It is a sensitive issue, all the more difficult with people you know.

Yet, regard for the other directors and respect for the culture of your board dictates that you do everything you can to insure that the board is the best it can be. Referencing is the way to learn the experiential qualities of your prospective directors. Talk to board members, for profit and not for profit, employees, and peers, who have worked with the prospective board member. In one case, we discovered that the reason the senior partner of a major law firm "retired" was because he was embezzling. In another, we found that the number two person in a top multinational finance firm was there because of marriage, not merit.

Often, referencing reveals important nuances of personality. If you bring on a bureaucrat who isn't used to the decision making process, who tends to drone on, it can fast destroy the process. So can a monopolizer, or a chronic naysayer, or the director who feels he has to say something about every subject that comes before the board. Or the director who micromanages and eats up the board's time, by going on about the layout of the brochure, the color of the packaging, the price of the software, or his ski vacation. One director we interviewed boasted about batting .500 in removing CEOs from the management team of the boards he sat on—not a quality that endeared him to the CEO recruiting him.

On the other hand, referencing can confirm strengths and address seeming weaknesses. A quiet person may be seen to have tremendous depth. An understated prospect may prove to have invaluable access. It is a time saver, a face-saver, and a courtesy to your existing board to do initial referencing before meeting a board prospect face to face. If an issue is raised, you can then address it in your personal conversation. If the references are negative, you can simply forgo any further discussion.

Here are some questions to ask references:

- Does she attend meetings?
- Does she contribute? How?
- Does he enhance the dynamic? Does he care?
- How does she move her thoughts into action?
- What differentiates him in the boardroom?
- What style does she use to express herself?
- Is she fair?
- Does he focus on the issues? Or does he just want airtime?
- Does she do her homework?
- How does he resolve problems and disputes?

- Why is he interested?
- What about his attitude? Does he always want to win his point? And, if he doesn't, does he become a Monday morning quarterback?
- What are his strengths?
- Where is she weak?
- What else should we know?

Remember that every director you recruit is a reason for others to stay—or to stay away.

The Case for Doing it Right

CEOs will tell you that the most formidable thing to do around the entire governance issue is to "fire" a director. Why not do your homework? Why not invest in the process instead of a failure? The most popular article in *Directors & Boards* is "How to Fire a Director."

Ultimately, you get what you ask for. Too often, it takes a wake-up call before a company pays attention to its board. Beckman Instruments is a good example of a company that was prodded into strengthening its board and implemented a proactive strategic recruiting process in response. The Bass brothers, who had invested heavily in Beckman, claimed that the company was not performing and that they wanted to put a director of their own on the board. That, says then director David Tappan, "convinced the doubting Thomas's they better do something differently." Beckman agreed to recruit four new directors. The company sought expertise from Wall Street, the health-care industry, someone familiar with the hospital side of health care and a strong drug company leader. First they wrote the specifications and detailed the expectations. "Before you go outside, you should decide what you are up to."

They contacted key suppliers, CEOs, management, security analysts, law firms, outside auditors and other directors and came up with a list of some 175 names. After evaluating their board matrix, the list was broken down into needed areas of expertise. "We were looking for four directors, so we needed a lot of names," says Tappan.

Working with a search firm, the directors whittled the list to twelve finalists, all of whom were acceptable to the board. It helps, says Tappan, "to have the search firm involved, so everything can be discreet." They then "handed the list over to the CEO, to see if there was anybody he couldn't tolerate." Next there were interviews with the twelve. And, after that, the CEO and search firm met with the finalists. The process took nine to twelve months and was, according to

Tappan, "a major effort. I was very skeptical that we would get four directors of the caliber and quality that we did, but I was proven wrong." A search for new board members doesn't need to take that long, especially if board recruiting is an ongoing process. But Beckman's process was effective. It validated Beckman's commitment to the board. And it attracted the best.

Using Objective Recruiters

Consider using an objective outsider to recruit for you. As David McLaughlin observes, "there is definitely a shift from cronyism and clubishness to a search process for selection. More thought is now being given to background and balance." Harvey Mackay says, "you should always go to two or three shops. When looking for advice, you should always have more than one opinion."

The advantages of outside recruiting are that it:

- Allows you to proactively recruit to your strategic plan, to your critical issues.
- Gives you access to the broadest spectrum of targeted best candidates.
- Allows you to move beyond your own circle of influence.
- Gives you access to a higher level of individual than through informal networks.
- Provides a choice among highly qualified candidates, who become multipliers for you, whether or not they come on board.
- Validates the board to potential directors.
- Validates the board to your constituencies.
- Provides objective referencing and interviewing.
- Provides confidentiality and discretion.
- Does not waste the time of the CEO and directors on less qualified candidates.
- Maintains the goodwill of candidates and constituencies.

Your time can be best used to select among prequalified, available candidates, focusing on the culture, the fit, and the vision. You validate the process, and, at the same time, you demonstrate your regard for your new board member. One obstacle in recruiting your friends and acquaintances on a personal basis is that it is awkward to objectively interview and reference them. Yet no board search is complete without a comprehensive interview and in depth referencing.

According to Doug Lecker, CEO of ProLink, "it was a huge smart move to employ somebody who has the network and can give you a lot of options for the board." There are a lot of smart people out there, Lecker says. "But, if you don't do the homework, you can bring on directors who are not right for your board. Doing the homework is a strategy session in itself—thinking about the culture, the personalities, what the strengths are, and then specifically targeting directors on that basis, as opposed to just bringing in the smart rich guys." The vast majority of companies are still controlled by their founder. If you want to compete and have the scope and will to grow, you will recruit a strategic board. Because great boards equal great companies.

PROVIDE COMPREHENSIVE ORIENTATION

You do a severe disservice to the entire process if you fail to educate new directors. How many boards collapse their orientation into some paperwork, brief introductions to other board members and management, and a summary of the logistics? Doesn't it make sense for your new director to know your space, your people, your facilities, and your issues before voting on policies affecting them? Even with thorough training, it takes about a year for a director to reach her capacity as a board member (see Chapter 9).

RECRUIT IN A CONTINUUM

The best boards continually upgrade and refine their board charter, the needs matrix and director profiles. And, they continually scour their resources for strong candidates. Most maintain a list of prospective candidates, a director in waiting process, although prospects usually don't know they are in line. As needs evolve, individuals drop off and new prospects come on. At Caterpillar, the CEO of Boeing was invited to join the board three years ago, but he was immersed in Boeing business. Finally, the Caterpillar board decided it had waited long enough and dropped him off the list. To be effective, as Bob Kile says, "recruiting must be a continuous process, not a series of isolated events."[21]

THE DIRECTOR'S CHECKLIST

The decision to join a board is as critical for the director as for the board making the offer. Perhaps more so. At stake are your resources and your reputation. You are going to pledge your commitment, your loyalty, access to your network, your time and your energy. What are the questions to ask?

- Where is the board on the strategic continuum? If it is more captive than strategic, do you care? Will it change?
- Why were you asked? How are you expected to contribute?
- Where do you fit on their needs matrix? Are you being pursued for your rolodex or your expertise?
- Is it a company whose business interests you? About which you know something? Can you learn to understand it well enough to accept the liability that goes with serving on the board?
- Is it a valued board with appropriate independent authority?
- Is there a majority of independent directors?
- Is there a board charter? Are there committee charters?
- Do the independent directors ever meet alone?
- Does the board evaluate the CEO? The board? The directors?
- Who determines board procedures?
- Is the board actively involved in key management succession?
- Is the board actively involved in long-range strategic planning?
- What are the ethics of the company? What are the core values?
- Is the company clear in its mission? There must be that passion to serve its constituencies—and a clarity of purpose. Why are they in business? How will the company move forward?
- Where will the company be in ten years? What is the exit strategy?
- What are the toughest issues facing the board now? Are there any unresolved lawsuits? Any major events or transactions?
- Ask yourself why you want to serve? Is it for the prestige? The camaraderie? The networking? The money? The opportunity to make a difference? Does this meet with the board's expectations?
- Who else is on the board? Why are the directors there? As Betsy Sanders says, "it's rewarding when they are there for their own personal integrity. They have reasons beyond prestige and pay. They are actively involved and they lay their gifts on the table."
- What is the board selection process? Is the process healthy? Does anyone other than the CEO/founder have meaningful input? What does the process tell you about the board? Does the CEO quietly invite you onto the board? Or is there a process that, in itself, testifies to the respect the CEO has for the board?
- What kind of time commitment is involved?
- What kind of D&O insurance and indemnification is provided? (See Chapter 12.)

- How are directors compensated? If it's at least half stock, that's a good sign. The money is not enough to compensate you for the responsibility you assume or for that one idea or introduction that catapults the company to success.

"The worst thing," says Roy Herberger, "is to get on a board of a company in trouble and the CEO is in trouble." The best director will be as thorough in her due diligence as the best company is in its recruitment process.

The bottom line is to proactively recruit, create a board charter, a needs matrix, a director profile, know what will attract a director to your board, cast a broad net, interview and reference in the context of your board and make the director search process a continuum.

Failure to recruit strategically is the first and perhaps the most common mistake made in governance today.

Begin moving up the steps of the strategic corporate staircase. If you can answer yes to all or most of the following, you are recruiting strategically. Score a one point as you begin your move up the strategic board continuum.

Do you have a strategically recruited board?

1. Is there a board charter?	Y or N
2. Is there a needs matrix?	Y or N
3. Are board processes and procedures defined?	Y or N
4. Are measurable profiles developed for each director slot?	Y or N
5. Do you know why directors will want to serve?	Y or N
6. Do you recruit proactively to each profile?	Y or N
7. Do you interview and reference potential directors in the context of your board?	Y or N
8. Do you provide comprehensive orientation?	Y or N
9. Do you recruit in a continuum?	Y or N

.

Step One: Recruit Strategically

Leadership
Value Added
Information
Diversity
The Money
Cronyism
Family
Conflicts
Insiders
Recruit

0   10   Strategically
Captive Board   *Strategic Board*

NOTES

1. Korn/Ferry International, *26th Annual Board of Directors Study*, 2000.
2. Thomas R. Horton, "Aim High for Your Dream Candidate," *Directors & Boards*, Fall 1998.
3. Korn/Ferry International, *26th Annual Board of Directors Study*, 1999.
4. Ibid.
5. SpencerStuart Board Index, 1998.
6. Korn/Ferry International, *26th Annual Board of Directors Study*, 1999.
7. Grant Thornton, *Public Company Advisor*, Summer 1998. Note difference in fees vs. total compensation.
8. Korn/Ferry International, *26th Annual Board of Directors Study*, 1999.
9. Ibid.
10. Ibid.
11. SpencerStuart Board Index, 1998, 7.
12. SpencerStuart, "Technology Board Survey," *Directors & Boards*, Spring 1998.
13. "Directors' Boards are Clueless about the Internet," *Computerworld*, 12 July 1999, 32.
14. John A. Byrne, "The Best & Worst Boards," *Business Week*, 25 November 1996.
15. Korn/Ferry International, *26th Annual Board of Directors Study*, 1999, 41.
16. Edward E. Lawler and David Finegold, "CEO Selection: Why Boards Get It Wrong," *Industry Week*, 17 November 1997.
17. Korn/Ferry International, *Advanced Technology Board of Directors Study*, 1999.
18. Russell Reynolds Associates, "Study Explores CEO Board Service," *Director's Monthly*, August 1999.
19. "Rockwell Semiconductor Builds a Board from Scratch," *Director's Alert*, December 1998.
20. Douglas L. Foshee, "How a New CEO Reshapes Governance," *Directors & Boards*, Fall 1998.
21. Robert W. Kile and J. Michael Loscavio, "Building a Better Board," *The Non-Profit Times*, November 1994.

Part II

The Conflicts
That Compromise
a Board

Chapter 3

◆

Insiders

The essence of strategic boards is independence. When you see a board loaded with insiders, it's a sign certain of indifference to and perhaps disdain for governance. At the least, it's a transparent signal that the CEO does not recognize or appreciate the tremendous strategic advantage he could gain from a proactive independent board. The best number of insiders is one, and, in some cases, two. Why?

1. Because an insider's allegiance is likely to be to her boss—not the shareholders. Shelby Yastrow, former executive vice president and general counsel of McDonald's puts it best: "How does an inside director challenge the CEO or Chairman when it might cost him his job? Does he embarrass him at a meeting? Secretly call other board members? Initiate a palace coup? If there isn't a 'safe' vehicle for dissent, he won't dissent, and dissent is part of his job."

You have the day-to-day benefit of these insiders' advice. You already know what the insiders think. And that thinking has been factored into the policies brought before the board. You can include them in board meetings, at dinner the night before, at strategic planning sessions. What gain is there in having their vote, unless it's to bolster management's position? As director Clayton Yeutter says, "you can get the insiders every day of the week. Why not get the benefit of outside expertise?"

"Make sure that the board is composed partly of outsiders and partly of officers," author and former CEO of Avis Rent-A-Car Robert

Townsend says facetiously. "Since all of the important questions relate to the performance of key men and their divisions, no important questions will be asked. To do so, would be a breach of etiquette, an insult to somebody at the table."[1]

"Let's face it," says George Aucott, former Firestone CEO, "you work for this guy. You are not going to down your boss in front of these outsiders. The more insiders, the less debate. The more insiders, the less opportunity to be critical of operations."

Insiders should be invited into the boardroom to answer questions and to provide an opportunity for independent directors to get to know them. They should not be board members. J. Keith Louden, pioneering authority on board management, said, "it is too difficult for an inside director to function as the subordinate of the chief executive officer every day and then, at a board meeting, become in effect his superior."

2. "Another problem is that those managers who do not serve on the board appear to have second class rank, and the manager-directors have a tendency to take advantage of this situation in normal day to day discussions and relationships," says Louden.[2] It creates a two-tier pecking order, with some management more "equal" than others and more privy to corporate information and corporate power. Further, what if you bring on an insider and realize you made the wrong choice? Or what if there is someone who turns out to be a better succession candidate who was excluded from the board?

3. Not only can the CEO intimidate insiders, but insiders can inhibit the CEO. One CEO was afraid to share a negative sales projection, because the director of sales sat on the board, and the CEO worried that the sales executive might leave the company when he needed him most. In another case, an owner of a $45 million company was afraid to tell his board about his cancer, because two employees were directors, and he didn't want word of his sickness to get out. So, the company was set adrift just at the time the board should have been strategizing succession and supporting the CEO.

4. With insiders, the board is more likely to get filtered feedback, almost certainly from the insiders, probably from the CEO. There are simply too many barriers to open and candid communication. Insiders tend to be wed to existing plans and policies, immersed in the day-to-day operations of their company—because that is what they are paid to do. In fact, if they are to succeed, corporate insiders must be unerringly committed to their strategic plan. How can this internal bias not dilute the objectivity that is a cornerstone of a good director?

5. In addition to inhibiting decision making going forward, inside directors also can skew the selection of a new CEO. Management gen-

erally prefers insider candidates, because they are less likely to change policies that those insiders helped create and execute, and also because an inside CEO is more likely to retain senior managers.[3]

Bart Brown, CEO of Brown Street & Main and former Circle K CEO, says, "I'm a firm believer that any board with a preponderance of insiders is making a colossal mistake. You are never going to have as effective a board as you ought to have." Instead, suggests George Aucott, encourage your insiders to be on an outside board. "As a CEO, you can call the other CEO and say, 'How's my guy doing on your board?' He may say 'he sits there and never says anything' or 'Wow, he's terrific.' It's a cheap training exercise." Michael Dell also says it well. "The board is supposed to be the outside input. We already know what the guys inside think."[4]

On the other hand, Tony O'Reilly, former CEO of H. J. Heinz, defends the practice of peopling boards with insiders. "If you have only one insider," he says, "the only person who talks to the board is the CEO, and every view is filtered through one mind to the board." But, this is true only if the board allows the CEO to be the filter and to restrict contact with other management. And, if that's the case, the board is de facto derelict in its duty of oversight, most glaringly in the realm of succession planning. It's revealing to note that O'Reilly is now out of office, largely due to public pressure against his failed governance practices.

The issue is not information. It is governance. Board members are there to govern. The primary role of a director is not to provide information. And, the board's primary purpose goes well beyond management training. Many CEOs think that the board is an excellent training forum for promising high-ranking corporate officers, and that this is enough of a reason to bring an insider on board.[5] Such was the case at Avon, where former CEO Charles Perrin's heir, Andrea Jung, sat on the board. "Having that exposure for her is important," said Perrin.

National Presto is a classic case of too many insiders. Melvin S. Cohen was chairman and a director since 1949. His daughter. Mary Jo Cohen, controls more than one quarter of the outstanding stock. Three of the six board members are company officers. Share price was languishing at around $40 since 1994. The New York Society of Security Analysts targeted National Presto as their first test case in how governance could be tied to returns. The company had over $29 a share in cash and marketable securities, which could be used to increase shareholder value. The Cohen's controlled 30 percent of the stock and were armed with "shark repellent" provisions that required a supermajority vote of shares to approve any change of control. The belief is National Presto avoided taking any action that might enhance investor value, because insiders control the board. [6]

Pascal Levensohn, investor and director, president of Levensohn

Capital Management, holds AMP up as a good example. When Allied Signal tried to buy AMP, whose stock had dropped 50 percent in the first 6 months of 1998, the AMP board did everything it could to stop the sale, despite the fact that 70 percent of AMP shareholders were in favor of the sale. Ultimately, AMP was acquired by TYCO. Levensohn implies that AMP could still be independent and says "the historic and continuing influence of former CEOs on the AMP board raised the emotional ante at the board level and inhibited necessary change." [7]

The erosion of Disney's stellar record of growth made it vulnerable to strident cries for independence, spearheaded by TIAA-CREF. Disney recently dropped off two inside directors and added at least two outside directors, according to Kenneth West, senior consultant on corporate governance for TIAA-CREF. But it still would have a mediocre rating on the Strategic Board Continuum.

A visible example of a good board is Ceridian, whose nine-member board has a single insider, CEO Larry Perlman. The board changed the directors' retirement plan to a stock option plan to align interests with the shareholders, and regularly evaluates the CEO, the board and individual directors. With improved financials, which many attribute to good governance the board was recognized as a best board by *Business Week* and *Chief Executive*.[8]

At Watermark, the two founders had grown the company to a certain point and realized they needed help to move forward. "They had the fortitude to set up an outside board—three of us," explained one of the directors, David McLaughlin. "The real issue was how to get the two founders to agree on strategic direction and to realize value out of the company. The board was able to catalyze a strategy to sell the company, which the board helped negotiate very successfully. "One of the nicest things about being on a board with good people is that your cumulative experience gets to be of some forty or fifty companies," observes McLaughlin. A passive board of insiders reluctant to challenge the two founders or a board without the right combination of experience could have vaporized the underlying value of the company.

There have been dramatic reductions in the numbers of insiders sitting on Fortune 500 boards, the majority of which have one or two insiders. The average number of insiders on Fortune 500 boards is two.[9] However, there are still a good number of well known companies where inside directors make up at least one third of the board such as General Electric (5 of 15 directors), Gillette (4 of 12), Heinz (9 of 19), Longs Drug Stores (7 of 13), Lockheed Martin (6 of 17), Marsh & McLennan (9 of 17), Republic New York (14 of 22), Synovus Financial (10 of 18), U. S. Surgical (6 of 13), Wendy's International (6 of 15), Winn-Dixie (5 of 11), and WorldCom (5 of 11).[10]

Smaller and midsize companies still tend to be overloaded with insiders. This is the next beachhead for independence. Significantly, inside ties and board inexperience characterize the directors of fraud prone companies. In a recent study of fraudulent financial reporting, about 60 percent of the directors of the some 300 companies cited for fraud were insiders or "gray" directors—outsiders with special ties to the company or management.[11]

Various studies are now documenting the positive relationship between independent directors and healthy companies. One such study of growth companies by *Inc.* magazine suggests that outside board members were even more important to success factors such as sales growth than were insiders.[12]

A case in point is Universal Technical Institute. In 1995, UTI was a $30 million, profitable private training school system, which had an inside board that focused largely on required and tactical issues. UTI was facing increased competition from community colleges and vocational schools while being squeezed by pricing and government regulations. Despite a remarkable placement rate of over 90 percent for their trained automotive mechanics and a wide-ranging sales program to potential students, enrollment was flat. CEO Robert Hartman recruited a strategic advisory board to focus on the challenges. He and UTI were ideally positioned to attract an outstanding board. The company was profitable with a reputation for integrity and excellence, and Hartman had the self-confidence and temperament to use a board well.

At the suggestion of the advisory board, the company switched from thinking of the student as the customer to thinking of the employer as the customer. Employers had a shortage of up to 70,000 technicians. Now UTI has contracts with power employers like Mercedes, Jaguar, Porsche, BMW, and Ford, who help reimburse student loans and offer high paying jobs and internships in return for access to precisely trained mechanics. Now, the company, with revenues of $100 million plus, has become attractive to Wall Street, and UTI is considering an IPO.

The board, says Hartman, "helped teach us the difference between strategic planning and tactical planning. We were solving problems, instead of positioning ourselves to be the leader in our sector and forming alliances. The board encouraged us to look at hard issues that we otherwise would not have explored. It was sort of a wake-up call. It keeps you out of your comfort zone on a positive, constructive basis."

The idea of refocusing on the employer was "heresy," confides Hartman. "Our focus was 'the student is the customer.' But, the deeper we go within industry, the more it benefits our organization and the students." In addition to the car manufacturers paying for student tuition costs, spin-offs include sponsored training, graduate programs tied to the industry, more donations and industry support, and an array of strategic partnership options. "There has been a dramatic change. Now we are seen as the preeminent automotive school in the country," enthuses Hartman.

Journee Software is another good example. As an outside director, Robin Curle helped identify a CFO for Journee Software and helped with the strategic plan, particularly the executive summary. "VCs will read the first page of the summary and won't go further unless it's good," Curle knew from her firsthand experience growing her own company. She also introduced Journee to key VCs. According to Curle, the board has worked as team to do a compelling business plan. Also on the board is Sam Smith, an ex-Texas Instruments officer who brought on former colleague Ron Harris, CEO and president of Pervasive Software. Board member Martin Neath, executive vice president and employee number twelve of Tivoli, has helped with sales and marketing expertise, Journee's alliance strategy, and setting up meetings with key potential partners. For example, he introduced Journee to IBM, which is Tivoli's parent. As Curle notes, "it's smart to get these kinds of people. None of them like to fail. Anything they touch, they take very seriously." Insiders could not have had the same impact.

FORMER CEOs ON THE BOARD

A pivotal subset of the insider issue is the common practice of former CEOs remaining on the board. Why is this objectionable? There are three reasons: the temptation to second guess the new CEO, the inclination to defend past practices on an emotional—rather than a strategic—basis, and the reluctance of the other directors to counter the former CEO or any of his policies. A major concern is slowed decision making, reducing the responsiveness of the board to the marketplace. In a 1998 study, 49 percent of directors believed that their company should require the former CEO to leave the board, yet only 30 percent of boards have formally implemented such a policy.[13] If an incumbent CEO wants the advice of his predecessor, a phone call or a meeting or a dinner does not require a board seat.

Insiders

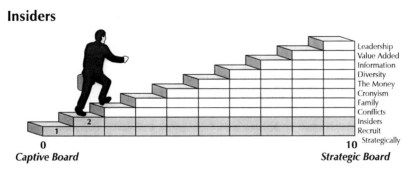

| 0 | | | | | | | | | | 10 |
| Captive Board | | | | | | | | | | Strategic Board |

Leadership
Value Added
Information
Diversity
The Money
Cronyism
Family
Conflicts
Insiders
Recruit
Strategically

As Doug Yearley, CEO of Phelps Dodge, who retired May 3, 2000, declared, "I don't stay one minute after my retirement, so my successor will have a clean sheet." "Ex-CEOs should walk out the door the day they resign or retire," insists Clayton Yeutter, who sits on at least one board chaired by a former CEO. "They should never come back again unless invited. It's a very hard decision. They spent years building the company to what it is and want to nurture it on into the future. And they are worried about what they are going to do with the rest of their lives. There's a lot of emotion involved."

"I don't believe in former CEOs being chairmen," says Chase Manhattan Chairman Walter Shipley, who retired as CEO in June 1999 and served as interim chair for a "short transitional period. The only reason I'm doing it this way, on a very short-term basis, is that two of us (at the top) were leaving in the same time frame. It was too abrupt."

"I really believe it [the CEO staying on] makes that very difficult," says Charles Perrin of Avon, because he recruited most of the board members. "When I'm done, I don't want the person following me to worry about my feelings in the board room," says Perrin of Andrea Jung, who succeeded him. "She has lots to worry about. The least should be to worry about the ex-CEO."

Melvin Goodes, chairman and CEO, of Warner-Lambert, makes it clear that ex-CEOs cannot serve on his board either. "This can be a harmful practice. I've seen a lot of instances on other boards where CEOs, by staying on, restricted new actions—trying to protect old business situations. When boards were talking about the need for tumultuous change, the ex-CEOs were inhibitors of change because they were less flexible. They conceived of the world as it was when they were CEO."[14]

"It is very difficult to move a CEO aside, have him remain a voting board member, and proceed to undo major projects that this person has previously done with the board's blessing. Retired senior executives have a natural tendency to glorify their exploits and to treasure past contributions as well as to protect one another and their reputations," points out Pascal Levensohn, president of Levensohn Capital Management. In most cases, the incoming CEO inherits a board, with whom the outgoing CEO has strong relationships. So directors are caught in the middle.

If you have no more than two insiders on your board, add one point to your strategic board continuum quotient.

NOTES

1. Robert Townsend, *Further Up the Organization* (New York: Alfred A Knopf, Inc., 1984).

2. J. Keith Louden, *The Effective Director in Action* (New York: AMA-COM, 1974).
3. Pascal N. Levensohn, "The Problem of Emotion in the Boardroom," *Directors & Boards*, Spring 1999.
4. "How Michael Dell Uses his Board," *Corporate Board Member*, Summer 1999.
5. Ibid.
6. Reed Abelson, "All in the Family? National Presto to Face Analyst Scrutiny," *New York Times*, 28 January 1999.
7. Pascal N. Levensohn, "The Problem of Emotion in the Boardroom," *Directors & Boards*, Spring 1999.
8. Susan Peterson, "How to Build a Board," *Star Tribune*, 5 January 1997.
9. Korn/Ferry International, 25th *Annual Board of Directors Study*, 1999.
10. SpencerStuart Board Index, 1998.
11. Mark S. Beasley, Joseph V. Carcello, and Dana R. Hermanson, "Fraudulent Financial Reporting: Implications for Corporate Directors," *Director's Monthly*, September 1999.
12. Roger Ford and K. Mathew Gillery, "Board Building in Small Companies," *Director's Monthly*, April 1999.
13. Korn/Ferry International, 25th *Annual Board of Directors Study*, 1999, 29.
14. Morris Goodes with Ram Charan, "Cross-Currents of Change: A Leadership Dialogue," *Director's Monthly*, April 1999.

Chapter 4

---◆---

Conflicts

◆ THE THIRD MISTAKE: TOO MANY PAID CONSULTANTS ◆

The Securities and Exchange Commission requires disclosure of con-flicted directors for a reason. A board's value always comes back to the quality of the individual. Not much else really matters. But, putting your consultants on your board means you are building in conflict. It is not illegal to have conflicted, "affiliated," or "gray" directors on your board. And, it is far from uncommon. But, you can do better.

Affiliated directors are sometimes referred to as "6b" directors be-cause of SEC Regulation 14A, Item 6(b), which requires that directors with such relationships be reported in a firm's proxy materials. Such relationships include:

- Employment by the corporation or an affiliate within the last five years.
- Any family relationship by blood or marriage closer than sec-ond cousin.
- Affiliation with a concern in the last two years that has had a customer, supplier, broker, or creditor relationship with the cor-poration.
- Affiliation with an investment banker who has performed ser-vices for the corporation within two years or will do so within one year.
- A control person (based on amount of shareholdings as detailed in federal securities law).
- Association with a law firm engaged by the corporation.

The list of affiliated directors includes your investment banker, your venture capital investors, your commercial banker, your lawyer, your accountant, your management consultant, and anyone else who stands to have his or her income compromised.

It is not considered a conflict if directors are compensated for extra time spent carrying out their board duties. For instance, at Pharmacia & Upjohn, Johns Manville, Aetna, and Levitz Furniture, directors earned extra compensation for time-consuming succession planning efforts. Committee chairs automatically receive extra pay, and audit committee members, who spend extra time, often receive "overtime" pay as well.

At a spin-off from a parent firm, any director who was associated with the parent firm is also considered to be an affiliated director. The Securities and Exchange Commission requires disclosure of all these relationships, but it can't regulate their effect. You already have the benefit of these consultants' commitment and expertise. Why pay for it again—when it is an obvious conflict? The appearance of conflict matters. Don't doubt it.

If a conflict exists, it is most likely to surface during the very crises the director is there to help resolve. A succession issue, an acquisition, a merger, or a major stock play all tend to jeopardize the conflicted director's income stream and test his allegiances. If not in fact, then in appearance. When the choice is between a director's pocketbook and the general shareholder welfare, it's a tough call. A good director will unfailingly choose the shareholder. But is her decisiveness slightly compromised? Does the conflicted director fail to ask that extra penetrating question or to make the persuasive argument at the board meeting that might influence other directors?

There are too many board members who provide business services for personal gain. The Securities and Exchange Commission does not require companies to disclose the dollar value of these fee-based services, but only to reveal their existence. There is no assurance that the terms of provider contracts are competitive, so shareholders cannot determine if the fees paid to the gray directors are fair market value.

Potential conflicts can range from an attorney whose firm provides nonrelated legal services to those who derive the entirety of their income from companies on whose boards they sit. According to David Bays, one board member only accepts directorships if he is assured a minimum number of hours of consulting contracts with the company. He makes considerably more money than before he "retired."

Actually, this is an all too prevalent practice. The California Public Employees' Retirement System (CalPERS), holder of 10.2 million Disney shares, withheld votes for Senator George J. Mitchell and for Robert A. M. Stern, an architect who has designed buildings for Disney and its Chairman, Michael Eisner, because Disney pays them consulting fees.[1] As director Roz Ridgway observes, "everybody is selling something to somebody." What about Henry Kissinger, who had a huge consultancy with American Express while he sat on their board? Even though it is disclosed, the conflict exists. Even if a consultant is no longer providing her services to the company, the special relationship of obligations persists with the CEO, and so objectivity is colored.

A classic example of conflicted directors is MBNA Corporation. Chairing the compensation committee was the CEO's college roommate, James Berick of Berick, Pearlman & Mills Co., the firm that provides legal services to MBNA. CEO Alfred Lerner took home almost $10 million in 1998. That same year, Berick served as Lerner's attorney when he purchased the Cleveland Browns football team. Six months later, the MBNA Board of Directors approved a ten-year, $30 million marketing agreement with the Cleveland Browns.[2]

In 1998, the Board at Telxon turned down a buyout offer from Symbol of $40 in cash or $42 cash and stock combined. Three months after Symbol withdrew its offer, the stock was sitting at around $19 a share. There may be legitimate reasons. But the veneer is flawed. Robert A. Goodman is a director and outside counsel. In fiscal 1998, Goodman's Cleveland law firm received nearly $1.7 million plus $159,000 in reimbursements for expenses from Telxon. Another director, Norton Rose, received a management contract worth up to $500,000 for several months work.[3] How can these directors not be conflicted when the time comes to vote for a sale—and perhaps the end of their income streams?

One more example: Twenty-five percent of Maryland based Lockheed Martin Corp's net income for the third quarter of 1998 was generated by an "adjustment" of accounting reserves and triggered a lawsuit. The former CFO, Vincent Marafino, a Lockheed Martin director, who received $250,000 for consulting services that year from Lockheed, was named a defendant in the shareholder suit. Former SEC chairman Rod Hills said, "Nobody in good conscience could possibly think that the former CFO, particularly if he's paid as a consultant, constitutes an independent director. It's not good corporate practice. It's bizarre."[4] Marafino is retiring from the board.

A conflicted board triggered a Lens Fund onslaught at Juno Lighting. Fund principals Nell Minow and Bob Monks sought board seats and secured a commitment to hire a headhunter to identify two independent directors. At the time, the board included the CEO, an employee, the company's lawyer and banker, and a friend of the CEO. The Lens Group sought to restrict the board to one insider and prevent the company from being acquired by an affiliate of Fremont Investors. Reasons for opposition included a low price, bad timing, inappropriate notice, and the Lens' stock plan that reserved almost 30 percent of new common stock for management. The board approved the acquisition.

At Nike, John Thompson, former basketball coach at Georgetown University, is a director of the board that awarded CEO Philip Knight $1.7 million in compensation in 1998. In turn, Thompson received more than $400,000 in endorsement money from Nike.[5]

Gershon Kekst, founder of Kekst and Company, leading public relations firm in the merger and acquisition arena, sits on one board, Loral. He is adamantly opposed to directors getting fees for services. "Anything I do for Loral, I don't ever put down on my time sheets. It is the only client in the firm that I have never reported a single billable hour for."[6]

Michael Burke is an attorney/consultant who sits on nine boards. He has opened a consulting practice as an adjunct to his law firm. Although he is not directly practicing law, his firm generates several thousand dollars in fees from the company of at least one board he sits on. Rather than being a negative, Burke insists the relationship is a plus for the company. "Would the CEO be slow to fire our law firm?" Perhaps, says Burke. But Burke says he and the firm are accountable in a conspicuous way as a board member. "We have to perform every day. It really comes down to whether you think I'm worthy enough as a businessman." insists Burke.

As with every gray director, the character of the director is what matters. In all such cases, a valid concern is that good directors may be disqualified because of what Curtis Barnette, speaking on behalf of the Business Roundtable, calls "mechanical independence standards."

INVESTORS

Interested directors in the form of bankers, venture capitalists, or angel investors are a muddier issue—increasingly important with the surge of start-ups and companies aiming for initial public offerings (IPOs).

VENTURE CAPITALISTS

With early stage companies, it is virtually a given that with money comes a board seat—or two. In fact, it is rare to see a fast growth or high technology company without an investor on board. Often investors make up the majority of outside board members. The first challenge, then, becomes selecting the best investors possible and resisting the temptation to go with the first offer.

Apply the same strategic recruiting yardstick to investors as you would other board members. As Robin Curle, CEO of Journee Software, advises, "the company ought to do a short courtship with prospective investors. Often, they are just so grateful to have someone give them money," that there is no courtship. The second key is creating a small independent board prior to funding to obtain the governance balance so critical to strategic boards.

Generally, the larger the company, the fewer the venture capitalists (VCs). In technology companies with revenues of $500 million or more, fewer than 7 percent of directors are venture capitalists, as opposed to 19 percent of directors in companies with revenues below $500 million.[7] A real advantage is the transferable experience these directors often have with other companies at similar stages of growth, often in similar or compatible industries. Another tremendous benefit is the access—usually to more money, but often to other proven resources as well. The other obvious value is the commitment of investors to the financial success of the company. Former Kidder Peabody investment banker Steve Bansak contends that venture capitalists "are tough, disciplined, bottom line investors I happen to like on a board."

The downside is that these directors may not be the best directors long term for your company. If you were to proactively recruit board members to fit your strategic plan, would these directors fit the optimum profile? How would they fare on your board matrix? Second, in times of crisis, or a major event, such as an acquisition, an IPO, or a merger, your interests may not be aligned. Just as with affiliated consultants, precisely when you most need the wisdom of clear objectivity, your directors may be conflicted by their fiduciary duty to their investors. They may well do the right thing, but that vestige of conflict exists. For example, in deference to the need to show quarterly earnings increases, a director might dissuade the board from spending money on capital expenditures or a new R & D initiative.

As investment banker Jock Holliman says, "we want to create shareholder value in the shortest period of time and seek liquidity for our funds. That typically is about a five-year cycle. So, we're interested in building the value as rapidly as we can as opposed to building a lifestyle company. Typically, as a syndicate, we'll have voting control. Or we'll have a contractual voice over the substantial acts, such as selling assets, taking control again, changing the board of directors, changing the articles of incorporation, changing the CEO, going public or a bankruptcy event. We try to form a consensus on the board to vote on those substantial acts"[8]

Venture capitalists are very conscious of cycle times—the length of time before an investment is liquidated. When Photometrics, a $22 million Tucson company, received an offer to sell, Holliman was the only director who dissented. Five directors voted in favor. It was a complex deal, a performance work-out that had a lot of downside and which could take considerable time. Holliman had more time than the other two venture capitalists on the board. As it happened, the deal become so complicated that the board came around to Holliman's position, and, in early 1999, a new deal was structured that resulted in the sale for $37 million in cash, significantly more than the original deal.

Many investors are not interested in having a majority of independent directors on board. In terms of composition for early stage companies, Holliman prefers a five-person board, two venture capitalists, two representatives of the common class, i.e. management, and one "independent industry guru." Steve McConnell, former CEO of Nu West, who has invested in scores of small companies, says he wants other investor/owners on the board with him—people who understand that things don't always go up. People who help in due diligence, people with skin in the game.

According to McConnell, if someone invests a minimum of $1 million in a public company or a substantial six-figure number in a private company—or if someone owns 10 percent or more—he or she is entitled to a seat at the table. "If our CFO mortgaged his house to buy stock, bingo, he's at the table. Because he showed me it's important to him. Nothing is more important than being an investor. Who better to give input than stockholders?" At a public board, "all I'm doing is representing stockholders. The only reason we don't invite all 2000 stockholders to our board meetings is the logistics. At small companies, I don't need anybody to represent stockholders. That's the essence of a board—to represent the owners."

Former general counsel and executive vice president of McDonald's, Shelby Yastrow, believes that "when a venture capitalist invests heavily in a company, there is a valid reason to have him on the board—he has to protect his investment. This gives him a slightly different approach to the job. Like the other directors, he wants the company to succeed, but, while the other directors have both eyes on the shareholders, he has one eye on the shareholders and the other on his investment. This doesn't mean they shouldn't be on boards—indeed, it's often a condition of the investment, but their position has to be recognized."

More than two venture capitalists are too many, warns attorney and venture capitalist Rob Dunaway. "Remember the hat the VC wears. Me and my investors first. Because his fiduciary responsibility to his fund is to exit that investment with as much money as possible, even if at the expense of someone else. It's a direct conflict with other shareholders." However, board seats are a standard deal point in venture capital fundraising rounds. "You are forced into it. And, there are many venture capitalists who do great things, because they have good and very applicable contacts for companies. They can be the people who bring the most to the table that way," Dunaway continues. "But, you risk losing your objectivity with too many. You have the risk of people running the company who have never run a company."

Robin Curle says "venture capitalists have one interest and one interest only—to produce good returns for their investors and funds. It involves selecting the right companies, helping those companies grow and getting a good exit strategy. They all want ten times return on their money." The company wants a high valuation and as much money for as little stock as possible. The VC wants the opposite. With a high growth start-up company, there is a built-in conflict.

Tom Emerson, former CEO of several venture-supported companies says "sooner or later, the VCs can't resist the temptation to meddle." Of course, as with every director, "it very much depends on the gifts and talents of the individuals." At one of his companies, an investor board member rather proudly announced that he had never had a real job, not exactly what a CEO seeking strategic operating advice wants to hear.

"If they are just financiers, they don't bring much to the table. They got on the board, because the company has been financed. At that instant, financing is not the problem. Operating is. The VC's interests are going to be represented very well with one or two competent VCs. You don't need three, four, or five of those kinds of guys. A concerned investor," Emerson believes, "generates a self-fulfilling prophecy. If investors become nervous about their investment, either because the company is slow on the upswing or because of inexperience or pressure on the investor director, he will often make demands that may not be in the best interest of the company. It is a very unhealthy way for directors to behave."

As Bobby Inman sums it up, representatives from venture funds bring advice from troubles they have encountered at other venture companies, but they are "oriented toward earlier liquidity." An example at the Evolutionary Technologies (ETI) board in Austin demonstrates both points. A $40 million, 230 employee company, ETI's product line, EXTRACT, automates data integration management. The ETI board consists of the two cofounders, Bobby Inman and several other venture capitalists. The cofounders were clear about their expectations. "We wanted a collaborative board that strategizes and doesn't point fingers. If there is a rock in the road, they will help us and not replace us," cofounder Robin Curle explained.

The company had just started marketing its software and generating revenue for the first time. According to Curle, the VCs were very nervous because ETI was several months later than projected in generating revenue. During a potentially calamitous board meeting, one young and new venture capitalist announced. "If you aren't getting

revenue, and we have to do a second round, you won't like the terms."
Bobby Inman turned to the venture capitalist and looked him straight
in the eye. ("But, he spoke to us, the founders," says Curle.) "Kay and
Robin, of course if it comes to that, I'll bridge you as I did the last
time."

"The VC was trying to threaten us," Curle says. "Bob was able to
nip the insurrection in the bud. Probably it would have spiraled into
an unpleasant meeting. The next month, ETI started getting a lot of
revenue, and everyone was fine after that."

According to Michael Burke, a Midwestern pharmaceutical company was projected to have a straight-up trajectory with an IPO in its
near future. However, its ascent was more gradual, and the IPO has
still not happened. A venture capitalist who put $20 million into the
company was having a very hard time divorcing the interests of the
company from his own self-interest. The company needed another
round of funding, and all the VC directors were more concerned about
their dilution than the long-term outcomes for the company. As a result, the board process deteriorated into form over substance. Proceedings are dominated by *Robert's Rules of Order*; board members bring
their lawyers to the board meetings; and now, to accomplish at least
some of the business of the board, there are meetings before the meetings.

Terry Lee, Chair of Bell Sports prefers to sit on boards in whose
companies he is invested. But, his approach is to balance the investors
in early stage companies with strong outside members. "In the end, we
have entrepreneurs who have done deals before and financial people as
investors. If you do a good job of picking investors, you'll find these
people have a wealth of knowledge. The outside (independent) board
members end up influencing the inside and investor directors in very
positive ways and visa versa. It's no different than rounding out a management team."

"For every strong investment oriented person, think about a
strong operating entrepreneur," Lee suggests. "If you have good quality people, they end up balancing each other, and you get good advice." In one case, after acquiring a company, Lee wanted to sell a
nonprofitable $50 million division, to avoid wasting more resources on
it. The bankers on the board were against the sale because it would
reduce the overall size of the company, so the spin-off was stalled.
Ultimately, after a year's delay, the division was sold. According to
Lee, the spin-off could have helped the company sooner. As Lee points
out, "there is a lot of give and take in these situations."

Another consideration is the success of the venture capital companies themselves. Crosspoint Ventures began as a seed fund with small
investments of $200,000 to $300,000, and its principals were very in-

volved in picking and coaching management. Then Crosspoint became the lead investor in eBay and made over $2 billion on that investment alone. Now a completely different investment strategy significantly impacts the attention they can devote to a smaller company. The pressure is on with many funds like Crosspoint to invest huge amounts of money in ever bigger deals. Those with money have as much pressure to invest well as the companies have to succeed. A strategic board is a great comfort to those investors who may no longer have the time or inclination to hand-hold smaller companies.

For early-stage companies, CEOs can make a preemptive strike by proactively recruiting several key directors before going out for money. Dennis Murphree, of Murphree Ventures, provided seed funding to Journee Software, an internet business services management company in Austin, and then pushed for an independent board before going out for further funding rounds. "Most VCs want a bunch of VCs that can drive in the direction that best suits their outcome," says CEO Robin Curle. Murphree understands that better visibility and better strategy is more important.

It is rare that founders start their company thinking about their board as a competitive advantage. As Curle says, "They start with their nose to the grindstone, not thinking how the board will look going forward and how strategically they will use it. By the time they are ready for their first rounds of funding, the VCs are driving things."

"I would have a board before the VCs come in," says veteran director Phil Matthews, describing such a situation with a successful restaurant company. "When you bring the money in, its better," Matthews says, "to already have your own board members who are bright and strong, whom you have confidence in." Bobby Inman recommends replacing investors as early as possible in order to bring on directors with broader experience to focus on overall growth, management, and liquidity.

Include strategic recruiting as part of your business planning. (See Chapter 2.) Sell that to your investors along with the rest of your plan, and then proceed to implement it.

PUBLIC COMPANIES

As James Kristie, editor of *Directors & Boards*, observes, "While intuitively it makes sense for a major owner to be represented, there are practical drawbacks—i.e., being privy to nonpublic information and other things that limit their ability to trade."[9] Former Federal Reserve Board governor and director Martha Seger asks, "Why shouldn't we realize there are different kinds of investors? Some like a lot of cash dividends. Some are 'hot dog' investors who don't really care, because they are in and out so fast. Why should they dictate what we do?"

There is a belief among many investors, for instance, that dividends don't matter any more. They do, she says. In many years, dividends are a significant portion of the total return to shareholders and can be crucial to retired shareholders with fixed incomes.

Roy Herberger has been in situations in which investors forced an early sale. "Where there are significant shareholders, sometimes people say it's time to cut and run and not wait for the growth and development of a company," he says. "It's difficult to prove. But I've seen a company sold prematurely."

However, Herberger believes it can be valuable to have an investment banker on board to monitor the investment banker you may hire. As he says, "That game is operationally very difficult to play, not a game for amateurs." Robert Lear disagrees. "Absolutely no investment bankers. How would you like to be an investment banker, and your competitor is on the board? Or, how would you like to be on the board and not get the investment banking job? It's a straight conflict. Are you going to criticize the CEO," he asks, when a huge deal is at stake?

For public companies, Stephen Draizin, Chairman of Rad Energy Corporation, believes investment bankers are a "terrible, terrible problem." For the most part, "they are there to generate fees through relationships. You're damned if you do, and damned if you don't. You are clearly an insider because you know about things. All that can happen is you are second guessed. If you sell out and the stock goes down. Or you buy at a particular moment and come under scrutiny by regulatory authorities, although it may be completely benign. Say," Draizin continues, "you own a big position in the company. Now you have new investors who join your group so you buy more shares, simply adding to your overall position. You . . . find out someone is making an offer for the company. You just hope somebody doesn't come at you and sees what purchases you made, accusing you of knowing or alleging that you should have known the offer was in the works."

If you have no paid consultants or no more than two venture capitalists on your board, add one point to your strategic board continuum.

Conflicts

0
Captive Board

Leadership
Value Added
Information
Diversity
The Money
Cronyism
Family
Conflicts
Insiders
Recruit
10 Strategically
Strategic Board

NOTES

1. "CalPERS to Withhold Votes for Two Directors Paid Fees by Disney," *The Wall Street Journal*, February 2000.
2. AFL-CIO Web Executive Pay Watch Web site, "Executive Pay Watch: Too Close for Comfort," July 1999.
3. Diane Evans Column, *Akron Beacon Journal*, 16 September 1998.
4. Stephen Barr, "Watchdogs or Lapdogs," *CFO*, May 1999.
5. AFL-CIO Executive Pay Watch Web site, "Do Deals with the Compensation Committee," June 1999.
6. "Gershon Kekst," *Directors & Boards*, Winter 1999.
7. "Technology Company Boards: In Search of the Differences," *Directors & Boards*, Spring 1998.
8. John M. "Jock" Holliman, III, Snell & Wilmer, Arthur Andersen seminar, November 1998, 1.
9. "Interview with James Kristie," *Equity Market Insight*, March 1999.

Chapter 5

———◆———

Family

◆ The Fourth Mistake: Too Much Family ◆

A family-controlled board triggers alarms, because it is perceived as impenetrable and intractable. When many of us think of family companies, we think in terms of the local art gallery, machine shop, deli, corner boutique, or gift shop. We think small. And, we think casual, inbred, and sometimes inept.

Actually, there are more than 300,000 private family-owned American businesses with revenues over $5 million and more than 45,000 with revenues over $25 million. More than 80 percent of all businesses in the United States and almost 35 percent of Fortune 500 companies are family owned, according to the Family Firm Institute. Richard Narva, consultant to family businesses, says that, "in terms of governance, family-controlled enterprise constitutes the new frontier."

Often, however, just as with other small and midsize corporate boards, the board at a family company is an afterthought. It is there because it is required when a company incorporates to do business. In private family companies, the board often is invisible. As Richard Narva says, "commonplace wisdom has it that family businesses range from secret to hermetically sealed, and that both fiduciary and nonfiduciary governance bodies are merely rubber stamps." Narva says the main reason for a lack of strategic boards is because there is "insufficient power in the family's relationships to tolerate the disclosures required for effective governance."[1]

The SEC considers family members conflicted and requires public companies to disclose such relationships. As Pascal Levensohn, advisor to high net worth families, puts it, "the governance structure that invites paralysis and the great emotional discord in the face of problems demanding action resides in the family board consisting exclusively of family members or including one or two passive outsiders." The toughest issue is that of generation succession, and the structure of the board has the greatest impact, "particularly when the board and the family are indistinguishable. By their very nature, families are closed systems and are therefore insular and exclusionary. . . . As a result they often lead to emotionally rooted business positions that create deadlocks with disastrous consequences for competitive success in a dynamic business environment."[2]

Imagine the tremendous value of a reasoned, independent board in this context, one that can diffuse the emotional agenda, a board committed to the success of the enterprise.

WHY BOARDS ADD VALUE TO FAMILY COMPANIES

Richard Narva, Principal of Genus Resources, says founding families establish independent boards "to enhance the quality of their companies' relationships, to preserve the values and culture of the family and to protect core financial assets." All companies deal with changes in ownership and management. What makes family businesses different is that succession is not an event. Transitions in ownership occur over time and are a process. In addition, when Ford, for example, changes CEOs, it differs from GM in one crucial way. The family must approve. "What exists before and after are relationships which may last one's entire lifetime," Narva observes. "This places a premium on the need for vehicles to develop consensus, resolve conflict and promote reconciliation as well as develop strategy and hold management accountable."

In other words, says Narva, "there is an independent and concurrent set of reasons why governance is crucial for family businesses over and above the rationale for strategic boards in non family businesses. A lot of people will tell you that you can't have effective governance in family businesses because the controlling party won't tolerate constraints on his or her power," Narva says. "However, where core values include a legacy and a family history a board can be that coherent force—a wonderful functional strategy."

As Narva points out, it's "really hard for family controlled enterprises to remain family controlled without effective governance." The family needs a place to assess their long term picture, to compare and contrast their vision with their core values. Whether the company is private or public is beside the point. Whether there is a mass of anonymous shareholders is irrelevant, Narva insists. If there is even one shareholder who is not in management, then "that owner deserves the same level of fiduciary care as all the stockholders of General Motors."

Recruiting and retaining the best people is always an issue for family firms because, according to Narva, "they fear the absence of checks and balances." A strategic board lends credibility to an owner's claim to all constituencies that decisions are *made in the best interest of the firm, not the family.*

Also, when the founder passes the business on to new generations, it leads to a complex system of siblings and cousins that trigger governance, leadership and continuity issues. A lot of boards are wrestling with leadership. Family governance expert Ivan Lansberg says succession is seen as "substituting for the founder, which is often impossible. Directors try to look among the siblings for a single individual, and they don't find her." Instead, siblings share the leadership role and balance authority in a way that creates a leadership team. "The founder made decisions on behalf of the family," Lansberg explains. "Now the families are unprepared to develop their own decision making capacity to speak with one voice vis-à-vis the board. Unless they learn to organize themselves as a business, a family's ability to govern the enterprise is quite limited."

And, there are more challenges. Family members tend to zealously guard their privacy and their primacy, so, as Lansberg says, "it is a leap of faith to be open about family concerns that creep up to the board." Also, it is vital to recruit independent board members who "see the family as a resource to having the overall system work," who cherish the special family culture so many nonfamily companies emulate.

How does an independent director decide to whom to give allegiance? There is a hierarchy of constituencies. "Which master are you serving?" asks Lansberg, "the family or Wall Street?" At a food manufacturing company, the family owners created a sizable foundation supporting cancer research after the founder's wife died of cancer. A vending machine company seemed an ideal acquisition, until the directors realized that part of the business came from cigarettes and voted against it.

The notion of treating the family as a total unit is fracturing, as families become more diverse, broken down into branches of the tree. "Using the muscle of majority control can resolve a particular issue in a point of time. But that can come back to haunt you." Because the law is based on a competitive model, "there are many instances in family companies where the combative process fragments the family in an unnecessary way," Lansberg points out. For instance, a family member may want to sell shares or family members who are also in management may want to reinvest dividends, but nonemployee family members who rely on dividends for income may resist.

Remember, advises Lansberg, that in the end families want to stay together. They still want to go to the weddings. Frequently, family members are perceived as a liability and treated as second class owners. Yet, as Lansberg says, "they are the cheapest capital any company will get" and are usually there for the long term.

However, as Richard Narva says, "being a member of the lucky sperm club does not automatically entitle family members to a seat." Too much family dilutes objectivity. So recruiting independent directors is essential. Just as in all companies, "unless the agenda is powerful, focused and real, directors will lose interest and the process will cease." The only thing a company can do wrong, says Richard Narva, is to fail to put the most urgent issues on the table.

The New York Times Company is an example of a company that languished under inbred, family control. For the last decade, the company has had disappointing earnings, while supporting one of the most inefficient newspaper plants in the world. "The family and management took the position, 'we run the company the way we want to run it,' " said Bear Stearns analyst, Mark Boyar. In 1998, The Times made substantial reforms and the Times' stock rose from $31 to $44, raising the equity value from $3 billion to $4.25 billion.

Boyar says much of the change is due to new director IBM CEO Louis Gerstner, who was instrumental in forcing management to focus on the bottom line. It is even possible that a nonfamily member will ascend to leadership when Arthur Sulzberger retires—something that would have been impossible a few years ago. Says Boyar, "Corporate governance is the most powerful catalyst we've seen in years."

Empire Machinery, a Caterpillar franchise for Arizona and parts of Mexico and southern California, transitioned its board through a new generation. "For three decades," CEO John Whiteman, son of the founder, explains, "the board was literally afraid of the owner. My dad was strong, dominant, enterprising, challenging. 'I'll tell you the questions, and I'll give you the answers too.' He was that kind of guy. He had a lot of brilliance, and he had a lot of creativity, but it can get you into trouble when you don't have a strong board that asks those tough questions," Whiteman says.

"We have been very successful, and we had some excess cash. My dad says, 'the IRS is probably going to tax us if we don't do something with it. Let's invest. I've got a friend who understands real estate.' The proclamation was that real estate never goes down. It plateaus maybe. So he brings this up to our board, and 'yes Jack, yes Jack.' In the first big deal, we make $5 million. Buoyed with the kind of confidence that comes with not knowing what you're doing and succeeding, we went ahead and really invested. We invested maybe $15 to $20 million. It's tough to sell when you buy high. So, we lost $50 million. Our annual revenues were between $350 and $400 million. So we paid the tuition."

The lesson, according to Whiteman, is "don't think you're smart in something else, because you are smart in what you are doing. If we had had a strong board, if we had a vision, if these guys understood our business, if we had a good strategic plan, they would say, 'this doesn't meet your vision.' " Whiteman also thinks it is essential to have family members on the board, so they understand the importance of reinvesting the money in the business.

A notorious Securities and Exchange Commission (SEC) case against The Cooper Companies, the contact lens and health care company, demonstrates excesses that can occur with a family-controlled board in place. Three distinct fraudulent schemes were perpetrated. One was a front running scheme for high yield bonds among Gary Singer, a Cooper director and co-chairman; Steven Singer, Gary's brother and chief administrative officer; and others. In the second scheme, Gary Singer fraudulently traded high yield bonds between Cooper's account and accounts in the names of his wife and aunt. The third scheme involved manipulation of debentures. Singer family members and Singer family controlled entities received about $3 million in illicit profits. At the time, four of the seven seats on Cooper's board were occupied by members of the Singer family. In 1994, Gary Singer was convicted of twenty-one illegal activities, and the board was judged to have failed in safeguarding the company's public statements and interests of investors. No member of the Singer family is currently an officer, director or employee of Cooper.[3]

A fascinating anomaly is Berkshire Hathaway, whose seven member board includes three Buffetts; Charles T. Munger and Ron Olson, both partners in the Munger, Tolles & Olson law firm; the chairman of a Rhode Island community bank; and the chairman of Level 3 Communications, which has some dealings with Berkshire. Yet, this is a company whose net worth surged almost $26 billion in 1998 and increased per share book value of stock by 48 percent, with an annually compounded growth of just less than 25 percent over the last thirty-four years. This is testimony to the power of a legendary leader, Warren E. Buffett, chairman and CEO, who has single-handedly amassed tremendous wealth for his stockholders. Could Berkshire benefit from one or two carefully, proactively recruited directors, perhaps visionary leaders in the industries in which Berkshire is acquiring holdings? No doubt that Berkshire could attract the best. What happens when Buffett is no longer able to lead Berkshire? Could a stronger, more diversified board optimize that transition?

What about the role of family on a board that is first among examples of good governance, Campbell Soup? The board is probably larger than it would otherwise be, says Bennett Dorrance, vice chairman of the Campbell finance committee. And, "I think we're more interested in what's going on. Family members ask more questions so perhaps the board meetings tend to go a little longer than they would otherwise. We peel the onion back further," says Dorrance, who, as the largest family shareholder, owns over 12 percent of the stock. "The company tries to keep us, the third and fourth generation, interested and informed in order to keep the family committed to long term growth."

On occasion, Campbell's officers make presentations just to the family, so they can think about issues before they go to the board. According to Dorrance, "the family is part of the reason we try not to make a major decision in a single board meeting." So a "big" issue will usually be on the agenda at several board meetings before a vote is taken. Sometimes, because of this approach, an opportunity is lost. In other cases, if a quick decision is necessary, the board will go along with management's recommendation.

As the family leader on the board, Dorrance generally doesn't find being a family member colors his role as a director. In fact, he believes that the family has "all made so much money" they can be more objective than others for whom the outcomes are financially important. He concedes it's probably tougher for Archie van Beuren, President of Campbell's Godiva Worldwide, a family member who has to prove himself constantly. "We are so dedicated to pay for performance."

Scripps is another major family-owned company which is maximizing the use of its board. . . CEO William Burleigh stepped down in September of 2000. The family's fourth generation is transitioning into power. "We are a formerly family owned company in which the melding together of outside board members and representatives of the next generation of the Scripps family become a happy challenge," Burleigh says. "We have a need for board members who are knowledgeable and yet broadly educated, so they can understand the universe in which all these changes are taking place." The majority of the voting stock is in family trusts, and twenty-eight members of the fourth generation inherit the majority. The family is led by Charles Scripps, the former chairman, who "decided to undertake a deliberate and carefully planned education program, where the fourth generation people can get up to speed on the business in which we are engaged and the history of the family."

A series of family meetings were a mix of reunion and educational sessions, bringing people in from the company along with an occasional outside expert. The majority of the family signed an agreement that, if any of them want to liquefy their holdings, they will first offer the shares to their cousins. Failing that, they will make the shares available to the company, before offering them to the open market. "This pretty much insulates us from mischief," says Burleigh. Additionally, the twenty-eight voted for two members of their generation, representing two branches of the family, to represent them on the board.

"Having the Scripps on the board," says Burleigh, is "helpful in letting the outside board members soak up the family legacy. They are very value centered, very decent folks who stand for the right things. The board members see that, and the melding takes place automatically." The question has come up, "we are outside board members, but the family has all the voting power. Do we really serve a purpose?" The answer, according to Burleigh, is "that the family looks to outsiders for direction and leadership, and the outsiders look to the family for the anchor and the values they represent. There is excellent chemistry."

Some companies turn to advisory boards to help them negotiate the pitfalls, instead of folding outside directors into the statutory board. A single, statutory board enables dialogue, synergy, mutual education, consensus building, and focus. A separate, advisory board allows the family to develop trust for the independent members, and the board can focus on strategic issues, apart from the family. In all cases, it is important to have family representation. If there are no qualified family members, either select an outside representative for the family or designate and train a prospective family director. Some companies have two family members sit on the advisory board, so the rest of the family knows that a single director hasn't been co-opted by outsiders.

Ivan Lansberg's preference is to have outside members "on line, with full accountability. There may be an intermediary step forming an advisory board, because the family is too scared. But, the real discipline of getting a board with real authority is part of what they are buying. If you form an advisory board, look at it as a transitional structure and not as the end game."

As advisory board member Bill Hawfield describes it, "the board helps the owner create the future he envisions. It's first about the owners, second about the shareholders and third about the company. The owner often creates the board, because he wants to create change in the company."

When the owner of a $25 million printing company in Diamond Bar, California, had a heart attack, he realized he had to formalize the company's structure and create some stability in the event he couldn't get back to work. His statutory board consisted of his mother, himself and his two brother employees, one in data processing and the other in marketing. A four-person advisory board was recruited, consisting of a director with marketing expertise, a director with finance credentials, a human resources expert, and a manager from a production company.

After a few meetings, the owner came in one day and told the advisory board that his doctors said he could no longer run the company. The board helped find a COO, who quickly became the CEO. Equally important, they helped the owner transition his two brothers out of the business in order to build a professional management team to increase the company's value. Through the process, the two other brothers learned that it was okay to be investors and not employees, and they both chose to leave. A package was structured for management as well as the family to participate in any sale of the business. Eight months later, as the family disengaged emotionally, the business was sold for more than twice revenue. Creation of a professional management team proved that the founder didn't have to be there for the company to grow and prosper. "The bottom line," says Hawfield, "is that the board is constituted to be an instrument of change. If change doesn't happen, the board ought to dissolve and go play golf."

At a $15 million trucking company in California, ownership is divided evenly among four brothers. There is a statutory board made up of the four brothers and their mother, an advisory board, and a family council that includes the brothers' wives. The advisory board was created by the brother CEO about five years ago, soon after his father died and anointed him first among equals. The CEO created the advisory board to make recommendations to him, which he then takes to the statutory board.

According to Bill Hawfield, the board helped define a job description, which defines the vital steps to success: creation of a strategic plan, a compensation and incentive program, and a strong organization to support the strategic plan. The board then negotiated the action plan for the year with the CEO with the appropriate measures, compensation triggers and results needed. The company is growing and profitable, and the advisory board can take a fair amount of the credit.

One of the greatest challenges for the trucking company is ensuring that there are real consequences for nonperformance. How does the CEO get his brother to improve marketing, which is a problem area? Can one brother really demote another or cut his pay? What right does the CEO have to tell his brother who owns 25 percent of the trucking company anything? In this case, the company hired a strong number two marketing executive.

According to Hawfield, who sits on the advisory board, a key challenge is deciding what to do with the company over the next twenty years. One brother believes the company's main purpose is to employ as many family members as possible. Another says, "no, let's run it like a professional company." This is where the family council comes in. One question posed to that council is "how do we define criteria going forward for new family members who want to come into the business?" The council has agreed that requirements will include a college degree and three years work experience outside the company.

"We're mainly there to help make the CEO effective," says Hawfield. "And to be there for the rest of the family—to create change through the CEO and elevate him to full CEO level." If the CEO chooses to maintain the status quo and opts in favor of employing as much family as possible, then the board's responsibility is to support that decision.

Ciminelli Development Company, New York, was formed in 1983. After the founder got the idea at a seminar, he created a board in 1989, when there were some twenty employees. With the transition of leadership from the founder to his son, Paul Ciminelli, president, the board has assumed increasing value. How? "It is a good sounding board. They hold us accountable for working not in, but on the business," says Ciminelli. The board, which meets three times a year with a fee of $1000 per meeting, has been "very effective" in structuring the ownership in the succession plan. The board has provided valuable advice on how to penetrate new markets and helped Ciminelli select investment bankers, because "they have been through that." Further, the board has helped redirect the strategy regarding expansion into certain geographic areas and deal with the family transition.

"Ironically," muses Ciminelli, "my father was afraid that the board wouldn't take their role seriously and challenge me enough." Ciminelli describes his father as a "classic entrepreneur, who depended on himself a lot, running a business from an operations perspective. I'm running it more from the perspective of being a strategist," Ciminelli says. The board is a group that "I can have a heart to heart with and get objective feedback. They have really helped me focus," says Ciminelli.

"Most important, they are people you can really trust, and they can challenge you. Without a doubt, things I am doing would not have been done without the board," he confides. The board has done a "good job in prodding me to find specific ways to work on the business from a family perspective. I get together on a weekly basis with my father and stay disciplined. These people have done a fabulous job of tackling the emotional issues that many boards would ignore." One of the issues in the transition has been whether Paul Ciminelli should have controlling interest of the development company. The board helped persuade the family that one person should be in control—Paul Ciminelli.

"At first," confides Ciminelli, "I was reluctant to talk about details and sensitive issues. But I sensed that the board knew exactly what was going on. It took about a year to become fully confident in the board. "When you look at a growing family business," advises Ciminelli, whose company now employs over ninety people, "you have got to look at where the company is going in the future and where it may be weak. Really put people on your board who are in the business you are going to be in in the future."

Add one point to your strategic board continuum quotient, if your board has a solid majority of strategically recruited, independent directors, and a ratio of at least three independent members to each family member.

Family

0   10
Captive Board   *Strategic Board*

Leadership
Value Added
Information
Diversity
The Money
Cronyism
Family
Conflicts
Insiders
Recruit
Strategically

NOTES

1. Richard L. Narva, Esq., "Creating Effective Corporate Governance in Family Businesses," *Director's Monthly,* June 1998, 6–8.
2. Pascal N. Levensohn, "The Problem of Emotion in the Boardroom," *Directors & Boards,* Spring 1999.
3. Legal brief. Report of Investigation in the Matter of the Cooper Companies, Inc. as It Relates to the Conduct of Cooper's Board of Directors, 12 December 1994.

Chapter 6

———◆———

Cronyism

◆ THE FIFTH MISTAKE: TOO MANY CRONIES ◆

An obvious conflict is one thing. But cronyism is an innocent thing, isn't it? What could be wrong with inviting your friends and colleagues to sit on your board? After all, these are the people you know best, the people you trust. These are the people who will support you, the people you respect. These are the people most like you. A powerful argument can be made for filling a board with people you already know—and it often is. Look at the overwhelming majority of corporate boards, and you will find friendships, alliances, interlocks, and a web of ties that weave through business, community and social activities. This is a real test of a strategic CEO and his board.

WHY NOT FILL YOUR BOARD WITH
PEOPLE YOU KNOW?

1. *You severely circumscribe your universe to your existing knowledge base if you do.* By restricting your board to your own circle, you immediately cut your options—without even having an opportunity to consider them. Your friends and colleagues may be good thinkers. But, are they the best? Your cronies may be successful at what they do, but is it relevant to your business? Is their skill set what you would pick if you were recruiting to your strategic plan? How do their capacities fare against your board matrix? Can your friends fast-forward your com-

pany? You already have the benefit of their friendship, advice and contacts. Do they need to be on your board?

Business Week lambasted Coca-Cola's board, where, in 1966, at least three directors were executives at companies to which Coca-Cola paid consulting, leasing, or bank fees, including more than $800,000 to SunTrust Banks. As it happens, SunTrust chairman and CEO James B. Williams sits on Coca-Cola's board and the CEO at the time, Robert C. Guizueta, sat on Mr. Williams' SunTrust board. Would Warren Buffett and Herbert Allen have had to call a meeting to tell Doug Ivester, after little more than two years on the job, that they had lost confidence in his ability to lead?[1] Would a more independent board have helped prevent the implosion that has since occurred at Coca-Cola, with the embarrassingly public unraveling of its management structure?

Consider ProLink the integrated golf course management company that installs its GPS plus distance-measuring software system in golf carts. More golfers than read *Golf Digest* are captive in golf carts for over four hours at a time, which translates into well over a billion minutes of internet time. "I'm really glad you hooked me up," says Roadrunner Hockey Team President Shawn Hunter of the ProLink board. "They are very smart people, especially in terms of technology. Everybody cares," he adds. "They have a lot at risk. We provide healthy insights that the original group [of investors on the board] couldn't." By recruiting outside his circle, the founder gained tremendous advantage.

2. *Cronyism tends to beget favors.* At the least, cronyism can divert—even diminish—the focus. And, it can temper the inclination to ask the hard questions. There is a temptation to substitute golf for governance. A strong leader can drive a company with a captive board through the sheer force of her charisma and will. But, when the crises come, the company is not well served.

Too often, board members are personal friends of the CEO and sit on the board as a favor to him. When it comes time to hold the CEO accountable for poor results or behavior, they hesitate until their reputations are on the line. The bonds of years of close friendships, respect for the legacy of a former executive, and deep ties of loyalty may cause the board to postpone critical decisions, to deliberate, to stall—and thereby to erode shareholder value.

"I have a strong aversion to relationships being too close," says Bobby Inman. "A board performs at its best when operating in an amicable environment where people are respectful of others, listen and respond civilly. I'm not an advocate of lots of time at resorts and at golf. I've had glimpses of clubby boards. I have not been dazzled by the governance in those situations. They don't inquire enough about what management is about."

There are untold numbers of companies "that have gone out of business strictly because of cronyism," according to CEO/author Harvey MacKay. "The CEO loads up his board with cronies who never tell him he's wrong, and he eventually gets in trouble."

There are too many examples of directors who are on board for nonstrategic reasons, who lack the breadth or will to offer proactive assistance. And there are too many directors who abuse their positions, an unhappy outgrowth of cronyism where the expectations are fuzzy. Remember when executive vice president of MacAndrews & Forbes Holdings Inc., took a call from Vernon Jordan—a board member for the firm's Revlon Inc. unit—asking him to talk to a "bright young woman" about finding her an entry level job in New York? A few months later, Mr. Jordan called Ronald O. Perelman, chairman of Revlon and its holding company, to enthusiastically recommend Monica again. Mr. Perelman then told the senior vice president who had interviewed Monica Lewinsky, "Let's see if we can be helpful. . . ." To be interviewed by a senior vice president for an entry level position is a huge advantage. Not surprisingly, Revlon eventually offered Monica Lewinsky a job, but later retracted the offer after learning of Ken Starr's investigation.

As Christina Duff and Joann Lublin wrote in *The Wall Street Journal*, "Mr. Jordan's calls to executives, and their subsequent quick follow-up, help make clear just how much the 'it's who you know' rule still applies in corporate job-hunting." The grand jury got the message. "If ever any of us needs a job," the jury forewoman asked Mr. Jordan, "can we feel free to come to you?" "Madame Forelady," Mr. Jordan responded, "my door swings back on welcome hinges to anybody on this grand jury."[2]

It is fully arguable that it is appropriate, even beneficial, for directors to funnel resources to their companies whenever possible. And, what resources are more valuable than excellent prospective employees? But, did Vernon Jordan have any idea whether Monica would actually be a good employee? Was his allegiance to his friend, President Clinton, or his company?

Should a director be trying to get a junior employee a job? Is this good corporate governance? Or does it waffle into micromanagement? Charles Elson, director of three boards, including Sunbeam Corp., sums it up. "To ask a CEO of a major corporation to hire someone for a low-level position who has no experience in the industry appears to be a quid pro quo. . . . It obligates the director to the CEO. It creates the kind of conflict that prevents oversight."[3] Most importantly, how does it serve the shareholders?

No one denies that access, whether it be for start-ups or Fortune 500s, is an invaluable, expected and appropriate director attribute. Vernon Jordan serves on ten boards and is in demand for more. In at least one case, his firm profits handsomely as well. He is not in demand for his operating experience, because he has none. But important people return his telephone calls.[4] Is that enough?

"Vernon Jordan comes in for a lot of criticism," observes James Kristie, Editor of *Directors & Boards*. "I'm agnostic about whether he deserves it or not. The CEOs know he sits on nine other boards. They don't have Vernon on the board to approve the quarterly dividend. They have him on the board for when the company runs into problems. The CEOs can call Vernon and say 'I need you to make a call for me.' Maybe you can criticize it. But it may be cheaper to pay $100,000 for director fees than to hire his firm for a couple million dollars."

In some cases, for some companies, directors like Vernon Jordan are valuable. Another new board member whose connections will be worth it is Melinda French Gates, who was named to Drugstore.com's board in August 1999; she is a former Microsoft employee, and also happens to be the wife of Bill Gates.

INTERLOCKING DIRECTORSHIPS

Interlocking directorships breed beholden directors. If I am on your board and you are on mine, a so-called interlock, will our allegiance be to each other instead of the shareholders? "Back-scratching can be a problem," says John Olson, attorney and governance expert. "I'm going to give you a salary increase and you give me one." The first thing he looks for in directors is how independent are they? How intelligent are they? Are they social pals of the CEO? A study by University of Illinois economics professor Kevin Hallock found that in companies with interlocking directorates, CEO compensation was up to 17 percent higher on average than in companies without interlocking directorships.

Another issue which applies to director CEOs in general is the "kindred spirit" phenomenon. Since CEOs do not generally like their boards criticizing them, they are disinclined to be critical of the CEO on whose board they serve.

A particularly incestuous relationship is at Grand Casinos and Rainforest Café, where Lyle Berman is CEO at both companies. In 1997, President David Rogers and CEO Joel Waller of Wilson's–The Leather Experts were the compensation committee at both Berman companies. As such, they gave Berman $6 million in stock options at Rainforest Café, and they repriced his one million stock options at Grand Casinos from $32 down to $11 per share. Berman and his president at Grand Casinos, Thomas Brosig, in turn make up Rogers' and Waller's compensation committee. One further interlock: Brosig, Rogers and Waller all worked for Lyle Berman at the Leather Express, a business founded by the Berman family.

Other boards that have had interlocks include Cisco Systems, Emerson Electric, Lucent Technologies, Honeywell, Citigroup, Hilton Hotels, and Walt Disney.[5] *Business Week* describes the board of Nations-Bank Corp. as oversized, with twenty members, and among "the most clubby and incestuous." Five NationsBank directors serve on the board of Bassett Furniture Industries, Inc. Another five are directors of So-noco Products Co. Three more serve on the board of Ruddick Corp, a diversified holding company in Charlotte, N.C.

NationsBank Chairman Hugh L. McColl Jr. was a director on five outside boards. The Chairmen of four of those companies for whom Mr. McColl sits as a director sit on Mr. McColl's NationsBank board. Five of the company's outside directors are top executives or owners of companies that do business with NationsBank. For example in 1995, NationsBank paid $15 million in rent to a joint venture partnership managed by a company of which director Thomas G. Cousins is chairman and CEO.[6]

Heinz has been described as a "textbook example of what a board should not be: a cozy club of loyalists headed by a powerful and charismatic chieftain." Anthony J. F. O'Reilly, Heinz chairman until 2000, and CEO until 1998 hosted the 15th annual three-day Heinz 57 Stakes in Ireland, when Heinz was laying off 2500 employees and about to embark on a shut down of some twenty-four factories worldwide. More than half of the 500 guests for the annual celebration were flown in from around the world and feted at lavish parties. O'Reilly's compensation placed him among the five CEOs cited by *Business Week* as giving shareholders the least for their money. In 1996, when the cutbacks were in the works, O'Reilly received a new options grant on 750,000 shares. As fortunes turned, TIAA-CREF, the pension fund with a $113 million stake in Heinz, and CalPERS, the California pension fund, took notice and began advocating reforms.

The Heinz board had all the signs of a toxic board. It included a former U. S. House speaker, Thomas S. Foley; former Coca-Cola president, Donald R. Keogh; former vice chairman of Mobil, Herman J. Schmidt; Richard M. Cyert, president of Carnegie Mellon University; and Nicholas F. Brady, chairman of Dillon Read & Co. Of the nineteen board members, ten were insiders. The CEO was chairman of the nominating committee. Three directors were ex-Heinz executives. The outside directors never met without the CEO, there was no governance committee, and no share-ownership requirement for directors. At least five of the outside directors were over 70 years of age, and three were in their late 60s. And, three outsiders were directors of Mobil Corporation, along with. O'Reilly. But, where were the outside directors as the company spiraled downward?

In contrast, Ashland Inc. decided as far back as 1996, that interlocking directorships are inappropriate. Their guidelines specify that the CEO and other principal officers of Ashland may not serve on the board of a company for which an Ashland nonemployee director serves as an officer.[7]

The reality is that, at the overwhelming majority of boards, the CEO and the directors have a personal connection. And, those connections diminish the likelihood of a fresh perspective. According to Michael Burke, "By definition, they are not at arm's length. You are not going to get the same injection of truth serum."

OTHER SOURCES OF CONFLICT

■ *Directors who sit on the boards or are employees of competitive companies.* More potential conflicts exist with the flood of mergers and acquisitions and with convergence, especially in the finance, telecommunications, and technology sectors. An honorable director will recuse herself in matters of conflict, but those are often the issues where the strategic thinking of all directors is most valuable. At some point, the lines begin to blur.

■ *Consultants who represent both sides of the table.* An example is Wells Fargo and Norwest's $34 billion merger in which both companies used Goldman Sachs to advise them in the merger. "The minute you enter a transaction where you have failed to establish the independence of your advisers, you have virtually assured a shareholders' suit," says the attorney who filed a lawsuit, Andrew Entwistle of Wohl & Entwistle, New York. On the other hand, NationsBank and BankAmerica decided against dual representation, although they each typically use Wachtell, Lipton, Rosen & Katz. "It doesn't create an unsolvable conflict of interest by definition, but there's a comfort zone if you avoid that situation," explained NationsBank's Dick Stilley.[8]

■ *Directors or employees of suppliers, competitors and customers.* It is tough to be objective when confronted with a proposal that would compromise your relationship or make it less lucrative. And, it is not easy to prioritize shareholders' interests, when your future is at stake. Further, are these the people you want knowing your numbers, your plans, and your problems?

UNIONS

If labor understands and aligns their thinking with that of management and the owners, the argument goes, relations will be bolstered.

The boards of Inland Steel and United Airlines are examples. North-west Airlines has three union directors. The challenge for the union directors is how to handle confidential information that could impact labor. To whom is their allegiance?

Governance counselor Ira Millstein, partner at Weil, Gotshal & Manges, recommended that the board of Delta not include a voting union member because of conflict of interest concerns. "We agreed that we don't want a director representing a specific constituency," says Gerald Grinstein, chairman of the Delta board.[9]

MERGERS AND ACQUISITIONS

Probably the most notorious case of a conflicted board in 1998 was at Cendant Corp., the result of the merger between CUC, which operates a discount shopping club business, and HFS, which owned Avis and Ramada Inn Hotels. Walter Forbes, the CEO of CUC, was to be Chair-man until 2000, when HFS' CEO Henry Silverman would take over. At CUC, phony club memberships were used to inflate sales and profits, resulting in a $300 million scandal that toppled Forbes prematurely. Forbes claimed that Silverman was distorting Forbes's role in the scheme at CUC to gain the chairmanship sooner.

The Cendant board numbered a whopping twenty-eight and was split evenly between allies of Forbes and Silverman. According to the New York Post, each faction was trying to freeze the other out. Both factions hired public relations gurus to take their story to the street. Ultimately, Silverman prevailed and Forbes and 10 CUC directors re-signed. In the meantime, the directors repriced stock options for senior management and, at one point, the $20 billion Cendant had no certified financial statements and could not access capital markets. The stock plummeted 46 percent, and more than sixty lawsuits were brought against the company.[10]

Forbes left with some $35 million in cash plus additional options. As of May 1999, the board consisted of seventeen directors, including five insiders, four investors, no women, the president and COO of America Online, and Brian Mulroney, the former prime minister of Canada. How does that payoff to Forbes or the money spent on fueling the feud help the shareholders going forward?

INSTITUTIONAL INVESTORS

CalPERS and a number of other pension funds have adjusted their by-laws to allow their members to hold board seats. Lens Fund Principals Robert Monks and Nell Minow vie for board seats on companies they target. Could this be considered a conflict? Will they be tempted to recommend investments in the companies on whose boards they sit? Or will they be tempted to bypass those companies when targeting companies for governance reform?

Further, there is rising controversy about board practices at these very organizations propounding best practices. For example, Paul Schnitt, *Sacramento Bee* staff writer, reported that prompted by controversy surrounding the re-election last year of its president, a divided governing board of the California Public Employees Retirement System voted to sharply limit written ballot statements in future elections, which offer dissenters an opportunity to explain their concerns.[11]

INDEPENDENCE

All these conflicts can color independence, the crux of strategic governance. The council of Institutional Investors, a coalition of over 100 pension funds whose assets exceed $1 trillion, defines an independent board member simply as someone "whose directorship constitutes his or her only connection to the company."[12] To minimize potential conflicts of interest, consider asking the following questions, recommended by two lawyers writing for *The National Law Journal*.

- Do you own, or are you an officer, director or employee of any enterprise that competes with this company? Information sharing is the issue.
- Have you or your immediate family had any interest in a transaction or proposed transaction with this company?
- Is the company indebted to you for any advance of money?
- Have you or your immediate family been indebted to the company?
- Do officers or directors of this company serve on the board of any other companies you own, that employ you or of which you are an officer of director? In other words, would there be any interlocking directorships?
- What percentage of your gross income will consist of the fees that you receive as a director for this company?
- Are you related to any member of the board of directors or to any officer of the company?
- In which charities are you involved? Are you employed by an organization that receives benefits from the company?
- Do you have any other relationship with the company that

could be construed to influence your ability to exercise your independent judgement as a director?[13]

No checklist delivers independence. Independence hinges on the integrity of the individual director. On paper, a board can look entirely independent. But, there are a lot of ways to connect the dots. The Blue Ribbon Committee on Audit Effectiveness believes that the current NYSE and NASD standards on independence allow too much discretion and should be fortified.[14]But, these are very difficult things to regulate. And, sometimes the rule can substitute for the reality.

As investor Steve McConnell says, "Some of the trickiest things to maneuver are conflicts of interest. I've found it in the most discreet situations. A director may have inside information on trades. You may see it in business areas." The SEC does not require disclosure of board interlocks between senior executives and directors that involve nonprofit and private companies, or of many professional, personal and financial relationships.

When a director makes a suggestion, McConnell says, "my first thought is 'why are they saying that?' Do they have a conflict of interest? You've got to dissect everything. People are in these things to make money." "Board conflicts are often subtle and difficult to assess," Ken West underlines. "You don't know whom outsiders play golf with." It is the undisclosed conflicts that can undermine the process.

Sometimes directors' only vested interest in their role is holding onto it. As Shelby Yastrow says, "There are conflicts every day. Insiders are conflicted because the CEO can fire them, so, of course, they vote with the CEO. Suppliers are going to be conflicted, because they don't want another product to take the place of theirs. Even an outside, independent director may be conflicted, but it isn't as obvious or problematical."

Many would say an independent director is something of an oxymoron in today's companies. The directors are selected by the CEO. The candidates run unopposed, and management counts the votes. "In the rare case of an opposing slate," according to Robert Monks, "management gets to use the shareholders' money to pay for their side of the contest. The CEO determines the directors' pay, and the directors set the CEOs pay. It's a very cozy relationship, and one that has been most profitable for both parties."[15]

Doug Foshee, the CEO who has revitalized the Nuevo Energy board, says, "I think it goes without saying that independence is the most basic of requirements for successful governance." How can management really look their investors in the eye and say they are only interested in the shareholders when their compensation committees are populated with former employees or other insiders? How can directors claim to be independent when their law firms provide significant services for fees to the company in question? How can a director claim independence when he or she has strong personal ties to the CEO?"

James Kristie believes "independence is a state of mind. You could have seemingly the most conflicted director turn out to be the most independent minded person on the board." Unless we sit in the boardroom, it is impossible to know whether a conflict is reality or fiction. However, the appearance of conflict matters. And, so does its commission.

According to the Investor Responsibility Research Center, about 150 directors of companies on the Standard & Poor's 500-stock index had conflicts of interest. By their measure, only a quarter of large U.S. companies have a majority of independent directors—ones that are neither former employees nor have personal or financial ties to the company. And, more than half still employ takeover defenses.[16] This excludes the web of less apparent ties that color independence. If you are proactively recruiting a board, why subject yourself to the increasing tempo of criticism against such conflicts, perceived or real?

If your board has no cronies, interlocks, or conflicted directors whose allegiance to your shareholders is compromised, add one point to your strategic board continuum quotient.

Cronyism

0
Captive Board

10 Strategically
Strategic Board

Leadership
Value Added
Information
Diversity
The Money
Cronyism
Family
Conflicts
Insiders
Recruit

NOTES

1. "What Really Happened at Coke?" *Fortune*, 10 January 2000, 114.
2. Christina Duff and Joann S. Lublin, "Board Games," *The Wall Street Journal*, 5 October 1998.
3. Ibid.

4. Dan R. Dalton and Katherine M. Daily, "What's Wrong with Having Friends on the Board," *Across the Board*, March 1999.

5. AFL-CIO Executive Pay Watch Web site, "Put Your Fellow CEO on the Compensation Committee."

6. John A. Byrne, "The Best & Worst Boards," *Business Week*, 25 November 1996.

7. Robert Stobaugh, "The Ashland Inc. Board Guidelines," *Director's Monthly*, April 1997.

8. "Beware When Bankers Work Both Sides of the Table," *Director's Alert*, August 1998.

9. "Why Did the Delta Board Reject a 'Union' Member?" *Director's Alert*, September 1998.

10. "Cendant Civil War Getting Personal," *New York Post*, 24 July 1998.

11. *Sacramento Bee*, 21 May 1999.

12. AFL-CIO Executive Pay Watch Web site, "Executive Pay Watch: Too Close for Comfort," July 1999.

13. Barbara J. Dawson and Patrick J. Barrett, "Director Conflicts," *The National Law Journal*, 7 September 1998.

14. "Report and Recommendations of the Blue Ribbon Committee on Improving the Effectiveness of Corporate Audit Committees," 1999.

15. Robert A. G. Monks and Nell Minow, Sears Case Study, 1996.

16. Daniel Bogler, "Corporate Governance Raises Few Hackles," *Financial Times*, 22 April 1999.

Chapter 7

———— ◆ ————

The Money

Accoording to James Kristie, "Directors are one of the last great bargains. They are underpaid for the work they do and the responsibility they assume." Constructive boards are responsible for untold millions going to the bottom line. The value of a single idea, of strategic succession planning, of risk avoidance, the value of one mistake prevented—is incalculable. These are the stories that rarely get told. Or measured.

DIRECTORS' COMPENSATION

In 1999, the average annual compensation for directors at public companies, exclusive of stock, was $38,216. This figure includes an annual fee of $30,131 and a per-meeting fee of $1357. Committee fees, paid by 91 percent of the companies, average $1058.[1] At small to midsize companies, the annual retainers averaged $10,000, and fees averaged $1000 for board meetings and $500 for committee meetings.[2] Pay is trending straight up. In 1998, those with the highest board retainers were Travelers Group, $100,000 (all in stock); Monsanto, $90,000 (part stock); Sears Roebuck & Co., $90,000 (part stock); and Alcoa, $85,000.[3]

There is some debate about meeting fees. Some ask why should directors be paid for doing the job for which they were hired. However, meeting fees not only encourage attendance at meetings, they also compensate directors for any extra time required in carrying out their duties.

DIRECTORS' STOCK

Most agree that stock ownership helps align directors' interests with those of the shareholders. Korn/Ferry reports that 93 percent of respondents to their annual survey believe directors should be compensated with at least some stock. And, 53 percent of surveyed companies require their board members to own shares in the company. At banks and insurance companies, that number is 66 percent, and it is 65 percent at insurance companies. Retailers are least likely to require directors to own stock, 31 percent.

Eighty-four percent of all public companies compensate their directors with some form of company stock. Forty-two percent compensate with stock options only, and 31 percent offer stock grants only. The annual median dollar value of stock given to directors is $12,500. All pharmaceuticals, 93 percent of the healthcare providers, and 86 percent of technology companies offer stock as compensation for their directors.[4]

According to Grant Thornton, the median small-to-midsize-company stock option grant to directors is 4750 shares, compared to 1000 shares for large company directors. One in four of the board members in small to midsize public companies own at least 3 percent of the stock in their companies. In contrast, less than 2 percent of total board members at large public companies own at least 3 percent of company stock.[5]

At least two studies indicate that an outside director with a sizable stake in a corporation may be more likely to question and challenge management's proposals. Outside directors who do not own significant amounts of stock are more likely to act as employees of the firm due to the compensation they receive.[6] Not only does stock tie directors to the outcome, it offers them an opportunity to profit in a significant way.

For the lucky few, that motivator can be powerful indeed. Companies whose directors earned the highest compensation in 1988 include:

Pfizer	$258,147
Seagate	$313,333
Dell	$343,017
Compaq	$362,448
Sun Microsystems	$409,500[7]

Attorney John Olson says "Some directors don't have enough skin in the game to hurt them. Some have huge net worths and very little money invested." According to Bill Crist, President of CalPERS, there is no magic number, but probably it should be in the tens of thousands of dollars in value. John Vogelstein, Mattel director and investment banker, believes there "are far too many 100-share directors engaged in determining the fate of multibillion dollar corporations."[8]

One guideline is for directors to be awarded the same multiples as are given to the CEO, about three to five times pay. The test is whether the holding can meaningfully impact an individual's net worth. The commitment to retain a significant portion of the stock while the director is in office is important also. As Intel director Arthur Rock says, "I invest a lot of money, and it helps. If I don't, I can't get my points across."

Nell Minow, founder of Corporate Library, talks about her "personal favorite moment." At the annual meeting of Stone & Webster when directors were elected, she asked each director to explain why they thought the stock was a bad investment. "I have a lot of stock," she told them. "I want to know why you don't." A director should believe in the company. If she doesn't think the company is worth investing in, how can she represent those who do?

An exception to the trend is Coca-Cola, which pays directors entirely in cash, plus retirement benefits, health and dental coverage, and life insurance, the type of benefits most companies are phasing out, because they tend to compromise independence.

When Al Dunlap, ousted CEO of Sunbeam Co., brought Stetson Law School Professor Charles Elson onto his board as the "corporate governance type," Dr.Elson was required to buy $100,000 in Sunbeam stock. When the stock price began to fall in 1998, the board was told that the bad first quarter was an aberration. But, the board learned that the second quarter would be worse and that the company was in trouble. The board voted to terminate Dunlap, and Elson said his equity position played a role in his support of that decision.

"The fiduciary duty was important, no question. But it had to do with the fact that each of us had had substantial investments that had suffered," said Elson. "If the boiler blows in a house you don't own, it's someone else's problem. But, if you own the house, it's your problem." Marjorie Fine, director of CREF, the pension fund, disagrees, "I don't want the directors to treat the company like their own property. They are overseeing it for other constituents."[9]

At Ashland, to avoid tying directors to the status quo, the board avoids any compensation elements that vest only after a specific period of service. Directors are required to own Ashland common stock having a value of at least five times their annual retainer within five years of their election to the board.[10]

What happens when companies fail to perform? Orthologix is an orthopedic devices company in Phoenix, whose 1997 revenues of $77 million collapsed to $41 million in 1998, with a responding stock plunge of 49 percent. Board member Jock Holliman, who owns some 100,000 shares of the distressed company, says "I can stand up at the board meetings and feel the heat with the shareholders."

Companies are aligning director pay more closely with incentives provided to executives. At Harnischfeger Industries, which makes heavy machinery for mining and papermaking, directors receive an annual retainer of $33,600 and committee and meeting fees of $1,250, with incentive compensation based on the same Economic Value Added performance targets used for the executives.[11]

ADC Telecommunications uses a return-on-equity (ROE) goal. Directors receive start-up grants of 8000 options. If the company achieves at least a 10 percent ROE, each director is awarded 8000 more options. If Bergen Brunswig Corp. achieves a 10 percent ROE, their directors receive a grant of 2000 options. Carolina Power & Light Company pays an $8000 retainer that is deferred in stock units. There are ten performance measures that the company must meet. The company matches 50 percent of the stock deferral if five measures are met and grants an extra 10 percent for each additional performance measure that is met. Directors can double their retainer if the company achieves all ten performance measures.

At Lincoln National Corporation, directors are eligible to receive a bonus and a service award based on total shareholder return compared with fourteen peer companies. The maximum award is $41,000 if the total shareholder return is the best of the peer group over three years. At Rouge Steel Company, no options are awarded if return on sales (ROS) is 2.3 percent or under. Options are awarded on a graduated scale, so that a ROS of 7 percent or more triggers an award of 1500 options.[12]

Retirement plans are being phased out, because they can color a director's objectivity. Kellogg converted their plan into a stock grant available to directors when they retire. As Bennett Dorrance, vice chairman of the Finance Committee at Campbell's Soup says, "In reality, a good board is worth the money. If you have a good board, and it is recognized to be a good board, it's going to put money in the stockholders' pockets." But the whole issue of aligning directors' interests with shareholders through stock may be overplayed.

Some argue that it is inappropriate to have directors set their own pay, and that this, in itself, constitutes a conflict. Most agree that the measure of corporate governance—and thus the reward—must be long term. TIAA-CREF President Bill Crist says the minimum stock award should be tied to a ten-year period.

What is not tracked is the number of failed companies whose stock compensated directors fail to be rewarded for their service. Many of those directors are compensated entirely in stock, so essentially they serve for free. Watch for a major "readjustment" as companies figure out how to compensate these directors.

Carl Hagberg says, "I feel personally offended by the theory that a board member who has a legally binding fiduciary duty to investors will do a better job of watching out for them if given stock. The evidence is that money is the last thing that influences someone to join a board. When you accept a position to be a fiduciary for thousands of people, it should override any personal consideration."

Richard Narva believes that if a director has "too great a prospect of making a significant financial killing, it's not possible to be independent. You take someone with a nice salary and put him on a Fortune 500 board, and the limousine picks you up at home and flies you and your spouse in the private jet, and the chauffeur takes your spouse around shopping. If you need one more year to cash in your options," he says, "you explain to me where the independence is." The danger lies in directors being perceived as privileged insiders watering at the trough they are pledged to protect.

CEO COMPENSATION

The most inflammatory governance issue is the massive surge in CEO pay, which many say is enabled by indifferent boards, at best, and conflicted boards, at worst. Igniting the controversy is the gaping disparity between pay at the top and pay for the average worker. In 1973, the typical wage earner was paid about $1/50$ the compensation of the Fortune 50 CEO. By 1998, the wage earner's pay was less than $1/350$ of the CEO's compensation. In 1998, CEOs of the top 200 companies were paid, on average, over $8 million.[13] In 1999, compensation packages for the CEOs of the largest public companies surged 24 percent, to about $9.4 million.[14]

Human capital has soared to 75 percent of the value input today. Thus, not only is it right, it is also sound business to incentivize all employees, not just the top layer. This issue becomes especially significant in the global context, where comparisons are stark and increasingly unavoidable as our economies merge across borders.

Because compensation is such a heady target, it has become a rallying cry for activists. Labor unions are joining other activists in waving this red flag in front of their members. Union web sites consistently harangue against pay extremes. Fifty percent of the resolutions filed by the International Brotherhood of Teamsters deal with director or executive pay. Institutional investors have led the charge and continue to amass ammunition against excesses. For instance, the Council of Institutional Investors challenged forty firms in 1998 on various pay issues, including retirement plans, option pricing, and golden parachutes. Groups such as the Interfaith Center for Corporate Responsibility are concentrating on linking compensation to social issues.[15] And, Nell Minow has begun Corporatelibrary.com to make CEOs contacts public.

Charles Collins, co-director of United for a Fair Economy (UFE), frames the issue in a particularly provocative way that demonstrates its potentially explosive nature. Using a ratio of 326 to 1, Collins invites audiences to imagine, "If the Washington Monument is 555 feet tall and reflects the average 1998 CEO paycheck, guess how tall the average worker's paycheck would be? Answer: 21 inches."[16] The campaign is on, and the public is responding.

A GE shareholder, Scott Klinger, brought a similar analogy down to earth. At the annual meeting in Cleveland in April 1999, he argued in support of a proposal by Trillium Asset Management Corp., which manages about $570 million. The proposal sought to cap the pay of Jack Welch, CEO of General Electric. Welch's 1997 compensation totaled about $40 million. In 1998, salary and bonus were $10 million, realized options gains were $46.5 million, and restricted shares were valued at $27 million. "Think of Mr. Welch's pay as the height of the Empire State Building in New York City," suggests Klinger. By comparison the pay of a U.S. factory worker would be only a few inches high and the pay of a Mexican worker less than one inch high, amounting to little piles of dust."[17] The cap was overwhelmingly rejected by the board. Here is a CEO icon, who has increased shareholder value in a tough market. Should this be the focal point of shareholder attention? Or should it be the larger, less framable issues of succession and competitive vision and depth of management?

Charles B. Wang, CEO of software firm Computer Associates, is a favorite example of pay that does not track the value. Wang's earnings from May 1995 to May 1998 totaled $1.1 billion for three years of work, or an average of $367 million per year. Shareholder return at CA over a fourteen-year period beat the S&P index by about two to one. However, on May 21, 1998 when Wang received shares totaling $670 million, the stock plunged nearly 31 percent in a single day.

Citigroup CEO Sanford Weil took home more than $52 million in compensation and exercised $156 million in "reloading" stock options. For the same year, 1998, the return to shareholders was minus 9 percent. At Rental Service Corp, stock performance nose-dived over 36 percent in 1998, yet Chairman and CEO Martin Reid's pay soared 592 percent to about $4.5 million.

In June, 1999, Simula CEO Don Townsend stood up at the annual shareholders' meeting, and touted the air bag and airline seat manufacturer's rapid growth since 1992, going from two products to fourteen, adding six factories and quintupling the number of employees. The company was poised, Townsend smiled, to report its seventh consecutive year of record sales. He ended his presentation with emotional anecdotes of lives saved by side impact safety devices. No one applauded. The stock had plummeted 66 percent during the last year. And Simula had failed to make a profit on $42 million in sales in 1996, $67 million in 1997, or $100 million in sales in 1998.

One shareholder said, "You don't add value to the company. You just add volume." Another shareholder, with a $250,000 investment, complained that, "Some of the directors do not own one share. How can you expect them to feel the same pain as me?" Seventy-eight-year-old retailer and community leader Walter Switzer said he was shocked to learn that executives received raises and bonuses in 1998, just because the company logged record sales. "My plea to you is: Please don't reward our executives for booking business that is not profitable. . . . If you cannot make a profit in 1999, don't come back with the same executives and board members with more excuses. Come back with the news that you have sold the company to someone who can make a profit."[18]

Ann McLaughlin, director at GM and former Secretary of Labor, says that "some CEO pay today looks like the Internet—bloated, cryptic and embarrassingly obscene. Obscene pay will continue as long as directors are willing to pay for it," McLaughlin believes.

COMPENSATION COMMITTEE

The burden of fairly defining pay falls to the board's compensation committee, although the responsibility is the full board's. Roy Herberger, President of Thunderbird, The American Graduate School of International Management, says, "without a doubt, the compensation committee is the most difficult board assignment. Despite its traditional laxness, the compensation committee must, by law, ensure that compensation bears a reasonable relation to services performed for the corporation. Any amount unrelated to services rendered constitutes a waste or spoilation of corporate assets and may thus be actionable by the shareholders."

So, the responsibilities of compensation committees are mushrooming, not only because of the complexity of CEO packages, but because of the need to synchronize pay throughout the company, including the board, and to then defend those packages to corporate constituencies. Most compensation committees lay out specific duties. Typically, they create their own mission statement and charter, detail committee responsibilities, and set a compensation committee calendar. Obviously, evaluation is an integral part of the process and is frequently included in compensation committee duties. (See Chapter 10.) The SEC has mandated that compensation committee members must be independent directors. With the spotlight on pay, compensation committees are starting to feel like real work. Some directors, in fact, are receiving double pay. And, probably with justification.

In the case of Computer Associates, did the directors on the compensation committee really understand how the payout to Wang would work? Compensation approvals used to be, and in too many cases still are, perfunctory. Whatever management and supporting outside consultants recommend tends to be approved. Worse, as Ann McLaughlin points out, the "manner in which compensation is set and by whom is often incestuous. It's meted out by people appointed by the people being compensated and the outside consultants retained by them."[19]

One prevalent abuse is the number of CEOs who sit on their own compensation committees. Since setting the pay of the CEO is the most important charge of those committees, can it be anything other than self-serving or, at best, a conflict? Before Donald Dye was terminated at Callaway Golf late in 1998, he sat on the compensation committee that awarded him some $16 million for the prior year. Other companies where CEOs served on their compensation committees include Carnival, Just for Feet, Mesa Air Group, SEI Investments, Sonic, Sterling Software, and Baldo Electric.[20]

Compensation Consultants

One problem is that consultants are used to validate pay scales and performance awards and thereby help to protect directors from lawsuits. Essentially, consultants are benchmarking existing salaries. The pay, then, moves up from there. Independent thought becomes a low priority. Roy Herberger says, "I can prove to anybody that the CEO in a financial services company is worth anywhere from $1 million to $5 million. I can prove it, anytime you want, by hiring the right consultant. Whether the CEO deserves that or not is another matter. Most CEOs have in their left hand drawers comparables on what other CEOs are paid."

Steve McConnell says he finds compensation consulting "distasteful" because "it isn't about getting to real answers. It's about getting more." Robert Monks, Lens Chairman, points out how difficult it is to "get any competent professional willing to get crosswise with any corporate management." Director and former Federal Reserve board member Martha Seger worries that there is "too much reliance on consultants. At the end of the day, it's the directors' job to make the decision. It's not the consultant."

It's a delicate matter. In one instance, when he was chair of a compensation committee, Roy Herberger and his committee recommended a raise for a CEO. The CEO turned it down, because he was insulted it wasn't more. On the other hand, Herberger has seen situations where CEOs don't protect themselves. "I ask the CEO to tell me how you think you did. And, then tell me what you think your package ought to be this year. I find out if we're really far apart." Despite the heated debate, many directors agree with Herberger who thinks compensation is a "grossly over exaggerated issue. I've never run into something that's totally egregious."

No one wants to think his CEO is worth less than his peers. Nor does any board want to send that message to the public or the markets. Everyone has an objective of coming in at the 75th percentile of the pay scale, says former Fluor chairman David Tappan, so "there is an endless ratcheting up of compensation." Further, no one wants to risk losing a star. "You have to look at your own CEO and make very sure that his compensation does not make him vulnerable. When you search hard and find someone who increases shareholder value," says Bobby Inman, "you have to look after him."

Attorney John Olson, who consults to Fortune 500 boards, agrees. "The board says our company management is as good an anybody else's. That's how these raises get to these phenomenal levels. The CEOs say, 'I'm going to quit,' and it's a never-ending spiral." There are only a couple of consultants, he points out, talking about the handful of compensation experts most boards turn to. "I've never heard of a consultant recommending that management get a decrease." It's better than it was, Olson says, because people are getting embarrassed. "The board should ask 'How does that benefit the stockholders?' Management should be compensated on whether the company does well over the long term and not on the basis of bringing in a consultant. Who brings them in the first place but management?"

Ken West, Senior Consultant for Corporate Governance at TIAA-CREF, agrees. "No self-respecting compensation committee wants to say it pays its CEO below the median. Many times they react as if they are trying to keep up with the Joneses. Most of the mistakes are in the stock based plans," West claims. "Directors often don't figure out in advance what the potential payoff could be. Is it really performance based? Or can the CEO get rich by just running in place? It's the megagrants that are the biggest issue."

"Everybody looks fast running past trees," Director Walter Auch remarks. "There are an awful lot of people who seem to be doing a better job than they really are." You should not have to pay more just because of a title. When a large bonus is on the line, Auch believes you are going to set objectives that are easier to meet, so the CEO can "earn" the bonus. "If you pay me a very generous salary, than you can give me objectives that are more challenging." Then, the bonus begins to live up to its name.

According to *The Wall Street Journal*, "CEOs were supposed to get top dollar only when they got top results. Now, many are getting top dollar—no matter what the results."[21] As Robert Monks says, "I couldn't begin to tell you what these packages mean. Compensation has become a political issue that can't be ignored. . . . It's a fairness issue. . . . There comes a time when people start asking 'where were you?' I think it's becoming an atrocity."[22]

Performance-Based Pay

A second issue is performance-based pay parity within a company, or at least for the executives. At Chevron, for example, the management compensation committee deals with the pay of the top forty people in the company. Only 25 percent of Chevron's CEO Ken Derr's compensation is guaranteed salary. Maurice Myers, Chairman and CEO, Yellow Corp., says, "If the CEO is really evaluated and the compensation committee really does determine his pay and incentives, it creates the right balance between the CEO and the board. The day I walked into Yellow Corp., I presented my goals for the upcoming year to the board. At the end of each year, I take those goals, and I write a letter to the chairman of the compensation committee in which I say, 'Okay, here are my goals and here are my accomplishments against those goals.' I then sit down with the compensation committee, and we discuss my letter. And then at the next board meeting, we go through the same process for the whole board."[23]

Campbell's Soup is intensely committed to pay for performance with "win" and "win plus" incentives. If Campbell's performs on a par with the top quartile of peer food companies, employees get something extra. If Campbell's is the top company, employees get something on top of that. "It's been good for us," says Bennett Dorrance. "We won't get anything this year on short term bonuses," he notes, referring to the downturn in Campbell's numbers under their new CEO in 1999.

"If you want a management team that preserves your job, a company alive and well and growing, in today's market, there is a market cost to that decision," insists Bill Franke, CEO of America West. The average employees want the best management they can get. They want management who provide stability and growth. And that requires competitive pay."

A new twist on performance-based pay is exemplified by Eastman Kodak Co., where employee satisfaction accounts for 20 percent of executive bonuses. United Airlines Inc., which is 60 percent employee-owned, began tying compensation to worker satisfaction in 1999. Unions are now lobbying companies where they own shares to key in employee satisfaction measures when they make decisions about pay. Next, labor unions will approach corporations where they represent workers asking them to do the same thing.[24]

The furor over lopsided compensation packages is fueled when shareholder value declines over the long term in direct inverse proportion to hikes in senior officers' pay. MagneTek, the Nashville manufacturer, missed its economic value-added goals in 1998. Nevertheless, David Reland, senior vice president and chief financial officer, was awarded a discretionary bonus of over $177,000. Two colleagues received $202,500 and $40,500. The justification for the disparity is retention.[25] But, then why call it a discretionary bonus?

Martha Seger points to Sears, where earnings dropped and CEO Arthur Martinez' pay went up. "When the market is booming, there is a disconnect between the stock price and earnings," Seger says. Because of the bull market, 1998 earnings of the 800 CEOs on *Forbes Magazine*'s list of most compensated CEOs surged 32 percent, while aggregate corporate earnings actually dropped 2 percent. If the stock price goes down, the top people should give something back.

Valuation

Should compensation be based on the valuation of the company by the Street? Or should it be geared to how a company fares against its peers? Depressed copper prices cut Phelps Dodge Corp.'s earnings in half in 1998, while CEO Douglas Yearley was awarded a $50,000 raise, a $400,00 bonus, and stock options valued at more than $1 million. Most agree that Yearley managed well in times of adversity and that Phelps Dodge is leaner and better run than at any time in its history. Taking advantage of low prices, Yearley engineered the high-risk acquisition of competitor Asarco.

At the end of 1993, Phelps Dodge ranked 12th between Coca-Cola and Disney in Fortune 500 company returns to shareholders over a ten-year period. As of March 2000, it ranked 479th. Yet, Phelps Dodge is outperforming all of its peer group, and as Yearley says, "doing things right on the governance front." Yet, he laments, "we're flat as a stock. Are we doing the right things? Will the market wake up one day and pay us for it? You can ask 'are you in the right business?' But you can't be a copper miner today and in panty hose tomorrow." When people on the street have the option to put money into AOL or Amazon.com as opposed to Phelps Dodge, it's an obvious call. The core question, given convergence, is how you determine who the appropriate peers are.

So, a key debate is whether the markets should be the primary arbiters of corporate success. Many argue that the markets are irrational and trendy. But Bennett Dorrance, cochairman of Campbell's Soup, says, "Yes, I am almost of the mind to say that you need to do well in the short term, if you are going to do well in the long term. In general, you can't sacrifice earnings for a year or two to shift gears. The CEO needs to work out a way that the new plan is integrated into the short term."

At what point does market price become a disconnect? What about fashionable industries like the dot-coms? Do their CEOs deserve more money because the street happens to like the sector, even though they make no money? Bobby Inman says, "Where I have trouble is when shareholder value is declining. Could circumstances have been controlled or anticipated? What steps have been taken to recover at what speed?" Gary Lutin says the "only thing that matters is if you can beat your competitors. All industries have cycles."

Director Roz Ridgway believes that boards are aware of their responsibility to do the best they can. If the directors vote to restructure, it is going to distort earnings per share. If they divest a line of business, they may take revenue down a few billion dollars, but leave the company in better health. You can accommodate two poor quarters, she says. "It's hard to see what makes a good board because the good board is making hard decisions for the long term that may not show up right away in the markets." As Ridgway observes, "You almost have to assume that these people of achievement and apparent value who are collectively sound, are responsible enough to do all the right things." Because you can't really know. The board and its deliberations are pretty much invisible.

A refreshing punctuation to the pay dispute is Pepsi Chairman and CEO Roger Enrico, who in 1998 and 1999 donated his entire $900,000 salary to fund scholarships for Pepsi employees' children. Obviously, his other compensation and accumulated wealth allows him to do that, but it is a gesture with resonance.

STOCK GRANTS AND OPTIONS

They call it wealth without risk. Options are popular because they purport to align management's interest with shareholders. However, in a bull market, even mediocre CEOs reap great rewards. Thus, some question whether options differentiate the good from the bad. Further, with options, there is no downside risk. Cofounder of Kohlberg Kravis Roberts (KKR), George R. Roberts, tells of several situations in which

CEOs refused to invest alongside KKR in an acquisition, because, with their options, they had no downside and couldn't lose. If they invested "real money," they stood to lose if the stock went down.[26]

"Instead of having to beat their competitors, CEOs with stock option fueled compensation packages are graded on a curve: the rising stock market."[27] The rate at which companies grant equity shares to their employees has reached an all time high. *Business Week* calculated that long term compensation, mostly from exercised options, made up, on average, about 80 percent of CEOs' compensation in 1998. Ninety-two CEOs of the top 200 firms received mega option grants, defined as $10 million or more in grant value. The average amount of shares granted was 2 percent, an 11 percent increase over 1997. CEOs with the largest option exercise gains were Weill, Travelers, $220 million; Grove at Intel, $49 million; Shapiro, Monsanto, $46.7 million; Purcell at Morgan Stanley, $36.4 million; and O'Reilly at Heinz with $34.8 million.[28]

Options alone now account for 54 percent of CEO pay, with average grants worth $5 million.[29] Not surprisingly, the average executive at technology companies with ties to the Internet made more than twice as much as her peers at other companies, due, of course, to rich options. For example, Timothy A. Koogle, chief executive at Yahoo, makes nearly as much as Jack Welch of General Electric, although G.E.'s $100 billion in sales is 500 times more than Yahoo's $200 million. In fact, Thomas Rogers, executive vice president of GE, was lured to Primedia, where he amassed well over 4 percent of Primedia's outstanding shares. In addition to his $3 million salary and bonus, his stock was worth about $143 million after about six months on the job.

Obviously, option windfalls are not limited to CEOs. When he joined eBay, the online auction company, in August 1997, Steven Westly, a vice president, was given options on about 2.4 million shares at just 7 cents each, exercisable immediately.[30] Executives sell most of their shares acquired from stock options prior to leaving office, which calls into question the entire argument that options help to cement long-term allegiance to the company.

As Robert Rock, President of MLR Holdings and Chairman of Directors & Boards points out, "Although touted as programs that make managers think like owners, stock option programs appear more like short-term bonuses, given the unwillingness of executives to retain their shares. The shareholder takes risk and invests money; the manager takes no risk but shares in the profits. By resetting the terms of stock options, a compensation committee is further advantaging the managers."[31] At Waste Management Inc., thirteen insiders sold heavily during their first selling opportunity since 1996. President and chief operating officer Rodney Proto collected $16.5 million at a share price over $51 in May, 1999. In July the stock closed at just under $34.[32]

According to Warren Buffett, CEO of Berkshire Hathaway, aligning management and shareholder interests by awarding executives stock options is an oversold concept. Options value increases by retention of earnings, rather than by superior deployment of capital. By retaining and reinvesting earnings, managers can report annual earnings increases without improving real returns. "Stock options thus often rob shareholders of wealth and allocate the booty to executives. Moreover, once granted, stock options are often irrevocable, unconditional, and benefit managers without regard to their individual performance." Better, as at Berkshire, don't give stock options. Exceptional managers can simply buy stock if they want to. If they do, they "truly walk in the shoes of owners," Buffett says.[33]

An interesting variance on option incentives is Colgate-Palmolive's performance options devised to incentivize CEO Reuben Mark. Regular options have strike prices set at the stock's current value. Strike prices for performance options are set higher than the current stock price. Mark was awarded 2.6 million shares in 1997, of which half, 1.3 million, vested immediately. The remainder vest through 2002 with an initial ten-year term. Mark only makes money when Colgate's share price moves above the premium strike price set for the year, which in 2002 is 50 percent above the current price. At Dell Computers, the board adopted a plan that allows 349 executives to exchange their cash bonuses for discounted stock options.[34]

The compensation committee at SunAmerica, provider of insurance and investment products, was equally creative in constructing performance options. CEO Eli Broad only receives options if SunAmerica's total return to shareholders exceeds the S&P 500's total return. Otherwise, Broad gets nothing. To collect, Broad not only has to exceed the S&P, he has to beat the highest share price he's hit before. And, his performance must be positive. The options have ten-year terms and cover a period when Broad will be retired. Thus, the value of his options will depend on his successor's performance and help motivate Broad to implement a strong succession plan. Broad already owns 10 percent of SunAmerica.[35]

At Borders Group, chairman and CEO Robert DiRomualdo and three key managers get paid only in options. As of mid 1998, DiRomualdo has a paper profit on his options of $34.3 million. Richard Fairbank, CEO of Capital One Financial, also traded in his salary and bonus for performance vesting options. At SYSCO, executives have five years to generate substantial increases in earnings per share, return on equity and return on capital. If they succeed, their options vest. If not, the options vest later and are worth far less. [36]

Repricing Options

Probably the most heated controversy revolves around repricing options, whereby the price of options is adjusted downward to help put the optionees in the money. Boards of companies on a downward slide often give in to the temptation to reprice options, especially those for officers and directors. Some boards say they must reprice options in order to retain their best people. However, most shareholders generally lose in repricings, because their shares are diluted, while their risk is not. Further, repricing perverts the concept of incentive compensation.

Shareholders can't reprice their investments after they lose value. But up to 10 percent of publicly held companies repriced options for management in 1998, including E-Trade, 3Com, Adobe Systems, Reader's Digest, Williams-Sonoma, and Sybase. Because of the tremendous demand for great executives and the sprawling volatility of the industry, technology companies are leading the pack in repricing, scrambling to hang on to executives who are driven by the game and the numbers. But aren't stock options supposed to be pay for performance? And, isn't the point to measure performance in the public markets?

"It's self perpetuating," says Bill Crist, "Tough independent board members will say, 'Let the guy go. No, we don't have to pay $18 million a year.' Give me a break here. You get some dude with a million options and the stock is underwater. 'Why don't we reprice these options?' says the board. 'He worked hard.' They forget the fairness of it. It's not right for the company. What good does it do to give the guy $12 million? You explain that to me. There are things you do because you don't have the guts to stand up."

Millions of options held by Circus Circus and Mirage employees were under water, until directors repriced them. At Mirage, after five losing quarters, options were repriced at $14³/₈ for CEO Steve Wynn and seven other executives. Wynn also was paid $3.9 million, including a $1.3 million bonus. His options lost $100 million in value, but were still worth $108 million at the end of the year. He sold additional shares for $160 million.

At Williams-Sonoma, stocks were repriced in early October, 1998, after the stock fell about 50 percent from midsummer. By the end of the year, the stock was back in the 40s. The lowered strike price boosted CEO Lester's options by $825,000. E-Trade's board repriced options of ten executives from $17 to $10, after the price fell to a low of $10 a share. Five months later, E-Trade closed at $98¹/₂.

Apple Computer has repriced options nine times since the 1980s, and Advanced Micro Devices has done so six times. Graef Crystal calls them "serial repricers." "Repricing to retain key employees is utterly hypocritical," Crystal says. "I think it's the most sleazy thing you can do with executive compensation, because boards are saying they'll pay executives a lot no matter what. Instead of aligning managers with shareholders, you're creating an abyss."[37] The message to executives is there is no risk for them, only for the shareholders. Does repricing mean that the directors have no faith in the company's ability to succeed? Does it means the directors believe the goals they agreed upon are unattainable?

Reforms are underway. At HealthSouth, the company is asking shareholders to approve a repricing, but only for nonexecutives. And, a number of companies are coupling repricings with share reductions.[38]

Bennett Dorrance, chairman of Campbell Soup's Finance Committee, is adamantly opposed to repricing and believes that, over the long term, the stock will reflect whether the company is well run. Says Dorrance, "It's not unreasonable to expect the CEO to meet or beat his objectives. Someone in a company that is repricing options may do better getting out anyway. Probably, it's not the last time the options are going to be repriced."

One way to help insert objectivity into the directors' deliberations is to exclude directors' stock from repricing. Another is to evaluate why executives work. If it it just the money, are they worth it?

Asymetrix Learning Systems Inc., a Washington developer of online training systems, went public in June 1998 at $11, but deflated to $4 as of June 1999, clipping the value of CEO James Billmaier's options to around $2 million from about $10 million. Although the company has not reset share prices, turnover is minimal. Says Billmaier, "The money is important, but it's somewhat secondary to the thrill of working on something revolutionary."[39]

Until 1999, repricings did not need to be included in proxy information. But, the SEC has ruled that investors have the right to vote on repricing plans. In 1997, the State of Wisconsin Investment Board (SWIB), a $60 billion plus fund, approached twenty-two companies on the issue of repricings, and eighteen of them agreed to adopt shareholder approval policies for repricing options. SWIB tagged fifteen companies for its 1999 anti-repricing campaign. One of the targets, Cambridge Technology Partners, is drawing tremendous criticism because its directors voted to reprice their own options.[40] Another threat to this tactic is the proposed change in rules governing how companies account for options, which would result in a charge to earnings if the stock price moves up.

A quirky variance on options are reload options, which allegedly help in retention and increase the amount of shares executives own. Created first by Fred Cook at Frederic W. Cook & Co., a reload allows an employee to exercise a valuable stock option before the end of its term, using already owned mature shares, without giving up the benefit of price appreciation on the full number of shares covered by the option. When the option is exercised using a stock for stock exchange, a new option is granted covering the same number of shares as those tendered to exercise the original option. According to *Director's Alert*, "Reload options are like the Energizer bunny—they keep on going. . . . They're making executives wealthier than normal options would. Compensation committees at Travelers, Toys "R" Us, Sara Lee, Bell Atlantic, and McGraw-Hill have awarded them to their CEOs. Critics warn that boards forfeit their control over the CEO's pay once they grant them."[41]

CREATIVE PAY—SOMETIMES MASQUERADING AS RETENTION INCENTIVES

So-called creative pay incentives sometimes masquerade as retention incentives. One example is transaction bonuses, which are used by Dean Foods, Mallinckrodt, and Rockwell International. When Compaq Computers acquired Tandem Computers, CEO Roel Pieper and six other officers each received cash equal to their salary and target bonuses as a reward.[42] SBC Communications, the baby bell, gave CEO Ed Whitacre a "retention incentive" worth $12.5 million. That's twice what he earned the prior year in 1998.

At Gillette, when CEO Alfred Zeien reached age 65 in 1995, the board awarded him annual retention incentives that, in 1998, included stock options worth $4 million and $500,000 cash. The directors wanted to compensate Mr. Zeien for postponing his retirement. Would Mssrs. Whitacre or Zeien have left the company otherwise? Fleet Financial Group's CEO Terrence Murray received annual pay of $6 million. In addition, he received $16.4 million in stock option grants, $3.7 million in stock option exercises and holds $22.2 million in unexercised stock options. In 1997, his board awarded him 825,000 additional stock options as part of a retention strategy. Apparently, the $22 million of unexercised stock options was not sufficient to retain Murray at Fleet, despite his seventeen-year tenure.[43]

Lockheed Martin tied a retention bonus to winning a federal contract to produce Joint Strike Fighters. Even if Lockheed doesn't win the contract, the executives will receive two-thirds of the bonuses. "Lockheed wants to ensure that executives who have special skills necessary for securing this contract don't leave."[44] In other words, it's a bribe.

Consolation agreements are another twist to retention pay. Essentially, they target CEOs in waiting and provide a consolation payment if the executive doesn't become CEO. The Medtronic board is using this ploy to retain Arthur Collins, COO, and entitles him to a consolation payment if he doesn't become CEO in May, 2001. AT&T's John Walter, COO under Robert Allen, left with $25 million when he failed to ascend to the CEO position.[45] How do these investments in failed succession policies help the company and the shareholders?

Golden parachutes are considered a retention tool. At US West, 39 percent of investors voted for an anti-parachute resolution sponsored by the Communication Workers of America. CEO Solomon Trujillo would earn $7.4 million in the event of a change in control, which could have made him eager to sell when an offer crosses his desk.[46]

Poison pills are becoming a favorite target of shareholder activists. In 1998, Wall Street arbitrageur Guy Wyser-Pratte sent letters to directors of the some 500 companies whose poison pills expired in 1999, asking them to make pills chewable or to submit their renewal to a shareholder vote. (Chewable poison pills provide that when the company receives certain types of offers the poison pill disappears and shareholders can vote on the transaction.) Explaining why the letters were sent, Wyser-Pratte said that "poison pills have been perverted. They've helped to entrench management when they were never meant to."[47]

TIAA-CREF, the pension fund giant, is challenging CEO supplemental plans. An example is 51-year-old David Coulter, forced to resign as CEO of BankAmerica in 1998. Coulter took home $19 million in stock and a supplemental pension of $5 million—every year for the rest of his life.[48] No matter how options and grants are configured, handing over additional shares dilutes the value of the stock held by shareholders.

Exit Packages

Even more jarring are *exit packages* such as Gil Amelio's $6.7 million from Apple Computer, John Walter's $26 million from AT&T, Robert Morgado's nearly $50 million from Time Warner, and Michael Ovitz's $90 million from Disney. During the two years that M. Douglas Ivester was at the helm, Coca-Cola's growth stagnated, earnings fell, and Coke endured the biggest product recall in its history, along with a racial discrimination lawsuit. Yet, Ivester left with a total of $17.8 million in payments and other benefits, as well as the release of nearly two million shares of formerly restricted stock worth just short of $100 million as of March 2000.[49]

How can these payments help those companies? In Disney's case, TIAA-CREF, the largest pension fund, withheld votes for five directors running for reelection and voted against Eisner's compensation plan.

Two inside directors are going off the board and at least two new outside directors are coming on.

Another creative bunch of benefits are "lifetime perks." Some are fun and imaginative—like the free ice cream for life that Ben & Jerry's Homemade Inc. gave to departing CEO, Robert Holland, Jr.[50] Less amusing, however, is that Jack Welch will collect an annual pension of about $6 million when he leaves GE, including lifelong access to company aircraft, cars, office, apartments, and financial planning services. As of April 2000, AlliedSignal's Larry Bossidy received company facilities and services comparable to those provided prior to his retirement, which include a car, an office, financial planning, and use of a plane— for as long as he lives.

Retired Citicorp Chairman and CEO Walter Wriston claims, "It's just wild. If they were retiring as paupers rather than having $500 million in the bank, it would be another kettle of fish."[51]

These retention and consolation packages pose two questions: Do these payments make a difference in the final decision of the executive to stay or leave? Ask CEOs today, are you doing your best? Are you working as hard as you can? Who will say no? Why, then, do we expect them to do better than their best if we give them still more money?

Pearl Meyer & Partners studied large corporations and found that salary made up only 14 percent of CEO pay at those companies.[52] The packages today are so cumbersome and intricate, it is almost impossible to tally the totals accurately, to evaluate all the options, and to predict the payouts.

Is CEO Compensation Too High?

Thirty percent of outside directors, 26 percent of inside directors, and 14 percent of the CEO/chairmen think compensation is too high.[53] These are not gadfly activists; These are the individuals setting and receiving the pay. "I think the pendulum has gone way too far under the guise of incentives," asserts David Tappan, former CEO of Fluor. "There is no way I would think some of these outrageous compensations are legitimate. There ought to be some caps or limits so it can't embarrass the board. I'm all for incentives," he adds, "but they need to be structured so they can't result in obscene windfalls. CEOs today are making two to three times what I experienced."

What's the solution? CalPERS president Bill Crist says awareness is not enough. "Everybody in the country knows Michael Ovitz's huge payout at Disney was not good. But if somebody like CalPERS doesn't stand up and say this is truly outrageous, it just goes on." What really matters is whether the CEO is succeeding. In actuality, the highest fees headlined in the business media are a sliver of the whole economic picture. Most CEOs deserve to be paid well. They carry the risk and the pressure of the marketplace. They deserve to benefit, not at the expense of shareholders but in concert with them. The key is to shrink the gap between top officers and the average employee—to share the upside with all the employees who have contributed to the success. The implicit contract that drives our economy is that if you work hard and contribute, you will participate in the benefits.

There are some promising signs. Companies are granting shares deeper into their organizations. Once achieved, the relationship should remain relatively constant during good times and narrow (from the top down) during bad times. Responsible Wealth, an organization of 400 very wealthy individuals including many CEOs and directors, filed resolutions in 1999 asking the directors at eight companies to consider linking CEO pay to the pay of workers by establishing a maximum ratio. Companies targeted are GE, AlliedSignal, Citigroup, Bank of America, BankBoston, Computer Associates, Huffy, and AT&T.

The most important question for the directors is "Does this payment benefit our company going forward?" "We are ignoring compensation absolutely at our peril," claims Robert Monks. "What happens if you, the owner, or the owner's representative, can't control your agent's pay? What does that say about your ability to govern?" If you cannot control the pay, you cannot control the power. And, the game is lost.

Some resort to the courts for resolution. But, the solution is not within the court's province. Courts are concerned that corporations be fairly operated, but what is reasonable compensation for its officers is primarily for the stockholders to decide. Consequently, the courts have been very reluctant to involve themselves in compensation disputes.[54] If abuses escalate, however, the potential for intervention by the judiciary and government is very real.

The even larger danger in this volatile issue is the potential for

The Money

0   10
Captive Board   **Strategic Board**

Leadership
Value Added
Information
Diversity
The Money
Cronyism
Family
Conflicts
Insiders
Recruit
Strategically

eroding public confidence in our corporate governance system. The public becomes mobilized against what is portrayed as a closed, self-serving, elite system. Pay is an easy, inflammatory target. And, the activists know it. If trust in the ability of directors to fairly compensate the leadership ebbs, this suspicion can spill over and pollute the entire governance pool. Once trust is discarded, it is virtually impossible to reclaim. Once trust is impaired, the entire system is in jeopardy.

Add one point to your strategic board continuum quotient if directors' and officers' compensation is independently judged, performance based, and fairly awarded in line with company-wide pay scales.

NOTES

1. Korn/Ferry International, *26th Annual Board of Directors Study*, 1999.
2. Grant Thornton, *Public Company Advisor*, Summer 1998. Note difference in fees vs. total compensation.
3. *SpencerStuart Governance Letter*, "Director Compensation," *Directors & Boards*, Fall 1998.
4. Korn/Ferry International, *25th Annual Board of Directors Study*, 1998.
5. SpencerStuart Board Index, 1998, 18.
6. Wallace N. Davidson III, Theodore Pilger, and Andrew Szakmary, "Golden Parachutes, Board and Committee Composition, and Shareholder Wealth," *The Financial Review*, November 1998.
7. "The Jungle," *The Wall Street Journal*, 1 June 1999.
8. John L. Vogelstein, "As I, an Owner-Director, See It," *Directors & Boards*, Summer 1998.
9. "How Do You Motivate a Director?" *Investor Relations Business*, 15 March 1999.
10. Robert Stobaugh, "The Ashland Inc. Board Guidelines," *Director's Monthly*, April 1997.
11. "Incentive Pay Bolsters Boards," *Director's Alert*, March 1999.
12. Mark Metzer and Remy P. Ash, "Compensating the Entrepreneurial Board—A Holistic Approach," *Compensation & Benefits Review*, July 1998.
13. Thomas R. Horton, "Betrayal of the Public Trust," *Directors & Boards*, Spring 1999.
14. Pearn Meyer and Partners, "The Jungle," *The Wall Street Journal*, 8 February 2000.
15. *Director's Alert*, February 2000.
16. Brenda Paik Sunoo and Craig L. Fuller, "Shareholders Revolt: Is Your CEO Worth $39 Million?" *Workforce*, January 1999.

17. "GE's Shareholders Vote Down a Cap on Welch's Salary," *The Wall Street Journal*, 22 April 1999.
18. Dawn Gilbertson, "Shareholders Underwhelmed by Simula Vows," *The Arizona Republic*, 20 June 1999.
19. Ann McLaughlin, interview with author.
20. "Put Yourself or a Relative on the Compensation Committee," AFL-CIO Executive Pay Watch Web site.
21. *The Wall Street Journal,* 9 April 1998.
22. Ibid.
23. Robert L. Heidrick, "How Do Boards Add Value?" *Directors & Boards*, Winter 1999.
24. "Bits," *Director's Monthly*, April 1999.
25. "The Jungle," *The Wall Street Journal*, 18 May 1999.
26. George R. Roberts, "Corporate Governance and the Power of Ownership," *Corporate Board,* September–October 1998.
27. AFL-CIO Executive Pay Watch Web site, "Runaway CEO Pay," May 1999.
28. "Recent Data Show Boards Grant Equity at Record Rate," *Director's Alert*, June 1999.
29. Gary Strauss, "Retaining Skilled Leaders Hinders Tying Pay To Results," *USA Today,* 22 April 1999.
30. "Are Stock Options Making U.S. Companies Shortsighted?" *New York Times*, 4 April 1999, 9.
31. Robert H. Rock, "The New Physics of Stock Options," *Directors & Boards*, Winter 1999.
32. Jeff Bailey, "Waste Management Insiders Sold Stock," *The Wall Street Journal*, 9 July 1999.
33. Lawrence A. Cunningham, "Warren Buffett on the Role of the Board," *Corporate Board*, July–August 1998.
34. "Dell Directors Dole Out Unique Bonuses," *Director's Alert*, March 1999.
35. "Sunamerica Touts Tough Option Plan For CEO," *Director's Alert*, September 1998.
36. "Tough Option Exercise Keeps Executives in Shape," *Director's Alert*, March 1999.
37. Graef Crystal, *crystalreport.com*, August 1999.
38. Gary Strauss, "Retaining Skilled Leaders Hinders Tying Pay To Results," *USA Today*, 22 April 1999.
39. Greg Ip, "CEOs Feeling Pain as Stocks Bottom Out," *The Wall Street Journal*, 28 June 1999.
40. "Investors Force Board to Cease Repricing," *Director's Alert*, March 1999.
41. "Should Your Board Give the CEO Reload Options?" *Director's Alert*, July 1998.

42. "Boards Increasingly Grant Transaction Bonuses," *Director's Alert*, June 1999.

43. Brenda Paik Sunoo and Craig L. Fuller, "Shareholders Revolt: Is Your CEO Worth $39 Million?" *Workforce*, January 1999.

44. "Your Career Matters," *The Wall Street Journal*, 27 April 1999.

45. "Unique Comp Clause Protects Execs," *Director's Alert*, February 1999.

46. "US West Investors Oppose Golden Parachutes," *Director's Alert*, June 1999.

47. "Directors Face Noisemaker's Ire Over Poison Pills," *Director's Alert*, September 1998.

48. "Pension Funds Target CEO's Supplemental Plans," *Director's Alert*, December 1998.

49. "A Hefty Farewell Package for Former Coke Executive," Business/Financial Desk, *New York Times*, 4 March 2000.

50. "All the Rage Among CEOs: Lifetime Perks," *The Wall Street Journal*, 6 July 1999, A17.

51. "For Some Corporate Chiefs, Perks for Life," *The Wall Street Journal*, 6 July 1999, A24.

52. "Unique Incentives Handcuff CEOs," *Director's Alert*, April 1999.

53. Korn/Ferry International, *26th Annual Board of Directors Study*, 1999.

54. Charles M. Elson, "Courts and Boards: the Top 10 Cases," *Directors & Boards*, 22 September 1997.

Chapter 8

◆

Diversity

Diversity means that you have access to the best, period. It means you are not arbitrarily limited to a single subset of your global constituency. Ken Derr, Chairman and CEO of Chevron, says "diversity in board membership is very important. By that I mean diversity not only in experience, but also in ethnic and cultural background."[1] Any CEO who has ten or eleven people just like him sitting around the board table will end up essentially talking to himself.

As Bill Crist, President of CalPERS, puts it, "You add water to water, you get water. It might be drinkable, but it's not joy juice." And Sheila Wellington, President of Catalyst, the nonprofit research and advisory organization working with business to advance women in corporations, observes, "A group of people with the same background, the same experience is going to come up with a predictable group of solutions to problems—not a good idea in the world we live in. Different points of views yield a wider approach to decision making."

"There's nothing like having five or six old guys like me sitting around the table," director and CEO of Main Street and Main Bart Brown says. "We don't need a meeting to know we all think the same way."

For TIAA-CREF, diversity is a key investment criterion, because they believe a diverse board will be less beholden to management. They divide companies into four groups: The "in compliance" group consists of companies that have at least one woman or minority director or is about to nominate one to its board. The "actively looking"

128

group consists of companies who have hired an outside consulting/recruiting firm to recruit suitable women or minority board candidates. "Passively looking" describes the firms seeking women or minority candidates without outside help. Finally, the "get lost" group is made up of companies who are not searching for women or minorities.[2]

Catalyst consistently finds a statistically significant correlation between the presence of women on corporate boards and in senior executive ranks. According to *Newsweek*'s Adam Bryant, "At companies where you find one, you tend to find the other. If there isn't a commitment to make it happen on one front, it's not going to happen on any front." The same is true of minorities.

Until we have meaningful numbers at the top, diversity will be shortstopped. Because we all want to clone ourselves, we like people who are most like us. We put people on boards because we trust them; we know them; we admire them; we identify with them. We play golf with them.

In 1998, between 73 percent (Korn/Ferry) and 86 percent (Catalyst) of Fortune 500 companies had one or more women directors. Sixty percent had ethnic minorities on board. That means that 40 percent of all Fortune 500 corporate boards have no minorities. And consider companies like Safeway and Borden, whose customers are largely women, without a single woman on their boards. (See Appendix 5, Fortune 500 Companies without Women Directors.)

But, even these statistics are misleading. Because most boards have tiny numbers of women and minorities, women now make up only 9 percent of the director population, and minorities about 4 percent.[3] Hispanics, who will constitute 13 percent of the U.S. population in 2005, account for barely more than 1 percent of the 12,000 board members in Fortune 1000 companies. Catalyst notes that only one Fortune 500 board has gender parity: Golden West Financial Corp. of Oakland. Three other Fortune 500 companies have 40 percent or more women directors: Avon Products, Beverly Enterprises, and Gannett Co. Among large corporate boards, 271 still have zero women. Almost half of high technology companies have no women on their boards. The smaller the high tech company, the fewer the women and minorities on their boards.[4]

At General Electric, Exxon, Intel, Compaq, and Philip Morris, there are no women officers. And, Catalyst found only 63 women among the 2320 top earning corporate officers in Fortune 500 companies—2.7 percent.

As companies demand more of their board members, as Fortune 500 directors become scarce, and, as stockholders become more active in governance issues, the pressures are intensifying to diversify and to broaden board membership.

"The first minority or women is a token, but when you start putting two or three on a board," says governance guru Robert Lear, "now you're getting somewhere." Yet, it appears that the number of women and minorities is plateauing. Why?

THE COMMON MYTHS

■ *Myth #1: There are no women or minorities who are on a par with our existing members.*

Often this is corporate speak for there are no available women or minorities who are CEOs of Fortune 500s. As Sheila Wellington says, "I cannot imagine how you can come up with a set of criteria and come up with the idea that no woman qualifies."

When Adam Bryant, then at the *New York Times,* asked twenty companies why they had no women on their boards, the Quantum Corporation, a disk-drive maker in California, said it would like to add a woman to its board, but that, over the last five years, it had attempted "targeted searches" for female directors with no success. As Adam Bryant wrote, "part of the problem may be Quantum's criteria: Michael A. Brown, the chairman and chief executive, wanted chief executives at a company with $6 billion or more in annual revenue. Clearly, not many women fit that profile. But then, neither do any other of Quantum's outside board members."[5]

■ *Myth #2: There are no women or minority executives at the appropriate level in our industry.*

There are women and minorities in key leadership roles in every industry. Further, all strategic boards have nonindustry members. Look again at your board matrix. This is exactly the argument T. J. Rodgers made on the front page of *The Wall Street Journal* not long ago when he ridiculed a nun asking for women and minorities to be represented on the Cypress Semiconductor Board. Rodgers was arguing effectively against tokenism, but in reality he found reasons to turn down a number of highly qualified potential female directors. Said Rodgers, "I'm not going to have someone who doesn't know anything about my business."[6]

■ *Myth #3: "The only qualified women and minorities are already over-committed."*

Not true. Those are the only potential directors known to the board, the directors who tend to be recycled because they are trophies, because they are safe. Carley Fiorina at Hewlett-Packard is undoubtedly overwhelmed with board offers. Two Hispanics were recently recruited to the Wal-Mart board, and their board books will fill up quickly. But, many productive, excelling women and minorities tend to be overlooked, because they are less visible as a result of focusing on career development and building their businesses.

One reason for the vacuum is the lack of contact women and minorities have with powerful decision-makers. They are essentially invisible. Their relative newness to their position, the fact that they tend to be younger and don't belong to the same organizations, the fact that they may have grown their own business, all diminish the likelihood that a CEO or director seeking a board member will know them.

- *Myth #4: We have someone in mind.*

The single candidate approach doesn't offer the board a selection of targeted, carefully qualified candidates. How do you know there isn't someone better out there?

T. J. Rodgers is right in that it makes no sense to bring someone on board for the wrong reasons. Vernon Jordan's wife sits on the Johnson & Johnson board; the artist wife of Michigan State University's black president sits on three corporate boards. The innate skepticism, the stigma of being different overlaid by inexperience, and their lack of relevant knowledge mean respect will be a scarce commodity for them.

"The notion that you have your woman (or minority)—the quota of one—has got to go," insists Sheila Wellington. "It's not an appropriate way to look at the contribution women can make. It is based on the assumption that a woman will only speak for a woman. The notion that a woman comes on a board and becomes a single-issue person is absurd to anyone who knows boards and how they function. Women don't want to be seen that way, and it's a great disservice. Does that mean a man thinks only as a man?"

"I hate the idea of a constituency," says director Roz Ridgway. "As a woman, what is your view of nuclear weapons? It's a genderless expertise. My background is my upbringing, my religion, my age. I am all of those things when I look at an issue." If you have monotony, "you're missing the variety of the world we live in, all the ages on either side of their age on the board, all the marketplaces. You're probably getting all the same politics. I find that dangerous. I've spent all my career being the first woman," Ridgway continues. "It was time, and I was happy to do it. I've never been treated as something special, which I would really resent."

There are always the special interests. Intel board member Arthur Rock was on a board in California, and a local senator vociferously complained that they were discriminating against Italian-Americans because there were none on board. "He was adamant," Rock says.

Craig Weatherup recently recruited a "more diverse board than I ever thought possible" at Pepsi Bottling Group. "It is why it is important to have the best people you can possibly get. The board is a collection of personalities. You don't want a board all on the same script, who do the same things in the same way," Weatherup says. "Diversity of perspectives is a mandatory element of successful boards."

A recent Conference Board study found that diversity on boards can enhance organizations' strategic planning processes. And, as Bobby Inman says, "This isn't charity work. [A diverse company] is able to attract and keep extraordinarily capable people, and it fosters even stronger companies." He tells of a large company on whose board he sat which hosted a gathering for a customer whose top officers were mostly women. "They looked out over the rest of us, and asked 'why are we doing business with you?' Contracts were not forthcoming," added Inman.

Martha Seger questioned the dismissal of the top woman at Fluor. "There are things worth challenging," she said. "The discussion elevates the awareness of the board." Tom Emerson, Director, Donald H. Jones Center for Entrepreneurship, Carnegie Mellon University, says that boards with women members have been the most effective boards he has served on. Harvey Mackay believes there should be no all-male boards. "A woman's perspective brings different touches and feels and pulses and sensitivities."

Betsy Sanders was the first women on a number of boards, including Von's. "Diversity in and of itself is not a value," says Sanders. "But representing internal and outside customers is. When I see what I've been able to actually contribute as a woman, I know that our value is not to make the company look responsible to whomever is rating us, but actually allows us to be responsive to the rich diversity of associates and customers."

When Sanders was a relatively new board member for a supermarket company, the directors discussed the failure of "apron droppers," advertising specials so enticing that women drop their aprons and rush to the store to buy the specials. The debate was whether to change the day of those sales or the placement of the ads. No one until Sanders thought to question the premise of the sales themselves.

THE GLOBAL IMPERATIVE

In 1950, 5 percent of American goods faced foreign competition. In the 1990s, that number soared to 75 percent. In the new millenium, virtually every company competes globally. Economics is blurring borders. Technology is erasing them. Keep in mind the picture of the world as a village of only 1000 people, where 546 of the people would be Asians, 210 would be Europeans, 86 would be Africans, 80 would be South Americans, and only 60—a mere 6 percent of the world's population— would be North American.[7]

"For a company that has (or should have) global ambition, a board whose members lack truly global business experience and cross-cultural insight can be a considerable handicap," says David Johnson, former CEO of Campbell Soup. "Frequently, the best response to a business challenge in the U.S. is dead wrong overseas, and vice versa."[8]

International members "add breadth of vision to your board," says Roz Ridgway. Plus, it testifies to your international commitment. The Delphi Automotive Systems board, a spin-off from GM, recently recruited three international directors, one from Latin America, one from the Far East, and one from Europe, because over half of its business is overseas.[9]

Toughest for international directors is carving out the necessary time and adapting to different board cultures. Those who do adapt well are in tremendous demand. Dr. David K. P. Li, chief executive of the Bank of East Asia, a cogent, powerful leader, sits on some twenty boards, including Rolls Royce. To claim some semblance of family life, his wife travels with him to virtually all meetings.

Despite teleconferencing and videoconferencing, directors are far more effective in person. "I've been on boards where people try to participate by telephone, says Melvin Goodes, CEO of Warner-Lambert. "That's not good enough."[10]

To ensure expectations are met, boards craft with the director a charter of expectations and goals with a clear definition of how the director is expected to contribute, including the time commitment. Dr. Li has agreed to attend in person five of Campbell Soup's eight monthly board meetings each year. Objectives can include feedback on political and economic trends, brainstorming with senior company officials in the region, meeting with regional employees, advising on potential business partners, and making introductions to the highest-ranking government officials.

In 1998, 35 percent of the S&P 500 companies had international directors. They came from the following regions:

Europe	58%
Canada	17%
Latin America	12%
Asia/Pacific	10%

Great Britain (21 seats), Canada (17 seats), and Germany (13 seats) were the most represented countries.[11]

INTERNATIONAL ADVISORY BOARDS

International Advisory boards offer a way to connect to disparate markets and to access powerful globalists who would not be available or appropriate for a statutory board. The boards are usually composed of senior executives and officials and meet once or twice a year. The focus is typically strategy or access: Conflicts of interest are not a concern; often board members are called on to share their insights on foreign policy matters and to make introductions. A recently formed international advisory board for Salomon Smith Barney, New York, includes two former defense secretaries.[12] Marsh & McLennan Companies' international advisory board has thirteen members, including the president of the IMG and the former ambassador of Brazil to the United States. George Shultz, former Secretary of State, and Jürgen Schrempp, Daimler Benz's chairman, sit on the J. P. Morgan international council.[13]

NCR has multiple international advisory boards for finance, retail and communications, for example, to which they have recruited industry experts. Advisors are asked to spend a couple days a year listening to and offering insights into NCR's strategy. The senior vice presidents run the boards. "It's been very fruitful for us," says CEO Nars Nyberg, who took the lead in strengthening those boards.

Joe Stiglich, formerly of Wells Fargo, is the only American on the NCR Finance Advisory Board, which meets quarterly. As the result of the advisory board's deliberations, NCR has supplemented its traditional product R & D with a "knowledge lab" that fosters out-of-the-box creativity. One direct result is an innovative microwave bank, which is a prototype for Internet banking applications wed to a traditional ATM.

GLOBAL BOARDS

As a market-centered model overtakes the global economy, the capital markets compel reform. The secretive, cumbersome, incestuous and ineffectual governance practices so prevalent outside the United States are vanishing. Given the context, the history, and the nationalistic pride that pervades so many boards overseas, international corporate practices are reforming with remarkable speed.

The Organization for Economic Cooperation and Development (OECD) has issued a set of principles to reform global corporate governance practices. They are guidelines only, but highly significant in breaking open the shell around governance practices outside the United States. The guidelines include disclosure of financials, accurate reports on ownership, independence and accountability of the board and timely reporting on corporate governance.[14] The Trade and Industry Ministry in the United Kingdom may seek legislation requiring shareholders to approve senior management's compensation packages.

As Bill Crist, President of CalPERS, notes, "All this talk of global is actually real. International is our new challenge." The need to succeed in the international financial community is the real impetus to change. And, riding on that wave, the shareholder activist community is refocusing some of its ammunition on companies overseas. For example, the Teamsters, CalPERS, and TIAA-CREF are all actively engaged in pushing for international reform. The Institutional Shareholder Services was successful in pressuring Gucci to change its stock option plan and to allow shareholders to vote annually on director compensation. According to Julie Welch of ISS, "The supervisory boards of European firms are waking up to the fact that they need to change their equity culture because U.S. and U.K. funds have the capital."[15]

In Germany, the two-tier board system—a management board of top executives which holds most of the power, and the supervisory board—made up of executives, union representatives (by law), and outside directors—which is usually quite weak. Because of this structure, reform in Germany has been systemically resisted. But, the OECD guidelines combined with the force of globalism are compelling change even in this bastion of rigidity.

An interesting, albeit bizarre, forerunner of change is Reinhard Mohn, the 78-year-old patriarch who, for nearly 40 years, has controlled privately held Bertelsmann A.G., the world's third-largest media conglomerate. In July 1999, Mohn turned over his voting rights to a new six-person board made up of Mohn, the CEO, one family member, one employee representative, and two outside directors from the supervisory board. Not an inspiring example of independence, except for one thing. Members of the Bertelsmann board, including the outsiders, will each have a veto on major strategic decisions [16]

Along with goods and services, we are beginning to export U.S. directors as well. Siemens A.G., the electronics giant, appointed former U.S. ambassador to Germany Robert Michel Kimmit to its supervisory board, and at German utility Bewag, Southern Company executive Barney Rush chairs the supervisory board as the result of an investment. Rush has taken a more active role than his German predecessors, for example, by visiting every Bewag power plant.[17]

Multinational companies can no longer be propped up by government subsidies, family money, and cross holdings. They need the financial clout that follows listing on the U.S. Stock Exchanges. And the U.S. exchanges require governance reform. A Daimler-Benz admission that it is a corporate advantage to be listed is very significant.

In France, the egos of CEOs are especially fragile when it comes to revealing executive compensation, which, as in the rest of Europe, is significantly and embarrassingly lower than U.S. pay. Grudgingly, French companies are finally releasing their compensation figures— but as a combined figure for all employees. The French are "getting very open about discussing their problems," says Bill Crist. "It never would have happened even three or four years ago."

Even emerging economies such as that of Kuala Lumpur are improving corporate transparency and governance practices. Listed companies must release quarterly financial results, and directors can not hold more than ten directorships. In Malaysia, the Finance Committee Report on Corporate Governance recommended mandatory accreditation for all existing directors of listed companies.[18]

Enflamed by the Asian flu, Korea has been a major target of shareholder activism. To discourage attendance, five affiliates of the top five chaebols (conglomerates) scheduled their general shareholders meetings for the same day in March 1999. At the 1999 annual meeting of Samsung, Activist Jang Ha Sun unfurled minutes that showed that seven of the twenty-six board members had not attended a single meeting, but still received salaries. Jang Ha Sun had planned to canvass for proxy votes from institutional investors in New York and London, but Samsung threatened to withdraw its business from any investor who helped Jang. Even so, Jang said the Samsung affair was "an excellent meeting" compared to Hyundai Heavy Industries, where activists were searched at the door and physically forced back into their seats when they tried to speak out.[19]

Even Japan, the second largest economy in the world, is stepping into the governance fray. Japanese boards traditionally have been a reward for loyal and honorable Japanese executives who have worked very hard all their lives. The boards are generally inert and some are as large as one hundred members. Most number over thirty members.

A fairly typical board is that of Ricoh, the printing company, which has tiers of boards, presided over by a six-person executive committee made up of the most senior Japanese insiders. One American, Jim Ivy, CEO of Savin Corporation, a subsidiary recently acquired by Ricoh, sits on one of the boards. He relates that virtually all decisions are made prior to discussion at the board level. Ricoh executives generate some six business plans a year, for various time spans, which they then meticulously refine and update. By the time information bubbles up to the board level, it has been thoroughly vetted and is largely perfunctory.

Yet board chairmen steeped in the insular, cross-shareholding board cultures are participating in governance conferences and will host a major international governance conference in Tokyo in 2001.

"I expect our holdings are around $5 billion in Japan, so we have an interest there," says Bill Crist of CalPERS. "There is nothing to be served by weak companies in Japan—any more than is the case in the United States. The old ways of financing corporate growth have been lost."

A classic reform example is Sony, which totally revamped its board because it is so tied to the U.S. marketplace. It has diversified in gender and race and allowed tremendous transparency. With Sony leading the way, Crist expects seven or eight of the largest Japanese businesses to follow suit. And, then the stage will be set.

Add one point to your strategic board continuum quotient if you have embraced diversity.

Diversity

Leadership
Value Added
Information
Diversity
The Money
Cronyism
Family
Conflicts
Insiders
Recruit
Strategically

0
Captive Board

10
Strategic Board

NOTES

1. Kenneth T. Derr, "The Chevron Way to a Strong Board," *Directors & Boards*, Fall 1998.
2. "The Influence of Institutions on Corporate Governance through Private Negotiations: Evidence from TIAA-CREF," *Journal of Finance*, August 1998.
3. Korn/Ferry International, *26th Annual Board of Directors Study*, 1999.
4. SpencerStuart, *Technology Boards of Directors* Survey, 1997.
5. Adam Bryant, "Business: Few Signs of Advances for Women on Boards," *New York Times*, 18 October 1998.
6. Ellen Joan Pollock, "CEO Takes on a Nun in a Crusade against 'Political Correctness,' " *The Wall Street Journal*, 15 July 1999.
7. Ann McLaughlin, Aspen Institute speech, Aspen, June 1998.
8. David W. Johnson, "Globalizing Your Board," *Directors & Boards*, Winter 1996, 37.

9. "How Is the New Delphi Board Being Built?" *Director's Alert*, September 1998.

10. Melvin R. Goodes, "Cross-Currents of Change: A Leadership Dialogue," *Director's Monthly*, April 1999.

11. SpencerStuart Board Index, 1998.

12. "Business Bulletin," *The Wall Street Journal*, 8 July 1999.

13. "Join an Advisory Board . . . and Hobnob with Heavies," *Director's Alert*, August 1998.

14. Institutional Shareholder Services, "The Friday Report," 7 May 1999.

15. "Big Investors Force Gucci Board to Cut Option Plan," *Director's Alert*, July 1998.

16. Edmund L. Andrews, "Bertelsmann Chief Turns Voting Control Over to a New Board," *New York Times*, 2 July 1999.

17. "European Companies Nab American Directors," *Director's Alert*, September 1998.

18. Corporate Governance, September 1999.

19. "Little Buy vs. Korean Big Business," *Christian Science Monitor*, 26 March 1999.

Part III

Using Your
Board Strategically

Chapter 9

◆

Information Flow

✦ THE EIGHTH MISTAKE: INFORMATION BLOCK ✦

The output is only as good as the input. If the board is not informed, appropriately, intelligently and comprehensively, it can't do its job. In fact, the courts have ruled that being only passively informed may make directors legally vulnerable. Yet, most companies either inundate directors with materials or selectively parcel out information at the last minute. It is a matter of trust—the board glue, that elusive ingredient that makes boards work. It means entrusting your directors, your confidants, with full information, good and bad, and trusting directors to do the right thing—the best thing that can emanate from a synergy of focused minds. As Doug Yearley says, "If a chairman is less than informative, if a board senses selective disclosure, this can be a terminal offense. There has to be that trust." It's not only a matter of presenting information, it's how it is presented, the context, the source, the amount, the pertinence, and the timeliness. And, it is more complicated than it appears.

TIPS ON EDUCATING DIRECTORS

- *What information should directors have?*

Information topped with a summary page for each corporate performance measure. The monthly package might include: financial performance, use of assets and their employment, cycle times, quality indices, development of new products and services, updated cash flow, capital projects, projections for the next eight or nine months, anything that is extraordinary, good news, problems, and the CEO's guess as to where the quarter will end up. Directors need access to employee and customer data, marketing and technology input. What gets measured gets done, especially at the board level.

"The more summarized the better," says Gary Lutin, governance expert and director. "Don't inundate the board with murky details. Provide quick financial reports with executive summaries and flash reports." At Campbell Soup, directors receive a tabbed, three-ring binder a week ahead of the monthly board meeting, with committee work noted, summaries, and pertinent, accessible information. For boards that meet quarterly, a monthly update letter with financials attached is valuable. Tom Ringer sits on a high-tech board that e-mails an issue update summary every Friday.

At Bethlehem Steel, the directors tell management the subjects they want and need to know about. There are numerous recurring subjects that "the board really wants to hear about"—such as technology, the environment, developments with accounting rules, the e-business, and corporate governance. "It's very challenging and imposes a real discipline on management," says chairman and CEO Curtis "Hank" Barnette. Bethlehem is constantly striving to refine and improve their materials. They transmit the materials with a summary explaining what is included, and organize them by subject and by committee. Barnette is especially pleased with an operating performance report with charts and graphs that tells the story of what is happening in their business.

Information should be drawn from a broad variety of sources—management, customers, other directors, analysts, employees, and other stakeholders. The best boards encourage and ensure free interaction with senior management. As a matter of courtesy, most CEOs expect to be informed if a board member has contacted their employees. Every time director Martha Seger goes to a board meeting, she tries to have breakfast or lunch with a different company employee. Many directors are comfortable enough to simply call anyone they feel like calling. A good policy is, if you are asking for written information, ask that it be sent to all the board members. The mandate is to avoid micromanaging and spawning rumors. Unless directors have free access, they are only passively representing shareholders. Make sure, says Robert Lear, "that board members don't just go to a picture show."

Constricted information flow is a signpost of a controlling CEO. At the newly merged Bank of America, board members receive an agenda and meeting minutes, in sharp contrast to the three-inch thick information packets David Coulter used to provide. At Black & Decker, board books were handed to directors as they walked into the board meeting. And they were collected again as directors left. George Aucott sat on a board in Florida where he was handed the board package as he walked in the door. "You sit there [in the meeting] trying to read it. You haven't thought one iota" about the issues.

At Inprise Corporation, directors must make written requests to CEO Fuller or other designated officers to get any information that isn't provided at meetings. Among other things, policies require directors to consult with the CEO before any communication is allowed with company employees. The employees, in turn, are barred from communicating with directors without prior CEO approval.

C. Robert Coates came on board in June 1999 after he agreed to withdraw an undisclosed shareholder resolution before the annual meeting. He and his company invested more than $18 million in Inprise stock for about 6 percent of the shares outstanding. The value of the shares declined to about $12 million, and Coates sued to overturn the communications restrictions, which were approved a month after he joined the board with one dissenting vote—his. The suit contends that an illegal "gag order" prevents Coates from carrying out his fiduciary responsibilities to oversee the company's operations. Coates alleges "these Orwellian measures establish Mr. Fuller as a corporate Big Brother."[1]

- *Expose directors to your industry and business.*

Subscribe to association newsletters and trade journals. Directors take responsibility for reading the general news, but companies should ensure that board members receive relevant special interest journals. For example, Wolverine directors receive *Footware News*.

Director CEO Craig Weatherup invites key individuals with whom Pepsi Bottling has a special relationship or who represent unique constituencies important to the company to the dinners the night before the board meetings. The Chairman of PepsiCo was on the docket for the Fall 1999 meeting. Include directors at trade shows and industry conferences. "Let them touch the customers," says director Tom Ringer. Some use video conferencing as a supplement to regular meetings. Others set the directors up on their intranets so they can interact with studies, reports, market data, newsletters, industry news.

- *Conduct new director orientations.*

Through your board charter and the strategic recruitment process, directors will know what is expected and how they will be measured. The orientation will introduce them to the specific issues, people and processes that make governance work. Meetings with key management and mentoring by seasoned directors help new directors acclimate. At Ashland, new directors meet on at least two occasions with each of the CEO's direct reports and visit at least two major facilities. Regardless of how capable a director is, it generally takes about a year for a new director to really understand the company, to contribute strategically. Without proper orientation, it takes longer.

John Whiteman has served on large public boards. Yet, the longest orientation was two hours. At Empire Machinery, "our orientation is two days, and I don't know if that's enough," he says. "How can your board be a strategic tool for you, if you don't give them the orientation of what's really happening in your industry and how your company works?"[2] Phelps Dodge has an intensive board orientation with site visits. America West has instituted a full day of orientation for new directors, with visits to the hangars and the gates and is considering extending it.

Briefing books are a valuable adjunct to the orientation and should include the following information:

- Organization chart with biographies.
- Mission statements.
- Strategic plans.
- Proxy statement and prospectus.
- Core strategies.
- Company history.
- Board materials, including the board charter, structure, needs matrix, directors' biographies, meeting dates, locations, committee assignments, summaries and processes, and profiles for any open board seats.
- Marketing materials.
- Customer profiles.
- Articles, information sources on the industry.
- Competition data.
- Financials.
- Insider trading policy.
- Analyst reports.
- Bylaws.
- Corporate calendar.
- Board and committee meeting minutes.
- Compensation.
- Evaluations.
- Succession planning.

When ABC television correspondent Dr. Nancy Snyderman was a new director of drkoop.com, a consumer health Web site company, she was embarrassed when her husband sold shares one month after the IPO, violating corporate insider trading rules and a lock-up agreement with the IPO's underwriter. Snyderman paid the company the $53,245 she made from the sale. As of August 1999, she still owned 367,500 shares; thus, it was a small portion of her holdings.[3] But, if Snyderman had been carefully briefed about her insider trading responsibilities as a board member, she could have avoided the incident.

A pivotal person is the "board's ghost in the corporate machine," usually the corporate secretary. This is the person with the power of the editor, who assembles the board book and agenda materials, the person who knows how to reach every director at all times, who makes the board run smoothly.

Often, directors representing large institutional directors will be provided exclusive access to information, such as briefing papers or analysts' critiques. Other board members will tend to defer to the investor directors in areas where this special information is relevant. Instead, those board members should insist on receiving the same information.

Increasingly specialized training is also provided for committee members. Pfizer, Seagram, Hewlett-Packard, and Niagara Mohawk provide formal training for their audit committee members. At Seagram, any director new to the audit committee engages in a daylong training session with key staff including the head of corporate strategy, the treasurer and the Chief Information Officer. At Hewlett-Packard, the comptroller explains financial benchmarks and reviews most recent financial filings in one on one sessions with directors.

- *Provide effective reports.*

Present managers' reports in writing before the board meeting. Crystallize the issues in a one-page summary sheet, so directors can come to the meetings prepared with relevant questions and thoughts. One of Shelby Yastrow's "pet peeves is having an executive at a board meeting read a lengthy memo out loud and verbatim—the same memo that I've already studied. Why twice? Does he think I can't hear or that I can't read?" Yastrow wants to know.

Betsy Sanders sits on one nonprofit board that provides two fat notebooks. "I spend eight to twelve hours reading and don't always know what I have. I appreciate well-articulated background material that people have prepared in order to do their own work. Then it's their thinking. If it's 200 pages, give me an executive summary, and I will pick and choose what I need to know more about."

Many chairs believe the way to inform the board is to cover them with data and information, says Roy Herberger. "The CEO assumes that, because you got it, you should have understood it. It simply doesn't happen that way." They leave it up to the board members, Herberger complains, "to weave through that traffic and come up with conclusions that relate to the points they are going to make." Much more effective is for the CEO to state up front what her conclusion is and let the directors make up their minds as they listen.

The art of information sharing is far more complex and challenging than it appears. How to be inclusive, yet provide bulleted summaries that clarify the critical issues? How to stay in touch, so directors don't read company news in the media before hearing it from you, yet not overwhelm them. David Tappan says that too often "you get covered up with details that you don't really want. It takes a lot more effort to synthesize the information that is really pertinent to the responsibilities of directors." In Tappan's view, the biggest shortfall is lack of information on competition.

Former Firestone CEO George Aucott says, "I don't want the financial guy droning on. I can't focus on a hundred numbers up there on the screen. Lead me through what I ought to be looking at," says Aucott. "You ought to use your board to help you solve your problems. Don't use them as a whitewash for everything." One all-too-common error is squandering board time on the financials. Some boards deal with all but the most complex financial issues in teleconferences and reserve the board meetings for strategic and succession issues. Each executive presenter has to be able to say, here's the headline, here's the highlight.

"Boards don't need or want minutia, "says Shelby Yastrow. "They have to focus on key issues, critical decisions and company direction. Right or wrong, outside board members spend limited time on the company's business." According to Betsy Sanders, "If the meeting consists of reading reports to the directors, there is no engagement of talent. We may [as directors] vote yes or no. But, we're contributing nothing. Nothing vital is happening."

Also, as Caroline Donnelly, editor of *Corporate Board Member,* observes, "often, the backgrounders laid before directors have been prepared by lawyers, bankers, or accountants, who are not always spellbinding writers. The information they provide may be designed to 'sell' a preferred outcome."[4]

- *Encourage site visits.*

The ultimate example is Home Depot, which requires directors to visit at least twenty stores a year. Anthropology-trained Johnetta Cole resigned because it took too much time. But it is a highly effective approach. Usually a two-hour visit ends with a session with employees, who are not shy about voicing their concerns. "When we have a board meeting," says Bernard Marcus, Home Depot Chairman, "we don't hit the directors with things they don't know. They know exactly what we are talking about, and they are a part of it. We have the most informed board of any I know," brags Marcus. Over the course of several visits, one board member learned that the training programs that were supposed to be so innovative and technologically advanced were not even in place. "It changed our whole outlook," says Marcus.

Meet the sales people, the R & D group, the information technology team and see if they are on the same page. Tour division offices over time, so that, as George Aucott observes, "when you sit in the board room you have some idea of what they are talking about. Otherwise your vision may not have anything to do with reality." "I won't join a board," Aucott adds, "if I haven't seen its facilities." As far as he knows, he's the only director who has visited the Korean facility of a company whose board he serves on. "You need to touch the territory," he insists. "If I can't afford the time to make those visits, then I'm doing a disservice to the company." When Cleveland Machine Controls made an acquisition of a troubled company in Denver, Aucott went there to learn. "What does this place look like? How does it feel?"

Some companies go to great lengths to engage directors in their business. McDonald's gave business cards with a checklist for directors to leave with storeowners. Wal-Mart gave directors credit cards to get them in the stores. Wal-Mart also held two board meetings in distribution areas, one focused on the retail side and one on the food side of the business. Every couple of years, Motorola holds a board meeting outside the United States where the board hears presentations by business leaders and tours facilities. The technology committee attends a major telecommunications show in Geneva.

Craig Weatherup has begun an innovative tradition with his new board at Pepsi Bottling. As a prelude to the second meeting of the board, a strategic retreat, the directors "got in a Pepsi uniform and went out for the day and did the business of the company." One director spent the day on a conventional truck route; another with a transport delivery driver; two went out on repairs; two on sales calls, one of which was a cold call and one a Wal-Mart call; two directors went with fountain vending employees, and one spent the day with a front line sales person to the grocery store business. Afterwards, the board had dinner to debrief.

The next day, at the strategic planning session, "the board had a working knowledge of what the business is," says Weatherup. "I wanted to get them engaged." For example, without experiencing it, it's difficult to appreciate the implications of the fact that some 20,000 Pepsi Bottling employees work unsupervised. A secondary, but powerful, spin-off of the field trips was that it "gave the board an instant common identity," Weatherup says.

- *Expose directors to your investors and analysts.*

Review the status of analysts' reports on a quarterly basis including those who stop or add coverage and who make any change recommendations. Pepsi Bottling sends quarterly reports to its directors. Meet with the analysts to learn firsthand why there is any change. Include directors in analysts' conference calls. Take directors on road shows. Arrange for directors and investors to meet privately without management present. David McLaughlin gets—and reads—every security analyst's report on the twenty-five to thirty companies in his company's industry.

Direct communication with directors helps shareholders and analysts understand the value of the board and validates the company in the marketplace. It helps educate directors about the analysts' opinions and focuses on what generates wealth. With the escalation of shareholder activism, more companies are creating shareholder relations committees to facilitate shareholder/director communication.

Increasingly, says Pat McGurn of Institutional Shareholder Services, "we ask to talk to directors. Nothing builds more confidence in your board. It's almost impossible to make an evaluation of directors when all you have is that one paragraph in the proxy." At Avon, individual directors and executives regularly meet with big shareholders. Chrysler directors met with forty institutional shareholders without management present.[5]

Director Bennett Dorrance has begun listening to telephone briefings with analysts at Campbell Soup. Gary Tooker moved the timing of the Motorola board meetings to coincide with the major annual security analysts meeting. "You don't get the same feel for the entire company, if you don't hear it in one setting," observes Tooker. In addition, the board sees key leaders of the business on their feet, making presentations to the analysts, fielding questions. Tooker set aside two hours for the Motorola directors to talk about the meeting, give their impressions of the analysts and the business presentations, and provide feedback on the questions directors were asked by the analysts.

- *Communicate between board meetings.*

Regardless of the frequency of meetings, every board member should ask herself, "have I talked to the company this month? Have I visited its Web site, made a site visit, obtained other information on my company?" Every year, Curtis Barnette, Bethlehem Steel CEO, visits each board member informally at the director's hometown. Craig Weatherup at Pepsi Bottling has dinner with the company's board members individually twice a year.

At Fluor, David Tappan talked to each director at least once a month between meetings. The CEO might talk to his favorites, but not each director on a regular basis. As a director, if the CEO does not get in touch with him, Tappan calls to check in or make a comment. "It provides continuity. There is a general deficiency in communications. I am amazed what you learn when you do that that you would not otherwise have heard." Mostly it is in the area of personnel, which is the most sensitive area. "You have to be accessible to be told someone is threatening to resign," Tappan says.

At least one meeting before bringing an issue to a vote, Doug Yearley tried ideas out on the board collectively and individually. "I do a heads up. Here's initial information. Give me your visceral feedback. Sometimes we will modify it, or it will be a crazy idea." At Home Depot, Marcus says the board is given pertinent information. "I've been on boards when they wait for the quarter to give us the financials. We need to know every single month what's happening out there, what the trends are." When meeting times begin to slide, it is often a sign that the CEO has better things to do.

- *Brief directors on technology.*

The headline in *Computerworld* does not overstate the issue: "Boards are clueless about the Internet." Some companies are hiring technology coaches for individual directors, who often have to unlearn old ways to embrace the new.[6] Too many companies are slow to respond to the technology imperative. Too often boards simply ignore it, says Bobby Inman, founder of the semiconductor consortium and the Austin technology incubator. "One frustration is the slowness in investing in technology." How can the board make a difference? "By insisting on tracking the technology. Including it as a measure of overall productivity helps," Inman says.

Motorola has begun a process where several times a year, the directors receive a paper from someone in management relating to a key technology, including how it works, who the competitors are, what are the implications, and why a particular acquisition was made by a competitor.

Eileen Birge, research director of the Concours Group, information technology consultants, suggests that directors ask the following questions about technology:

- How does our technology allow us to be flexible?
- Do we present a consistent and personalized face to our customers?
- Are we connected to the marketplace? Consolidated Edison saved $150,000 by setting up a system for vendors to go online to see when they would get paid.
- What are our competitors and customers doing with informa-

tion technology? Wal-Mart got Johnson and Johnson to consolidate its billing instead of having each J & J unit submit separate bills.

- How can what we do help you be better?
- How strong are our IT capabilities?
- Does our IT group generate innovative technology-enabled business solutions? Or do they wait to be asked?
- Can our organization absorb and embrace the changes enabled by new technology?

In 1998, Delta Airlines made more money in Priceline.com than in moving passengers, according to Eileen Birge. At GE, Jack Welch assembled his sixty unit presidents and threw up a slide showing "destroyyourbusiness.com." How, he challenged them, are you going to compete with the company that is online with the sole intent of destroying your business? Yet, how many of us ignore it? The *Financial Times* of September 29, 1999 reported that a full 50 percent of United Kingdom board members never had a technology briefing at their board—and that 48 percent never intend to have one.

- *Plan your meetings.*

Schedule board meetings at least twelve months ahead. Do so with as much detail and specificity as possible, including place, times, special topics, and guests. Is there a meeting each year always devoted to succession, one focusing on strategic planning, another on finance or technology? Develop similar calendars for each committee. There is a natural cycle to committee activities. Directors can prepare throughout the year and multiply their value.

Information

- *Hold unstructured meetings.*

Dinner the night before the board meeting provides an "informal download," says Jock Holliman. "You come ready to make decisions the next morning. It's tough to get the pulse every ninety days." Topics may arise that need to be discussed but are not on the formal agenda. A culture is created and nurtured.

- *Allow no surprises.*

Bart Brown sums it up. "I don't want any surprises, and I don't want my directors to have any surprises." Directors need information before they hear it through the grapevine or the media. At E. W. Scripps, CEO William Burleigh sends directors progress reports, very candid, very confidential, in the interim between the quarterly meetings. "I hope we don't do things that surprise the board," Burleigh says. "Communication is everything. The board has every right to expect that we communicate thoroughly and often."

Of course, surprises happen in the best of companies. As Ken West points out, the chairman can't pick up the phone and call the directors every time something happens. The true test of information flow is communicating with directors upfront about a major event, such as a merger or acquisition, an IPO, a sizable capital expenditure, a sudden management change, the loss of a major customer, or a new product opportunity. Bobby Inman suggests board members review their decision making process after such an event. "Did we have the right information, enough information? Is there something that didn't go well? Sometimes a decision is not as well thought through as it might be, because of a lack of information."

When there was a major fuel leak at a publicly traded California utility, the responsible manager gave a report to the board shortly after the leak occurred and made absolutely no mention of it. It was awkward for at least one board member who had to field calls from the media and respond to inquiries—all before any communication about the crisis to the board.

A card and party supply company was, as Bart Brown says, "rolling along. All of a sudden, it ran out of money and nobody knew. The CEO was hiding it. He knew it was coming, and he didn't want to tell anyone. Just like a kid. If I don't tell, maybe it will go away." The company had gone public and the CEO became "enamored of going to New York and Boston and Chicago, doing the road shows. He quit running the business," said Brown who often serves as a turnaround director. The board had two meetings with the dilettante CEO, expressing concern. "I personally would have fired him the second time." Instead at that second meeting, the board voted 4 to 3 to keep him. New, dismal numbers came out just before a strategic planning retreat. Instead of strategy, Brown says, "we spent several hours debating whether to let him go and voted 5 to 2. We shook hands, and he was gone."

As former MCII and Firestone CEO George Aucott says, a CEO should want his board to be as knowledgeable as possible, so they can help him. "If you are afraid someone is going to one-up you, it's no good."

Add one point to your strategic board continuum quotient if your board has open, unrestricted, and effective communication.

NOTES

1. Don Clark, "Inprise Director Sues to Overturn Rule Limiting Ability to Get Company Data," *The Wall Street Journal*, 20 August 1999.
2. John O. Whiteman, Snell & Wilmer, Arthur Andersen Board Roundtable, November 1998.
3. Danielle Sessa, "ABC Reporter Will Give Back Her IPO Gains," *The Wall Street Journal*, 20 August 1999.
4. Caroline Donnelly, "Editor's Letter," *Corporate Board Member*, Summer 1999.
5. John Byrne, "The Best and Worst Boards," *Business Week*, 25 November 1996.
6. "Directors' Boards Are Clueless About the Internet," *Computerworld*, 12 July 1999, 32.

Chapter 10

◆

The Role of the Directors—Value Added

What is it that directors actually do to make a difference and add value? The soul of a great board is independence—members whose directorship constitutes their only connection to the company. Yet, the corporate landscape is littered with passive boards made up of technically independent directors.

Independence really translates into the intangibles. The most difficult issues facing directors are value and ethical questions, not technical in nature. As Ann McLaughlin says, the hard challenges revolve around "questions about which there is no objective truth." So directors must have the integrity, intelligence, vision and commitment to represent the shareholders for the long term.

Directors sat idly by at seemingly invincible corporate giants like General Motors, Eastman Kodak, Sears Roebuck, Coca-Cola, and IBM as their companies deteriorated. Only when those directors were stampeded by public outcry and forced into what *Business Week* calls "governance by embarrassment."[1] did they begin to assume responsibility.

Arthur Levitt asks, "Is the board simply going through the motions or has it demonstrated awareness of its important role by having some form of independent leadership that can act without relying on management's initiative?" Is the board still relegated to a "legitimizing function that is substantially different from the role of policymaker and guardian of shareholder and public interest as contemplated by

153

the law of corporations?" as Justice Arthur Goldberg warned several decades ago.

Executive/author Robert Townsend was particularly cynical about the value of directors. "Most big companies have turned their boards of directors into nonboards. In the years that I've spent on various boards," Townsend wrote, "I've never heard a single suggestion from a director [made as a director at a board meeting] that produced any result at all. While ostensibly the seat of all power and responsibility, directors are usually the friends of the chief executive put there to keep him safely in office."[2]

In moments of candor, most directors will tell you that fewer than half of the directors on any board add real value. But there are strong signals of a new governance. David Tappan, who was CEO of Fluor, describes "the incredible evolution" of their board over twenty-nine years. Fluor started with a "totally captive, subservient board. The change in responsibilities is dramatic. Now it is not something to go into for kicks and status. Now," says Tappan, "being a director is work with financial exposure. It is serious. If you are going to stick your head in the noose, you had better pay attention."

The question is who works for whom, does management oversee the board or does the board oversee management? If the most important thing a board does is evaluate management, and, in public companies, hire and fire the CEO, then the board oversees management. But if the chairman of the board *is* the CEO, how can the CEO oversee the CEO? How can the oversight be independent?

Empire Machinery CEO John Whiteman says that in a private company, "you don't have any authority, and that's a big deal. If you don't give a board authority, and if you don't have a strong board, you're in trouble already and you don't even know it." The best boards are a balance, a partnership at most times. Only in times of crisis is the question called.

WHAT DO GOOD DIRECTORS DO?

The following section discusses twenty-three distinguishing characteristics, duties, and responsibilities of proactive, independent, and strategic board members.

KEEP THE FOCUS

The board has a broader responsibility to long-term shareholder value than the CEO, who is necessarily focused on day-to-day operations. There are too many boards that overlook more than they oversee.

There are too many that substitute CEO directives for independent initiative.

"People forget why they are there," says Shelby Yastrow. "You are the shareholders' watchdog. Instead directors end up working for the CEO. 'Oh, I don't want to offend the guy.' There's a lot of hypocrisy about whom the allegiance is to." As Betsy Sanders emphasizes, "A board only focused on what happened last quarter isn't serving anybody. What we're trying to do is look forward."

A good board, as George Aucott puts it, "keeps dragging the CEO back." The CEO may be focused more narrowly on people, systems, product, or culture. Another "has his options and wants to make his hit. It's the directors' responsibility to keep the CEO focused."

Prioritize Ethics and Values

Ethics, shareholder value and the public trust are inextricably woven together. As Bobby Inman says, an independent board needs to be conscious of stakeholders, not just the current price of the stock. Seeing to the health of employees, for example, "is critical to long term value. Individuals are entitled to private lives, but not to lie to the board. The board has to demand high impeccable standards, and that applies to all executives."

When General Motors director Ann McLaughlin was speaking to the GM corporate legal staff, she reminded them that "winning in the global marketplace does not justify winning by any means or at any cost. The board expects you to win with integrity. I recognize that it is a part of my fiduciary duty to be assured that the company is conducting its business honestly, ethically and with the highest regard for compliance with the complex array of national and local laws. One of the most difficult roles a board has to play is to look far enough and deep enough behind the words to have a sufficient level of assurance that integrity is really practiced in a company and not just preached."[3]

One Fortune 500 director tells of a CEO of a public, Midwestern manufacturing company, who was married with three children of her own. His administrative assistant was a divorced mom with three children, dependent on her job to support them. Their affair was so disruptive that it was brought to the board, and the immediate reaction was to fire the assistant. The director said, "if anyone goes, it's both of them," pointing out that if the assistant were fired, she would probably sue the company—with good cause. The response of the other directors was, "we'll get a law firm." The dissenting director captured the truth saying, "we don't need a law firm to tell us what's right." The assistant was kept on, relocated to another building, and six months later was back at the executive offices. The dissenting director soon resigned.

Know the Business

You should be learning continuously and eager to do so. At IBM, at least five directors didn't even use a personal computer. You don't need to be an expert, but you need to build the context in which to understand the critical success factors.

Prepare

Plan. Do homework. Read the material. Know ahead what issues to raise at the meeting. George Aucott says up to half of most directors don't read the materials and often ask "stupid questions. If you can't read it, get off the board." "I'm generally well impressed with what I see in the board room," counters Roz Ridgway. "All the boards I'm involved in work very hard." She described a complex issue a board had been working on for a long time. "There were all the materials for the SEC and the proxies. I read them all. If you're going to sign stuff, you better read it," she advised. She estimates that she spends about two hours preparation time for every hour in a committee or board meeting.

Attend Meetings

As Roz Ridgway states, "The hallmark of a good director is you make the meetings, including the committee meetings—period. By and large, this is a 100 percent commitment. Not 'Gee, I'll make it when I can.' You read the materials and you read them well and arrived prepared and already have some things you'd like somebody to explore more. You may already know the answer. But, you may want to see that person in the context of succession. You should be prepared horizontally and vertically. You give meetings all the time you need. You're prepared to do more than sit there. You are prepared to keep topics alive to be sure people have really thought them through and are not treating you like potted palms."

If you miss a meeting, sit down with the chairman, lead or other director, and/or management and get a full briefing. At Coca-Cola, two members missed over 30 percent of the board meetings in 1996, and at NationsBank, directors Delta CEO Ronald Allen and Slane Hosiery Mills President John Slane failed to show up for 25 percent of the board meetings.[4] Shareholder activists are beginning to tag and publicize offenders who slack off. Institutional Shareholder Services withholds voting authority to companies whose directors don't attend at least 75 percent of the board meetings.

Listen Well

This seems obvious, but it's not so easy for CEOs and others at the top of their game. Many leaders have lost the habit of listening well, of being willing to change and adapt. Directors can be tremendously insensitive, interrupting presentations and publicly embarrassing the presenters.

Ask the Right Questions

"It's all that a board can do," opines Robert Monks. "You can't have the knowledge. Keep asking questions and require that they be answered." Ask privately those questions that do not apply to the full board. Get to know the thinking behind something, how realistic it is, what the cushions are for failure. Ask a lot of 'what if' questions." Martha Seger feels directors have a particular obligation to ferret out the impact of consulting "fads. Consultants take off and often are not accountable." She wants to know "what makes you think this approach will work?"

"I ask tough questions," says Roz Ridgway. "I listen carefully to a proposal and the train of thought. I'm very good at asking have you thought it through and 'where do we go from here, and what if we don't' and what if we do. And how will we measure success? I'm a person," she observes, "with years of experience in strategic thinking. It's easier for me to ask some questions. People don't expect me to know everything, because I'm from government, not a business background. I can say 'take me through that again.' If they start throwing initials around, I can say 'would you stop and tell me what those initials stand for?' I don't have to know everything." Many directors think they do, of course. Too many directors think that if they ask a question for clarification, it will be seen as a sign of weakness. "I always ask myself, how will this look in public, how will we explain it to the employees? I believe deeply there are no such things as secrets," adds Ridgway.

John Whiteman reminds us that usually "the directors were invited to be on the board because they liked the chairman and the chairman liked them. As a result of that friendship, the new board member, for the most part, doesn't like to tell his friend his baby's ugly or his idea is ugly. That's common nature. Second, there's a lot of patronizing. You patronize the chairman, and you don't ask the tough questions."

Tom Horton, NACD chair, says asking the right questions means asking very "trenchant, unusual questions" in a "tentative, tactful way, such as 'this is something I don't know very much about' or 'I don't know whether this applies here, but we had a good experience with this approach.' "

If management and the CEO feel you are putting them on the defensive, your questions won't matter. "If you are just unpleasant," says John Olson, "they don't pay attention to you. Only when you have management's confidence, can you have constructive skepticism about what management is proposing. 'Have you considered this?' 'What if that happens?' 'Do you have the right person, the resources you need?' 'Suppose projections are off by 10 percent to 25 percent, then what?' 'Do you have the capital to carry out your plan?' 'What are the risks?' Management sometimes misses one of those questions, and directors bring a fresh perspective."

"If a relationship of trust is there," adds Bill Hawfield, "I can ask almost anything." Well-framed questions allow the owner of an idea to defend her point of view and to explain so other board members understand. William Burleigh, CEO of E. W. Scripps, praises the director with "that X quality who understands what management is facing and the quality to ask a question to penetrate the fog to get to the core of the matter. He asks the question that gets you [the CEO] to strip out all of the incidentals to get you thinking about the strategic direction, to see fresh the question you should be asking yourself. It is valuable in illuminating the dark corners we didn't see," Burleigh continues, "the artful question that summarizes so much, but has an edge on it that demands an answer. Such questions enabled me to be decisive about our strategic direction and what moves we should and should not take."

DON'T MICROMANAGE

Distinguish between policy and operations and respect that difference. Don't second guess management, even if it is an area in which you have specific expertise. The temptation is to help solve problems. Instead, assess management decisions against the strategic plan. Doug Young talks about the too common failing of "tactics in search of a strategy." At General Motors, when the board became engaged in removing the CEO, there was a risk of micromanagement. "When you meet a lot," observes board member Ann McLaughlin, "you've got to find something to do, so you start to ask questions and get involved when perhaps you shouldn't."[5] "It's not important for me to know in detail how to make automobiles. It is important for me to know the numbers, the trends, the policies, succession, to know the strategy," says McLaughlin.

David Tappan describes situations when marketing presented new product programs to various boards, and the directors digressed into a debate on pricing. "It's not a board decision at all, but you would be amazed how everybody steps in to say something about pricing." Someone has to speak up and say, "look, we're not being asked to price this."

CONTRIBUTE

On one hand, there are board members who don't say anything—ever, just collect their checks and move on to the next board meeting. "There were guys at Firestone," says George Aucott, "who never said a word. They were old friends of the CEO and were not going to make any waves. He may have had private conversations with them. But, you do a disservice to other board members by keeping your ideas quiet. If you sit there quietly," Aucott observes, "you never have the debate. Sharing ideas, hearing other points of view, gives other board members an opportunity to tailor their own ideas. It encourages debate and free thinking as to how to handle a particular problem."

On the other hand, as Roy Herberger points out, "board members can have the knowledge, but they don't have to comment on every item that comes up. Most people have a habit of believing they must demonstrate their own expertise. Many people talk too much. A three-hour board meeting shouldn't take six. Most egregious," he says, "is in the area of marketing, because everyone is a marketing expert. Another time waster is tactical diversions. A director will bring in an advertisement or flyer from a competitor and say, 'I've never seen this from you guys.' Those are not strategic things," complains Herberger. "It is a habitual flaw in the way boards are governed."

At his first board meeting, a new director made a suggestion and an old timer dismissed it as a "stupid idea." George Aucott went to the criticizing board member and said, "there are no bad ideas, no stupid suggestions. The only stupid idea is no idea." The important thing is to use the idea to grow other ideas in the forum of the boardroom.

BE WILLING TO TAKE A POSITION

The thinking should be, "I'm going to give my opinion. You have to be willing to talk and not be afraid to make a mistake," George Aucott insists. "A director has to be readily available on the phone, think about issues and give advice. A director should not say 'I don't have an opinion.' " The CEO doesn't need to take the advice, but she needs to hear it.

Director Walter Auch remembers when "directors used to show up and listen to a presentation. Then too big a percentage would wait to see what the CEO was asking for on a vote, looking for a tone of voice" so they could pick up on it and vote with the CEO. "They would cast their votes, get their lunch, pick up their check and go home."

SET PRIORITIES

Don't confuse taking a position with what Terry Lee calls "destructive controversy. You want controversy to get the best thinking on the table. But, it's bad to get the guy who thinks he's smarter than everyone else and tries to prove it." Great directors pick their field of battle and spend their time on important issues. They don't create a lot of animosity by getting killed on little issues.

The best directors "have a keen sense of their role as a director," says David Tappan. "They know when to meddle and not to meddle and when to ask the question. They have a sixth sense of when they are getting a snow job. They don't take up board meeting time by talking about the last cruise they went on. They are broadly relevant. They don't say this is the way we do it at company X. They say 'this is my experience at company X. These are the pros and cons and, of course, these would be modified.' " A good director, according to Tappan, doesn't try to dominate the discussion, but steps in when the discussion needs to be diverted, or adds newer thoughts if others have had their say.

BE A CATALYST TO ACTION

Director Doug Young likes to "frame issues as a problem to generate a good debate. Don't wait for the CEO to say, 'Here is a problem.' A good board member will say 'I think we have a problem here.' The CEO then has to do the strategy work. But, a good board can be both a catalyst and a participant. The board can help find the right problem, the key to strategic solutions, and then they can bless the strategy."

BE CREATIVE

There are a myriad of ways directors can contribute. When Bell Sports board member Rick Winter was business school dean at Pittsburgh, he would bring together some of his brightest students with CEO Terry

Lee, and they would brainstorm marketing ideas. He sent letters about specific marketing programs that the company might try. In one case, Winter used Bell Sports as a beta site for a new software system that instituted better forecasting.

After a few board meetings at a New York Stock Exchange company, a director wrote a note to the chairman and said he had no desire to go to four or five meetings a year and second motions. "I want to be a part of the company," he said. "I would like the freedom to stop by and chat with the CFO or COO. I would like to think if they have a question I could answer, that they would call me. And, when you go to New York to talk with underwriters, I'd love to go with you."

Universal Technical Institute was a profitable, $30 million private company, facing increased competition from community colleges and vocational schools while being squeezed by government regulations. Despite a student placement rate of over 90 percent, and an aggressive sales program, growth was fairly flat. At the suggestion of the advisory board, the company began thinking of the employer of their technicians as the customer, instead of the student. . Employers had a shortage of up to 70,000 technicians. Now UTI has contracts with power employers like Mercedes, Jaguar, BMW, and Ford, who help reimburse student loans and offer high paying jobs and internships in return for access to precisely trained mechanics. Now, the company, at $100 million plus, has become attractive to Wall Street and is considering an IPO.

Avoid Group Think

Passivity is passé. "My directors will not allow someone to steamroll," says Doug Yearley, former CEO of Phelps Dodge, "even though it's my board, and I've brought the directors on. I'll play golf with them. We're good friends. But there is a level of respect that says 'I know if you don't agree, you'll tell me.' There has never been a time when it's been us against them," he adds. "Part of the heads up is that the directors are my boss, and I treat them that way."

Gerber had 75 percent of the baby food market and one of the most trusted brand names in the United States. They generated positive cash flow, but were not growing fast enough. So Gerber decided to diversify—into trucks. Despite the utter lack of synergy, Gerber bought a trucking company with hundreds of truck terminals. The business lost money and was sold, except for an albatross of thirty to thirty-five terminals with such large scale environmental problems that the cost of remediation was more than the value of the terminals. Where was the board to advise that trucking and baby food don't mix?

The danger is going along. The mistake is thinking "if this is what the group wants, then I won't rock the boat." "You can't avoid group think," insists Robert Lear. "Just fight against it all the time, rather than have it lurk in the background."

At Campbell Soup, an independent board helped dissuade the company from making a major acquisition in China. When a trucking company in southern California failed to produce adequate financial information, the advisory board held a special session and identified three or four key indicators the company should watch, such as on-time delivery and sales and safety records, because the company was delivering hazardous materials. The company had been measuring the wrong things. The founders of the company came out of Dupont, where safety first was everything, so they had prioritized the number of accidents. The new indicators are now the centerpiece of growth and strategy.

SUPPORT MANAGEMENT

Remember, this is not an adversarial relationship. Once the board endorses a CEO, the board's job is to support him—privately and publicly. That, says Chris Augur, "gives that person the mandate and the confidence within the organization and externally to do what's necessary. Then bold actions can come out of that CEO."[6] As Betsy Sanders says, "In any company, you have to realistically be able to implicitly trust the excellence of each person working there or you can't do your job. You have to trust that the people are the best."

This is where the board's responsibility for policy versus operations comes into play. As Terry Lee points out, "management sleeps it, eats it, owns it. Management is accountable for solving problems. The board is responsible for giving good advice and ultimately taking action if things get out of whack." At Caterpillar, the board firmly supported CEO Don Fife when the United Auto Workers were threatening to strike. "He had the courage to carry though despite a lot of risk. The UAW could have shut down the company," says director Clayton Yeutter.

CEOs are more willing to take social and professional risks when they can rely on the loyalty of their boards, according to James Westphal.[7] But supporting management doesn't mean support management blindly. "In most boards, it's considered a mark of failure if you don't have unanimity," says Robert Monks. "Who's kidding whom? Reasonable people will disagree."

BE POSITIVE

One of the most destructive things you can do is go on a board and destroy its purpose by constantly disagreeing. If you can't support the board's efforts and the corporate mission, don't stay. Bob Hartman says the UTI advisory board gives "guidance, encouragement, challenge and constructive criticism. I find the board very supportive. I am amazed how pleased they are with the things we have done. I thought they would be more critical than they are."

CREATE AN ATMOSPHERE OF ACCOUNTABILITY

Chris Augur, former CEO of SpeedFam, says "You're doing the CEO a favor by doing that. You are causing that person to crystallize the issues and to create a forum where he prepares and analyzes and then presents his view of the company and where he is taking it. If the atmosphere on the board is too cozy, that sense of accountability is reduced, the analysis and the exercises and the work the CEO conducts is often less and insufficient," Augur warns. "It becomes more of a day-to-day CEO paradigm, which can be dangerous."[8]

MAINTAIN A GOOD BEDSIDE MANNER

This molds the culture of the board. This translates into the finesse and tact that is such a cherished boardroom commodity. An incompatible board that doesn't communicate well together, a board peopled with even one divisive director, or a board that breaks up into cliques is a recipe for inertia. An infighting, bickering board with directors jockeying for attention spells disaster. Anything that eats into the trust and honesty of a board's culture can only mean trouble for the company.

The quality of a board's dialogue enables the strategic synergies that elevate companies. "There is a fundamental requirement of collegiality," emphasizes Roz Ridgway. This means resisting the temptation to say I told you so. At Phelps Dodge, according to Yearley, "so many of my board have been in the chair. They know not to impose their experience on us whether it is in compensation or data systems. A good director will say 'let me share our experience in this area.' "

Robert Lear served on twenty boards, and he is convinced their effectiveness hinges on how the chemistry works in the company. "You don't need scorecards. These are people of achievement. But, sometimes there are good boards that just don't work," he says. He offers AT&T as an example, where "Bob Allen had them buffaloed. There were good men on the board who did dumb things." Steve McConnell says, "When you have bad governance, issues get squelched. Things go unstated. There are hidden agendas. A board enables resolution of differences. If greed and ego overwhelm the discussion, you get bad decisions."

The challenge is to distinguish between getting along and going

along. Nell Minow believes that if you "graded directors on a psycho-
logical test, they would all get 100 percent. They can walk into a room,
size up the norms, and fit in. They are all good consensus builders,
who work well with others. Seldom are they iconoclastic. Rarely are
they boat rockers. A tough CEO," she adds, "is likely to turn into a
pussycat on someone else's board, because he is thinking 'I wouldn't
want someone telling me what to do.' "

Be a Coach

The smaller the company, the more important the role of director as
coach is—to the CEO and to senior management. "Some people are
good players," observes Terry Lee, "Some are good coaches. A good
board member was, in his day, a very good player, but has learned to
be a very good coach."

Experienced directors can do much to model the performance of
less experienced directors.

When Roy Herberger joined one of his first boards of directors, he
sat next to a seasoned director who mentored him, explaining which
important points should be made and why and other subtleties of the
process. Herberger asked for feedback on how he did. "Did I focus on
the right things," Herberger wanted to know. "New board members
can be confused by the legislative nature of the board relationship. It
sounds formal so they don't want to say anything."

Think Full-Time Job

Every month Bill Hawfield spends an afternoon visiting retailers who
sell the products of his company, and then shares it with the company.
"I'm calling at least once a month. It's a gentle accountability. I'm
showing I care and that I am engaged. I use e-mail a lot." Hawfield
stresses the importance of "asking about the whole person. Genuinely
caring about them promotes a high level of trust. You have to be available whenever they need you—whenever that is." As Betsy Sanders
says "the board doesn't just own me for the meeting."

Limit the Number of Directorships

As a general rule, acting executives should not serve on more than
three boards, including their own. Retired individuals should serve on
no more than five at the outside. As Ken West of TIAA-CREF says,
"just keeping up with the times is a big challenge. To have the necessary breadth of knowledge is much tougher than it used to be. Which

is a very good reason someone shouldn't be on more than three, maybe four boards. A complex company requires thirty or more days a year of its board members' time in one form or another."

When he was CEO of BellSouth, John Clendenin sat on nine boards, including Coca-Cola, Equifax, and Kroger. Robert Guizueta, CEO of Coca-Cola, sat on seven boards, including Eastman Kodak, Ford Motor, and SunTrust Banks.[9] There is no way these CEOs can be 360-degree directors.

Exercise Independence

Exercise independence and a healthy balance of power with the CEO. According to Nell Minow, if the independent members meet separately and own stock, "it's like murder suspects who have motive and opportunity. The motive comes from having stock, the opportunity comes from meeting in executive session." She believes independent directors need to take time following every board meeting to respond to what they heard. Such sessions have a rolling agenda with "perpetual" issues, which include evaluation and succession. It doesn't work if you have to ask for a special session, Minow says. It's too awkward. If directors reach an impasse with management, you want a process whereby discussions can get a clear airing and the majority will make the best decision.

A major signal of independence is when independent directors control the board's nomination process.

Be Willing to Disagree

Deliver bad news privately and good news publicly. Generally, if you are concerned about a critical issue, it's best to first approach the CEO privately. If you are still dissatisfied, tell the CEO you plan to bring it up with other outside directors. If necessary, raise the issue at the board meeting. If you are not willing to do that, you are a liability. Ultimately, if you disagree over a substantive issue, and it is not being addressed, you should resign.

"Most CEOs are there because they are tough and self confident," Shelby Yastrow points out. "These are not guys you want to say 'you're doing this wrong' to," because "you get thrown off the board. Then, you don't get the money. You don't get to say you're on the board."

"How does the board dissent?" asks Shelby Yastrow. "Every board has a leader. Every board has two or four people willing to stand up and be counted." The CEO has to know he is going to be challenged and is getting the best thinking. After all, a director should be encouraged to direct."

When the Spreckles Sugar company came out of bankruptcy, a new board was brought in. Bart Brown, a director, describes it. "We had really dedicated directors, seven people form totally diverse backgrounds, who gave a lot of time and energy. Hard to imagine, although the directors had never met, from the first day, there was substantial unanimity between us. . . . From the day I walked in, the pressure was on to sell the entire company. Even though we were pressured constantly for three years, the board thought that would be a terrible mistake."

The sugar company was losing money, but Spreckles had a profitable manufacturing division. Within four months, the independent board members created a strategy with a plan to sell the sugar company. The CEO's strategy was to do the reverse and sell the manufacturing company, which would have netted about $12 a share. Shareholders threatened a proxy fight in support of the CEO, so the independent directors brought several of them on board. The shareholders, said Brown, "became enthusiastic supporters for the plan we had." The sugar company sold first, and the valuable manufacturing company was later sold separately. The stockholders received $26 a share.

What happens when the board disagrees among itself? You keep the question open, says Roz Ridgway. "Everyone continues to make their case. Some minds change. Maybe the case is poorly presented. Over time, the inability to make a decision is the decision."

Because directors should be representing the shareholders, logic insists that they, therefore, share mutual objectives. Disagreement occurs only on the means, not the end. Gary Lutin subscribes to this concept and believes that differences come down to personal preferences.

One of the best tests of a good board member is your willingness to step down. Betsy Sanders left a health systems board where there was an "enormous clash of egos" and the board was unable to function. Walter Auch sat on the board of a manufacturing company with an "exciting new product," whose CEO felt he had to penetrate the market quickly. "He was more interested in getting the company spread far and wide, than in running the business." He consumed working capital faster than he could raise it. Auch resigned. The company went out of business. "There are lots of wonderful new products that never get to market," Auch laments. The company "could have survived and prospered."

Bobby Inman's first board was Western Union, which he joined just after retiring from the government. He had been actively recruited by the CEO, who told him that he wanted Inman to help with strategic planning and that he would create a special strategic planning committee when Inman came on board. Taking the CEO at his word, Inman spent a couple days visiting facilities and the other board members thought it was a good idea and went along. The company had approved acquisitions of three new products, and, during their visits, the board discovered there were major issues with working capital needs and the ongoing developmental activities necessary to complete them. The CEO said that the directors were intruding into management prerogatives. Inman resigned, realizing he was brought on, not for strategic planning, but "for my name and the publicity." Ultimately, it galvanized the board to ask questions, and seven months later, the CEO was discharged.

TIMES OF CRISIS

The board member is there as an insurance policy for the dreaded and inevitable eventuality when something goes wrong. He has to be there to stick his finger in the dyke. As Shelby Yastrow says, "There are times when the responsibilities are gut wrenching, as during severe financial problems, hostile takeover bids or 'life and death' litigation. It's at those times when a board member earns his pay and loses sleep, knowing that the shareholders and employees are relying on him to protect them from serious harm. If he's not prepared for these situations, he shouldn't be there."

"Don't bother me with the nitty gritty," says Roy Herberger, "I've got to be there to protect the CEO from his own avarice, protect the shareholders and the employees. You really find out how good you are in a crisis. When things are good," Roy Herberger adds, "it is comparatively easy. When you run up against the wall, you earn your keep."

According to Bob Inman, "I'm a more demanding board member, a more probing member because of my experiences. It's not from the good news that you learn. It's from the bad news."

ACQUISITIONS

One of the toughest challenges for a board, according to Bennett Dorrance, is approving acquisitions. "The prices are so substantial. We looked at a lot of acquisitions and didn't make any last year." As Warren Buffett observes, "acquisitions are thrilling. They give the CEO enormous psychic benefits by expanding his dominion and generating more action. The governance problem," according to Buffett, "is that most acquisitions do not come to the board for discussion until the process is substantially underway" and until after the CEO and key managers have invested substantial personal capital in it. To reject a proposed acquisition at that stage is embarrassing to management and can be interpreted as a rejection of the CEO who brought the acquisition to the board. Buffett believes that "more dumb acquisitions are made in the name of strategic plans than any other."[10]

Roy Herberger agrees. "The sale of an asset is where the liabilities really are. Some things you can't protect yourself on, such as a discussion of the probability of a sale and being sure it is open to outside bidders. You never do that, because you can't divulge any details because you would sour the deal. It's supposed to be a free event, but it's truly manipulated." This is where seasoned board members are valuable, Herberger adds, because there are "predatory people waiting to file suits."

The management of Phelps Dodge approached their board about an important merger. The board members knew the culture of the merger candidate well. "It won't work. We think you should step away from this transaction," the board said to CEO Yearley. He took the board's advice and ended discussions. At the time, the stock price ratio was 1 to 2, Phelps Dodge versus the merger candidate. A downturn in copper prices soon after upended that ratio to 4 to 1 in favor of Phelps Dodge's stock value.

When United Airlines made a pass at America West Airlines, says CEO Bill Franke, "the board was very methodical in requiring the lawyers and investment bankers to satisfy them that the price was fair and that we would actually see the money. The directors took a lot of time to consider the impact on different work groups. By acting slowly and methodically, the board kept management from getting stars in their eyes. The board coalesced and provided tremendous advice and support." The value provided was "worth far more than we pay them for the year," Franke adds.

In an example of a board that failed its shareholders, at Foxmire drugs the board was made up of two co-CEOs and three independent board members. Despite the fact that Foxmire was in trouble, the co-CEOs persuaded the other board members to pass $100 million to the $3 billion parent for dividend payouts. Sixty-seven days later, Foxmire went into bankruptcy and eventually totally disappeared. Holding onto the $100 million could have prevented it. "The board didn't stand up and ask the hard questions," says Bart Brown. "The board did what was in the best interest of the parent without regard for the future of the company.

Bart Brown has served on the boards of nine troubled companies. "Most of the people on the boards had a relationship at one time or another with the CEO. They've known him a long time. They trusted him. Signs of trouble arose, and they said, 'hey, he'll take care of it.'

They didn't have all the facts. It's not that anybody is trying to hide the facts from them," Brown observes. "It's simply that nobody wants to admit that things are as bad as they really are. Things slide and they get worse, and they get worse. Even when directors realize there's a problem, they vacillate. They don't want to make hard decisions. Finally, when they start to take steps, they take tiny steps. They kind of limp along, instead of hitting it and hitting it hard."[11] The disservice is to the shareholders, the employees, and ultimately the CEO himself.

A happier story is Circle K, which, when Brown came in as CEO for the turnaround, was "a company built to be sold, not operated. The view was that if Circle K, the convenience store company, accumulated enough stores, some big oil company would want to buy them. However, the industry was going in a totally different direction, "By the time they got where they wanted to be, nobody wanted what they had." So Brown inherited some 5000 locations and closed 2500 of them. It took three-and-a-half years to figure out which the good locations were and to work with the creditor constituencies. Said Brown, the "board totally supported us—to give us time to prove it was a viable business."[12]

At Excite Elect, a hostile takeover offer galvanized the board into addressing the situation at the under performing company. "It's never an easy thing to evaluate," concedes director Dave McLaughlin. "It takes place over time. The board struggled with the state of the company and performed superbly." They organized into an independent committee, resisting the easy route of accepting that first hostile offer.

The stock was around $11, up from $2 or $3, and Excite Elect was being offered around $19. Instead, the board decided to go into competitive bidding. It was, as McLaughlin recalls, risky, because the price could collapse, and "we would all look like fools." The offer crystallized the thinking of the board that maybe the way out was to sell the company, but only if "we could deliver significant return to the shareholders. To the surprise of everyone," McLaughlin says, "it galvanized management and they ended up with five offers on the table. The company sold for $29 a share. "Everyone was a winner. Management retired with some funds and their honor; shareholders wound up with a respectable return, and the board was able to insure that the company realized its potential and didn't hang in there just to protect jobs."

Directors must be alert to signs of trouble such as debt-to-equity ratio deterioration, market share downturns, same store sales declines, cash flow problems, resignations of key personnel, and morale issues. As Carter Pate, Price Waterhouse partner says, CEOs have invested tremendous emotional and intellectual capital into a management strategy that is failing. To change direction means admitting failure—with all of its ramifications. In turn, directors find it hard not to trust the CEO and admit the company has developed problems on their watch.[13]

As Bart Brown says, most of the time the board and management have time to study, test, improvise, retest, and go through a one or two year process to create strategy. "In troubled companies, you don't have time to do all that. Forget about the long-term strategy. Only when he's stopped bleeding, do you stabilize the patient and start thinking what's the long-term goal."

"You've got to save the company first. Do the best you can. But you've got to do something. You can't just let things simmer until you have things 100 percent correct. You've got to educate the board that 'we can't study this to death.' You've just got to find out what needs to be done and how it needs to be done. Get together with the CEO and outline a game plan with a tight, tight time schedule. And, either he does it, or he needs to understand that we'll go find somebody else to do it."

If directors are not informed and engaged, they often head for the door. If a company could be heading into trouble, it's important to talk to prospective directors candidly up front, before they come on board. Do they have experience with troubled companies? Remember, no surprises. Rural/Metro CEO John Furman, the attorney who came into the troubled company as its stock nose-dived, says, "It's a difficult situation. Nobody pays attention to the indemnity agreement or the indemnification provisions or the D&O (directors and officers insurance) policy, until the first lawsuit hits. And, then what starts to happen, and it drives the lawyers crazy, is that everybody wants exactly what they said put on the record. They don't want there to be any misunderstanding that they voted against whatever it was that might have a problem." It's at this point, says Furman, that you need to have "heart to heart conversations with people that take that position. If they want to get off the board, let them get off the board, because they'll cause you more problems ultimately."[14]

Unless you are sitting in a boardroom, it's tough to tell what boards and which directors are performing well. Directors rarely publicize their reasons for leaving a board, making it nearly impossible for stakeholders to know what prompted a resignation. As Ken West of TIAA-CREF says, "some good looking boards don't do very well, and some bad looking boards do pretty well. A board that has tolerated poor performance without changing management is probably a dead giveaway of a board tolerating mediocrity and less." Another sure clue is "some company with a full arsenal of takeover defenses, saying, 'even if God came down with a fistful of cash,' they wouldn't take it."

A key test of a CEO is, indeed, how she manages though adversity. When a company takes a nosedive, Bobby Inman wants to know if the directors could have foreseen the downturn. What was done to get costs down? Did they do that humanely? Was there concern for the stakeholders? Did they avoid "another Christmas Eve massacre?" If they have done their job well, they should know ahead if layoffs are required and not wait until the holidays to dismiss everyone in order "to do something ahead of the fiscal year." Inman is convinced that leadership in these tough situations can be learned, "if you are interested in people in the first place. Otherwise you come across as false. It's just a joy to watch superb leaders," he says.

THE AUDIT COMMITTEE

The Federal Deposit Insurance Corporation and the New York Stock Exchange requires all listed companies to have a minimum of three audit committee members—all independent. Audit committees are responsible for reviewing the company's annual audited financial statements: appointing external auditors, interacting with internal auditors and reviewing internal controls.

Audit practices and compensation are the two lightning rods for regulators. Perfunctory audits, lax director oversight, and occasional outright fraud have toppled the complacency that has prevailed. "Certainly," says Arthur Rock, lead director on Intel's board for many years, "the audit committee is the most important committee on the board." As Arthur Levitt says, "Directors need to understand the quality of annual reporting and disclosure practices, so they can influence those practices when—in their judgement—they fall short of meeting investor needs. Management and the outside auditor may find these questions inconvenient. They may even be embarrassing. This is a small price to pay. Every time directors ask a tough disclosure or financial question, thousands of shareholders will benefit."[15]

Areas likely to command increased audit committee scrutiny include environmental matters, internal controls, computer related controls, insurable risk management, interim reporting, regulatory and legal compliance, and budgets and forecasts.

Too many audit committee members are inept, ill informed, and financially illiterate. One well-known auditor says he is appalled by how much time is frittered away in board meetings by directors asking what he calls "stupid questions." One overdone question is "Can you tell us any questions we should be asking you?"

Often, members don't know essential, basic information such as what the internal controls are, what kind of systems are in place and how management knows whether numbers from the field are accurate. Other core issues about which audit members are often in the dark are what drives profitability, how R & D decisions are made, budget comparisons relative to forecasts, how capital spending is done, how management reports back, and what the critical success factors are. At Waste Management, for example, a director needs to know about internalization, which is the percent and amount of garbage delivered to wholly owned landfills.

MANAGED EARNINGS

One of the practices provoking the regulators' attention is managing earnings. The pressure has magnified as a result of short-term market myopia, with companies riveted on earnings per share. When stocks are punished by missed earnings expectations of even a penny and, with compensation increasingly tied to stock prices, the lure of managed earnings has soared. And, so have the abuses. "It's just human nature that executives are going to do whatever they can to meet expectations," says Gary Illiano, Grant Thornton's eastern regional director of professional standards.[16]

For example, managers pressing for bonuses often try to get revenue in as quickly as they can, when it should be deferred, says Arthur Rock. Audit committee members need to know about depreciation policies and think about the interests of long-term shareholders.

Another red flag is excessive write-offs taken during mergers. AOL had to restate its earnings twice after the SEC questioned write-offs related to research and development in a company that AOL acquired. Network Associates was questioned about a $220 million write-down on two recent acquisitions. Don Kirk, former chairman of the Financial Accounting Standards Board, says that directors should question the wisdom of using the same auditing firm to consult on the merger and also do any valuations.[17]

According to a Committee of Sponsoring Organizations of the Treadway Commission (COSO) study from 1987 to 1998 of nearly 300 companies involved in alleged instances of fraudulent financial reporting, smaller companies seem to be more vulnerable to fraud than the larger, more closely monitored companies. In 71 percent of these cases, the CEO was named and, in 43 percent of the cases, the CFO was associated with the financial statement fraud. Audit committees of the fraudulent companies generally met only once a year, and one-fourth of the companies did not even have an audit committee.

Further, about 60 percent of the directors of these companies were insiders or "gray" directors with special ties to the company or management. The average financial misstatement of assets was $25 million, a big number in light of the relatively small sizes of the companies involved. Over 50 percent of the sample firms were bankrupt/defunct or experienced a significant change in ownership following the disclosure of the fraud. One out of five of the companies was delisted by a national stock exchange.[18]

The abuses have prompted SEC Chairman Arthur Levitt Jr. to chastise inappropriate accounting practices. The practices most often used to manage earnings:

- *Big bath restructuring charges:* Establishing large, inappropriate reserves today to prevent lower earnings in the future.
- *Miscellaneous cookie jar reserves:* Using unrealistic assumptions to estimate liabilities during good times to manage earnings during bad times.
- *Creative acquisition accounting*: Immediately expensing unrealistic amounts for in-process research and development to lower future earnings.
- *Materiality*: Intentionally recording errors to meet earnings forecasts and then arguing that the effect on the bottom line is not significant.[19]

New Audit Rules

The result of these disclosures is a revolutionary, much debated set of audit committee best-practice recommendations driven by the Securities and Exchange Commission and the major securities markets. The result, regardless of the specific outcomes, is to make audit the focal point—and the symbol—of change and the new dynamic.

The framework of the Blue Ribbon Committee on Improving the Effectiveness of Audit Committees, issued in February 1999, emphasizes disclosure, transparency, and accountability. In December 1999, the Securities and Exchange Commission (SEC), the securities exchanges, and the Auditing Standards Board adopted new rules in response to the Blue Ribbon Committee Report and recommendations:

1. Define independence more rigorously.
2. Require independent audit committee.
3. Mandate minimum audit committee size and increased financial literacy.
4. Mandate a written charter detailing responsibilities and duties.
5. Mandate annual public disclosure of audit committee activities.
6. Clarify oversight responsibility for outside auditor's engagement.

7. Mandate discussion with outside auditor regarding independence.
8. Require outside auditor to discuss quality of financial reporting with the audit committee.
9. Include a report from the audit committee in proxy statements.
10. Mandate interim review of quarterly financial reporting.[20]

AUDIT COMMITTEE MEMBERSHIP

Membership is limited to independent directors who meet a more restrictive definition of independence, and are financially literate. Must include at least three members, at least one of whom has an accounting or related financial background.

ACCOUNTABILITY

The outside auditor is accountable to the board of directors, which selects, evaluates and replaces the outside auditor as appropriate, and which ensures the auditor's independence. The auditor will be required to provide an interim financial review and to discuss the quality, not just the acceptability, of the company's financial reporting. Further, according to Ernst & Young, independent auditors are now required to communicate certain matters, including significant adjustments, management judgements and accounting estimates, significant new accounting policies, and disagreements with management.

TRANSPARENCY

Audit committees would have a written charter detailing their responsibilities and must disclose the charter and verify that they have done so in their proxy. Other disclosures are required in the annual report and Form 10-K.

One area provoking intense controversy is the mandate to discuss quality. Many say that such judgments are so subjective that they are meaningless. The other major concern is the risk of liability such specificity may provoke. As John Olson, senior partner of Gibson, Dunn and Crutcher, asks, "Will implementing the recommendations make a difference in improving the quality of financial reporting and preventing fraud?" More basic to the recommendations is the question of available sanctions. Other than publicity, there doesn't seem to be an alternative to delisting, the "atomic bomb" sanction that punishes shareholders—the very group the rules are designed to protect.

No doubt that audit committee members will work more hours, engage more resources, be more proactive in their oversight, and become more accountable. Along the way, they may also earn more pay and incur added liability. As John Olson points out, courts have held insider directors to higher standards than other directors in meeting their duty of care. Unfortunately, a number of courts have carried this perfectly valid principle over to outside directors who serve on the audit committee, arguing that those directors have special access to inside knowledge.

Olson believes the requirement for a certification type report makes audit committee members especially vulnerable to liability allegations.[21] But, Arthur Levitt Jr. dismisses this objection saying, "I refuse to believe that more information, more public disclosure, and more active and diligent oversight creates greater legal exposure."[22] The new regulations may take a toll on membership. As one director, former investment banker Stephen Bansak, says, "It is a no win to sit on an audit committee today."

"I wish we had all been able to get there voluntarily," Bill Franke, CEO of America West Holdings Corporation, adds. "Apparently, the SEC became convinced we couldn't. I hope that nobody ordains the rules." "The Blue Ribbon Committee recommendations are an invitation to plaintiffs' lawyers and went too far in seeking to establish additional formality and a mandated process as a substitute for the responsibility of the board as a whole and management," Edison CEO John Bryson believes. "I don't think lapses of audit committees should be written to a universal mandate." Most agree.

"The greatest danger," warns Olson, who counsels Fortune 500 audit committees, "is that audit committees will be pushed toward an unhelpful focus on disclosure and accounting details, spending more time being briefed and reassured by lawyers and auditors, and will spend too little time in meaningful financial oversight discussions with corporate management. The audit committee should focus on the big issues—the key areas of business and financial risk to which the enterprise is exposed. For this critical function," Olson believes, "the best qualified will often be those with practical management experience as opposed to those with a finance or accounting background."

He also warns of the danger of audit overload and the importance for audit committees to look forward, not back—not so easy in the new environment.

CEO EVALUATION

The number one responsibility of directors is management succession and the hiring and firing of the CEO. Easier said than done. Directors must always be thinking, Is our CEO the best for the company—at this time, at this place? Are there gaps in expectations, goals, and commitments? If so, is the CEO addressing them? Does she understand them? Has the board specifically discussed the measures and has the CEO responded—and understood? If there are too many no's, the board has to act. The spate of forced CEO departures at American Express, General Motors, IBM, Kodak, and Westinghouse in the early 1990s catalyzed the process and set the stage for more.

Seventy-two percent of boards have a formal CEO performance review mechanism in place,[23] and almost 80% of directors think they do a good job. (See sample CEO evaluation form in Appendix 6.) "If I were CEO," asserts Shelby Yastrow, "I'd want each board member to give me a performance review unsigned. I don't want it to say 'you are great.' Say, here are the good and the bad points."

Robert Lear looks for three ingredients in an evaluation: 1) formal procedures to see how new technology is embraced, 2) how the CEO deals with global competition, and 3) how well the CEO does with creating and implementing the strategic planning; for example, if he got rid of an old product line that has been losing money. Simply put, says Lear, the CEO and the board should agree on what the CEO should get done during the year. And, then over the course of the year, see how he is doing. What happens all too often is that "the CEO says to hell with you, I'm rated every month by the financials. That's my rating." And all too often, he ignores the board.

At Campbell Soup, "most important is the care and feeding of the CEO," says Bennett Dorrance. Each director completes an evaluation form, and the chair of the compensation committee compiles them. Directors rate the CEO on performance goals on a scale of one to five with an option of a "qualified response" indicating the director does not have sufficient information to be definitive. The full board then discusses the feedback. "It takes a lot of time for the committee chair to do that and get a fair response on all the different issues that come up," Dorrance says.

According to Clayton Yeutter, "Caterpillar does the best job on CEO evaluation of any company I've been associated with." Every January, the CEO sits down with the relevant committee and lays out the objectives for the coming year. It involves some twenty to thirty objectives that are carefully delineated, each of which can be measured and evaluated. He comes back a year later and summarizes his view of how that has worked out and what he has accomplished. He lays out the list for the following year and then provides an opportunity for interchange. Although it is at the committee level, all outside directors are invited. According to Yeutter, it was relatively easy for Don Fife, who was a "world class CEO, to lay his guts on the line."

At Beckman Instruments, the board was concerned about the performance of the CEO, who was immersed in day-to-day operations and who ignored the strategic, external responsibilities of a chairman and CEO. The company was stalled and needed to generate growth. As David Tappan, a director at the time, said, "we had to do something big." Tappan was charged with leading the evaluation and feedback process. "I talked to each independent director and had the responsibility for blending opinions into consensus recommendations" to share with the CEO. The board "couldn't believe he would change his spots. But, it was an amazing thing," says Tappan. At the board's prodding, the CEO appointed a president/COO and concentrated on the big issues. And at the CEO's urging, Beckman acquired Colter, a merger of equals, and a "big acquisition. Every year, the CEO reported back on his progress. It was a remarkable thing. I didn't think he could change."

The time the board acts most decisively is when it decides it has to change CEOs. It is a challenge to be sure that you have the right CEO, says Robert Monks. "I've been a director of a dozen public companies, where we tried to understand the health of the CEO. Being a CEO is a tough job. It's not surprising that people burn out. It's a fearsome commitment to make."

The mediocre CEO is the board's nemesis. A terrible CEO is much easier to confront. "We have a saying at Warburg Pincus," James Vogelstein, president of E. M. Warburg, Pincus & Co., says. " 'We have never fired a bad CEO too soon.' " [24]

The board has to be alert to warning signs. All too often, a rising stock price will be the test of doing well and declining earnings the test of doing poorly. As Vogelstein notes, "But how many times have we seen a combination of clever public relations, clever accounting, and short term expediency—cutting research and development, for example—produce a rising stock price while a company was deteriorating internally." And, how many times has the market punished management for putting long-term strategy ahead of instant profits? [25]

The catalogue of indifference, ignorance, ineffectiveness and inertia in dealing with ineffective CEOs is legendary. But it takes only one director to catalyze the board, to break through an impasse. One study documents a strong relation between the percentage of outside directors and the frequency of outside CEO succession. It also establishes a positive relationship between the appointment of an executive from outside the firm and the number of outside directors. Third, evidence from stock returns indicate that, on average, shareholders benefit from outside appointments, but are harmed when an insider succeeds a fired CEO. [26]

Cleveland Machine Controls was a private company that had

grown from zero to about $40 million. It was stagnating and "drowning in overhead" under the 72-year-old CEO, who owned 80 percent of the stock. George Aucott came onto the advisory board, which included seven outsiders. When he realized the scope of the problems, Aucott called the other board members and found they all shared his concerns. "We decided to bring in a new CEO or resign from the board. The CEO resigned, and the company prospered," Aucott says. "We sold it and made a lot of money."

When Genentech was negotiating with Roche, it was learned the CEO was doing some under-the-table negotiating in his private interest without discussing it with the board. David Tappan was one of four outside directors assigned the job of evaluating the extent of any abuses. As the investigation unfolded, the directors learned that while they were negotiating an operating arrangement with Roche, the CEO was trying to negotiate several million dollar loans to pay for the mansion he had bought.

As Tappan points out, it is typical for directors to be indecisive in these situations and wait until their hand is forced. In this case, the directors "all had personal doubts about the way things were being run" before this incident. "We said why shouldn't we be the exception to the rule and take action," Tappan says. Over a two-week period, the four directors spent fifteen-hour days looking into the situation, investigating the CEO's performance and the ethical questions, and interviewing the top fifteen executives within the company. With the help of the full board, the committee negotiated the settlement of fifteen class action lawsuits, let the CEO go, and selected his replacement. After a full day's discussion, "there was not a contrary view," says Tappan, "and the new CEO is there right now doing an excellent job."

The board must be proactive. There is no one else to deal with the inept, ineffectual, or the some 15 to 20 percent of the CEOs who are alcoholics or drug abusers. Union Pacific Corp announced a medical leave for prominent former Secretary of Transportation, Drew Lewis. Forty-seven-year-old CEO Loren Ansley of Microtel died of a heroin overdose.[27] Venture funded firms frequently replace senior management during their tenure, because it is so tough for founders to metamorphose into visionary managers who can lead their companies through the multiple transitions of growth.

In a turnaround in 1998, the six-member board of Multiple Zones International in Seattle replaced the chairman, the president, and the CIO. As Bobby Inman points out, "when the founder is involved as CEO, it's a different world. It's toughest of all. In a company built by the founder, there is enormous loyalty. You can plan what to do, if something happens to him. But it's infinitely harder for a board to quietly ask the CEO to step aside."

Dave McLaughlin agrees that it is critical to "evaluate the CEO and nudge a transition when necessary. When you look back over a year, at a new venture that is still struggling and not much has changed, I start escalating the conversation at the boardroom. At a smaller company," McLaughlin says, "the identity of the company is intertwined with the people at the top. They are friends. They've gone through hell together to get to a certain point." When you get into situations where you are considering the future of the company, "your exposure to the company has got to be more than simply sitting in a boardroom with people coming in and making presentations," McLaughlin insists.

"In some ways, it's an onerous task to serve on a board," he says, "always preparing for that emergency. Often, there are big issues looming in the financing of the business and some strategic call or assessment of technology, while, at the same time, it isn't at all clear that the right person is in place." At the same time, adds McLaughlin, "you have a group getting to know one another and trying to work together in a limited time frame and learning to trust each other and function in a way that leads to effective results. They really work at it pretty hard," he continues. "It's not like a suit they put on. They worry about it and read and try to get prepared. When there are issues, there is a lot more communication among board members than people realize."

These are some of the broad benchmarking questions directors should be asking as they evaluate the CEO:

- What does the CEO have to do to succeed? Is he doing it?
- Do we have the right CEO? Why?
- Is a strong succession plan in place? Do we pay enough attention to succession issues?
- Are the proper strategies in place?
- What two or three strategies can affect the company, such as price increases, changes in the product mix, adding value to products?
- Are things getting better or worse?
- Where is new top line growth in the company going to come from?
- Does the CEO develop, attract, retain, and motivate an effective management team?
- Is there high quality, cost-effective management of the operations?

SUCCESSION

The average CEO's tenure is four years. The selection of the CEO and her team is profoundly important, yet often, just as with director recruitment, the succession process is haphazard and reactive, confounded by personalities and egos and passive or captive directors. Often, the selection process is antiquated, backward looking and devoid of critical assessment. This is where opportunity cost ratchets up. The wrong person can be a disaster. This is where boards earn their keep—and lock in or erase the success of an enterprise.

Common pitfalls are:

- Board passivity where directors cede their responsibility to management.
- Cloning.
- Isolation from succession candidates, both internal and external.
- Failing to recruit for the future.
- Reactive recruiting at the last minute.
- Outside candidates may be proven as CEOs, but you will never know how they really fit your culture and your company. The reverse is true with internal candidates.
- Selecting form over substance.
- Entrenched CEOs and founders.

Nearly 10 percent of new CEOs leave within the first eighteen months.[28] Over half of all Fortune 500 CEOs have been in office less than six years. The pressure is intensifying. Boards are giving CEOs less time to establish themselves. And competition is mushrooming, with powerful global ramifications. Israeli companies alone will hire more than 3000 senior executives from 1998 to 2001. Six hundred Internet companies emerge every single month, just in the "Silicon Valley."[29] Each year, for the next ten years, some 5500 new top executive jobs will be created. The pressure to hire right—and to do it fast and first—is immense.

As Dave McLaughlin says, "It's hugely difficult to select the right CEO. I've seen a company lose billions of dollars in value when it makes a mistake, and it doesn't get corrected easily. Years were lost. And, I've seen situations where the right person has revitalized what looked like a hopeless situation." Most important for the directors, McLaughlin says, is to understand the performance and growth strategy of the business and to insure that the right leadership is in place to address the strategy.

Edison's CEO John Bryson spends a good deal of board time on succession and management development, talking about the company's effort to identify younger talent, introducing senior managers to the board. "The board's most important role is selection of the CEO and the evaluation of the executive team. And the readiness to act, if necessary, to make a change."

At Motorola, there is an increased focus on the management development committee. "This is where the team spends time one on one. Two board members talk to a particular senior manager without anyone else there, an opportunity to see an individual two on one," says former CEO Gary Tooker. In his case, the "board knew I didn't want to continue past age sixty. Bob Galvin [the former CEO and chairman] put a succession plan in place a long time ago, and we try to make changes with the least amount of frustration. The management development committee reviews the organization within the company and knows our life plans."

At Bethlehem Steel, directors are actively involved in succession planning. They are encouraged to visit subsidiaries and spend time with management and division presidents, go to dinner with them and their spouses, and get to know them. "We open the process up totally," says Chairman and CEO Curtis "Hank" Barnette, who relies heavily on his board.

The board focuses on an eighteen-officer group, three people deep. Directors see their objectives, receive their reports and performance ratings, visit regularly with them, and discuss succession several times a year, holding "very detailed discussions." Candidates are ranked A or B to indicate their state of readiness. In August 1999, there was an A candidate in place for all current officers. At NCR, which has a new board, directors are extremely active in addressing succession. Fifty to sixty people are discussed at the committee level, which ends up in a book that is reviewed in an annual session of the full board.

"The old fashioned way of CEOs anointing successors is out the window," says William Burleigh of E. W. Scripps. For the board "to abdicate that responsibility, however well meaning that abdication is, is to function in an irresponsible way. Once you're given the job, it's the most important thing you have to do." The process, according to Burleigh, involves the board talking intensely over a long period of time, assessing the needs of the company, putting personality to need. Burleigh, who retired in mid-2000, says the policy governance committee is the immediate agent with whom he deals. Once when Burleigh went overseas, he recommended a successor in a sealed letter that he does not think was ever opened. "Since then, events have eclipsed the content of that letter. I may have a recommendation when the time comes," he confides. "But, the board has to live with the consequences. The last thing you want is a board that is hanging fire."

Done well, succession is a process, not an event. Ideally every direct report can identify her successor. "Make sure you keep on asking, 'Who have we got? Who are the up and comers? Who will replace whom? How will we go about this?' " says Arthur Rock. Independent board members should interview insiders for the job just as they would any other candidate.

Ann McLaughlin emphasizes the importance of "alone time" talking about the business with the key officers. "You need to know what they would do and how they would do it over a period of time." It's not enough to see key managers report at the board meetings. Yet, at some boards, you don't see anybody at all, says Arthur Rock. From the day he moves in, every CEO should be thinking about who will take his place.

At Fluor, the CEO was compelled to take early retirement. After considerable conversation with each of three internal candidates, the board made a judgment that none of the internal candidates were ready to take over. The CEO search was coordinated exclusively by the board. In the interim, the three ranking internal executives held the office of chair to manage the company. "We were lucky" that Shell, which happened to be Fluor's biggest client, had a policy requiring retirement at age 60, says director Inman, because Phil Carroll was not ready to quit working. He came on with a unanimous vote of the board in July 1998 and is "doing a superb job." In retrospect, the Fluor board was remiss in its succession duties, because they were not prepared for an early retirement.

At Phelps Dodge, the board began a formal succession planning process well ahead of Doug Yearley's retirement. One board meeting each year focuses on succession and, every other year, Yearley and the board met without any other insiders at dinner to discuss succession. Development people present a formal "what if I'm run over by a truck" scenario, which is supplemented by informal meetings and discussions. The transition was "smooth," says Yearley, whose successor Steve Whisler had been named more than a year prior to his succession. "They did not have to drag me to the altar screaming. They did not have to initiate the process," Yearley explains. "It was my style." Whisler joked that Yearley had until he retired to get the copper price back up.

The succession process at Phelps Dodge goes well beyond the CEO position. "I am amazed how directors perceive people differently," says Yearley. "I've been persuaded by the board to change focus at the senior level," he says. In one situation, they had been struggling with an individual who was competent in all ways, and who was slated for promotion moves in courses in line with the process. Phelps Dodge had a slate extending for three years, and the board said 'let's talk about that. We're not comfortable with that promotion.' In response, Yearley says, "We went on a tighter watch. In one case, a senior officer was asked to leave. The board does and should play an important role," Yearley believes. "All directors are judging people every day. They have a great perspective. This is where a CEO's job gets a little lonely."

Director Clayton Yeutter's most vivid experience of a board making an impact was at Texas Instruments, when CEO Jerry Junkins died suddenly of a heart attack in Stuttgart at the age of 58. A succession plan was to come to fruition seven years later. The board determined to stay with an internal candidate. But, after interviewing the candidates, the board "torpedoed" the succession plan. From the four or five real contenders, the board selected 44-year-old Tom Engibous, deciding against the candidate at the top of the list. Because Engibous was relatively young, the board went to Jim Adams, a director who had retired recently as president of Southwestern Bell, in order to have a veteran executive in place as well. For two years, Adams took on a lot of the outside responsibilities and mentored Tom "in a significant way, and it worked just as we had hoped," Yeutter says. "Tom has totally restructured TI, creating more shareholder value since then than even Intel or Microsoft." Yeutter says the process was extremely positive, although the internal candidate who was passed over took early retirement soon after the initial decision.

Compaq, which has been lauded for its governance practices, stumbled badly when it came to succession. Two very public firings signal something is amiss with succession planning, if there is no candidate in waiting and directors have to take the reins twice to fill in until a replacement can be found. In the most recent case, with the search for a successor to Eckhard Pfeiffer, the saga of at least two candidates who spurned the CEO position was sprawled across the media. The company ended up with an insider, whose position was seriously undermined before he even began. Much preferable would have been an agreed upon outcome before Pfeiffer left. Pat McGurn believes that the board has been micromanaging and is "not living up to the ideals of good governance they have always stood for." Compaq is not alone. At Disney, does Michael Eisner have a successor? Is the next level so strong so they can run the business well without Eisner? Did Waste Management have a plan in place when their CEO went into the hospital?

Don Jackson, CEO of Sitek, a $40 million fast growth semiconductor company, remembers a cartoon with a just fired CEO hanging on the fence of his company looking back in. "I really do believe the board is responsible for management, and, if you take that seriously, everything derives from that. I want to know (from my board) if there is something I need to learn," Jackson adds, "This is where entrepreneurs fall on their swords."

CEOs can block the succession process and often do, simply ignoring succession or discouraging it or misrepresenting it. It is a jarring fact to face your own mortality and tempting to ignore it. The CEO who succeeded David Tappan at Fluor stifled succession planning at all levels, by implying that he was taking care of it. In fact, he did not. As Bobby Inman says, "when the CEO is reluctant and the board is reluctant, it does the company a great disservice."

Robert Monks of the Lens Fund is skeptical of the entire succession process, which he thinks should be far more independent than it is. "Can you find any company that has, as a matter of practice, a process whereby directors are given an opportunity to meet potential candidates for succession—not nominated by the CEO?" Are there any sources of candidate information not controlled by the CEO? Is there any opportunity to talk to candidates who are not recommended by management?

TENURE

A board with no plan for removing directors is another indicator of a passive board low on the strategic board continuum. The red flags of entrenchment include an aging board, unequal voting rights, and a controlling CEO.

If strategic boards translate into added value, if directors are recruited to strategic needs, and if needs change over time, through the phases of corporate growth as well as the dynamics of the economy, then shouldn't new directors with the needed skill sets be rotated onto the board? And shouldn't directors who have contributed, but whose skills and vision are less relevant, be rotated off the board? Not just for cause, but because they, for any number of reasons, have outlived their usefulness. How can entrenched, captive directors evaluate the CEO's performance with complete objectivity? When you bring directors onto your board, make it clear it is for a term and not for eternity. One approach is to invite directors to serve a year at a time. Then invite only those who are appropriate for your next stage to continue. There is nothing wrong with thanking someone for her contribution and moving on.

No one who sits on a board will pretend that every director is contributing at 100 percent. Everyone has a story about the director who falls asleep, or digresses, or babbles, or doesn't do his homework, or monopolizes, or micromanages. But, they rarely tell. And, more important, they rarely instigate that director's removal from the board, although there is no doubt it would be to the company's advantage. Howard Christensen suggests that as many as 50 percent of all directors are ineffective. Many agree.

At Firestone, a good friend of a previous CEO was a small retailer. "He knew how to sell clothes, but he had not one clue what the business was about," says George Aucott. Soon after Aucott became CEO, the retailer resigned on his own volition. Eventually, "somebody's going to call you to task. A stockholder is going to ask 'why did you go along?' Will you say, 'I did it because I wanted to collect my fees?'"

Somehow directors seem to assume the mantle for life. David Tappan is very much in favor of doing away with that concept. He describes the "culture among corporate boards, especially the big ones in New York where it is all kind of a club anyway, in which it is considered a real disgrace if someone is asked not to stand for reelection." Board membership has become a trendy badge of honor, and being removed can be a crushing ego blow. As John Olson comments, "there are some directors I'd love to get rid of, those who contribute little or nothing to the board's deliberations. But it has to be pretty bad before you ask someone to resign." On the other hand, "it's so tough to get a good director. When you do get him, you want to keep him."

The removal of a director is a delicate, uncomfortable process—a process that most would prefer to ignore. And, it's gray. At Phelps Dodge, if a director loses confidence of the management and the board, he is asked not to stand for reelection. Doug Yearley remembers one director who, for three years, did not say a single word. It is such a filmy dynamic. "You don't want people holding up their hand to look good," Yearley says. "You hope it's not a popularity contest. At Phelps Dodge, it is the responsibility of the chairman of the Committee on Directors to talk to a disruptive director, to say 'you're dominating a bit.'"

Michael Burke tells about sitting on a board with a former executive of a large national department store chain who never read the materials and could not comprehend the income statements. "If you've got a board member who can't read a financial statement, look out."

One director with twenty-three years of board service and a finance background has said to his board, "Any time you need a different skill set, come to me and say we don't need you anymore. We have enough finance guys. Come to me and say, 'you know what? You've done a great job for the company. We need to make room for someone else.' I'd be injured because I wouldn't want to leave the board. But, those ground rules should be set in advance."

Bill Franke, CEO of America West, says dealing with underachievers at the board level "is the most difficult part of a CEO's life. You need all the directors to be happy campers. It is a very difficult conversation. These are essentially your peers. There's no good news to it. "Frequently, the directors know it, before you hardly get going [in the conversation]." But, in one case, when Franke suggested to a director that he resign because he was not contributing, the director refused.

Many boards, such as Phelps Dodge, Nuevo Energy and Campbell Soup, ask directors to submit a resignation if there is a change in status, a job change, if there is a health concern, if a director becomes involved in a potential conflict of interest, or becomes unable to spend the required time. Whether those resignations are accepted or not is another matter. Campbell has not let anyone go, although they have told directors whose employment status changes that they need to have another position to meet the qualifying criteria. In 1999, according to Korn/Ferry, 54 percent of all boards asked a director to resign—for poor performance or due to a change in position.

AGE LIMITS

The stale, tenured, predictable board is an anachronism. New directors can change the tempo, the tone, the synergy and the dynamic of a board. Some board members should be steeped in the history, in the nuances of the company's heritage, values and mission. Some board members should know the intricacies of the audit committee, the market approaches, the strategies. But, other directors should be younger, with their roots in technology and change. They should be hungry for the future and diversified. What board could not profit from an entrepreneur or cross-fertilization of ideas?

In recognition of the need to embrace change at the board level, increasing numbers of companies are mandating age limits. Because boards have such a difficult time removing directors except for extreme cause, age limits are seen as a relatively painless way to accomplish a rotation of directors. In fact, however, age is a rather cowardly, arbitrary way of culling board members—a process that should be based on merit. George Shultz, at age 70, was rotated off the Bechtel board. The former Secretary of State was positioned to bring tremendous value to that board, but the arbitrary age limit swept him aside. Yet, there are directors who, at age 50, are utterly inept.

Director Betsy Sanders says the chair of the compensation committee at Wolverine, Dan Carroll, "is a brilliant man, the most insightful director I've ever served with. He understands the issues and the intricacies of the comp programs, reminding us how they worked last year. Dan simplifies what can be convoluted and obscure." Dan Carroll is 75 years old.

"I'm not a term limitation person, and I don't think there is an age at which you cease to give good ideas," says George Aucott. "There is room for continuity." But there needs to be value added. "You have worked with these people for years. They have become your friends," he continues, "But either they are giving you something or not. As CEO, you have to have guts, if you have fifty or five thousand people depending on you to make the hard decisions. There are ways to do it that are humane."

Some companies confer emeritus status with reduced pay. Directors know when they are not contributing. At a Midwest manufacturer, one of the directors had sleep apnea and kept dozing at meetings.

TIAA-CREF looks at age and time served on a board as a critical indicator of good governance. At H. J. Heinz, the average age of the directors was $73^1/_2$. No new director under the age of 65 had been added for a "long, long time," says Ken West. "Where is the new blood? The new thinking?"

Phelps Dodge imposes a 72-year age limit. One CEO thinks such limits are misguided. He thinks people are hiding behind an age restriction, because they won't face up to the performance issues. There are, however, strong and reasoned arguments in favor of age limits, grounded in the practical realities of what is. Bobby Inman is an advocate of age limitations. "It's hard to remove someone during her term except for malfeasance." "When you get to a certain age, faculties change," says Gary Tooker. "If you don't use age, what do you use? You don't want a situation where you are embarrassing people."

Pepsi has an age limit of 70 and requires registration with a material change in circumstances, at which point the board will decide whether to renew the board position. "It gives the board flexibility to keep refreshed." David Tappan is in favor of what he calls "mandated senility." But he feels people ought to have the courage to make exceptions, and he has been on both sides of that. He says some of the worst boards he has seen are when directors get more senior and lose their business contacts. "No matter how hard they would like to be of use, they don't make a contribution."

America West has an age limit of 72. "I think," says Bill Franke, "that some directors, like CEOs, run out of gas. They lose energy. They are not the same. They don't have new ideas. But you can't totally generalize," he says, noting that he has been on the Phelps Dodge board for nineteen years and considers himself a valuable member.

Carl Hagberg tells of an extreme case when he served on a closed end mutual fund board whose directors were all friends. The average age was in the high 70s or low 80s. Three directors came with oxygen, others with their nurses and wheel chairs. "I used to be embarrassed," Hagberg confesses. The day the SEC passed the 75 percent attendance rules, the board changed. "The directors had been coming to one or two board meetings when their nurses could get them out."

Phil Matthews adds a different perspective. The tough part is "making the call before a director turns 70. It takes years to get up to speed with a director. You're better off getting directors more effectively involved instead of starting over. It takes a long time to get to know the players, the industry and to feel comfortable. In my book," he adds, "it takes close to incompetence" before removing a director is justified. With most directors, "if you focus on the right skill, they can really add value and excitement." Matthews describes a "systems guy with not much to say at board meetings. Once we got him involved in his area of expertise, he became chairman of the audit committee and developed into an active, invaluable board member."

"Turnover is a careful balancing act," says William Burleigh of E. W. Scripps, where retirement is required at age 70. "Turnover for the sake of turnover can strip a company of valuable experience and history. Companies, like nations," Burleigh believes, "will be condemned by history if they don't understand what happened."

TERM LIMITS

Only about 5 percent of boards have term limits. Bobby Inman is "not inclined to terms because there are some great advantages to continuity." He prefers staggered three-year terms, where you can look at a third of the board each year. It leaves continuity on the board, he contends, and it forces you to evaluate. The other directors who are not being considered can help in the evaluation. Mandatory term limits," says one CEO, "are crutches people hide behind."

MERGED BOARDS

The year 1998 alone saw a trillion dollars' worth of acquisitions and mergers. Increasingly, merger and acquisition activity ends up with disparate boards coming together in bloated, ineffective, often factionalized entities. Too often, in a merger or acquisition, the board is simply forgotten, until it becomes a clumsy afterthought. Because few are willing to resign voluntarily, often every director from all the merged entities ends up on the combined board. Instead of using the board members proactively during the process and then carefully considering who has the best talent to govern the merged entity, many companies simply pile the boards of the merged companies together.

Cendant is an example of an entirely mismanaged process that demeaned the interests of the shareholders. When Time, Inc. and Warner Brothers merged into Time-Warner, the merged board of twenty-four became impotent. Finally, two directors, one from each side, were elected to take responsibility for dislodging the impasse. With the twenty-four directors assembled, they asked two things of everyone. Will you abide by our decision? And, will you each agree to step down if we ask you to do so? The directors, forced to do so in public, agreed, and the logjam was broken.

Another striking example of the governance fallout of the merger and acquisition mania is in MGM Grand's $3.5 billion bid for Mirage Resorts. "We made it quite clear that this is a friendly offer," said James Murren, President of MGM Grand, commenting on the unsolicited offer. "We invite the entire (Mirage) board to be a part of the board of the combined company."[30] How can a board with a combined membership of 23 people be of much use?

Key Questions: Is there some means by which directors are rotated off the board when they are no longer contributing 100 percent in terms of the company's needs? Is fresh, new thinking being rotated onto the board on a regular basis?

BOARD EVALUATION

No board is truly strategic or deserving of a score of 10 on the strategic board continuum, if there are no measures of accountability. (See Appendix 7 for a sample board evaluation form.) How else to know that decisions are made for the right reasons, in the right time frames? Governance has been a sideline issue, so its secrecy has been tolerated. But, in the 21st century, corporate governance will be a mainspring of corporate success. Because the system rests on trust and integrity, checks and balances are an imperative.

The great boards are those which proactively govern, help avoid the big mistakes, strategize and most important, ensure that the best leadership is in place with the resources to lead. How can shareholders know the directors are doing their job, if the board doesn't at least measure itself and tell the shareholders the results?

Slightly more than one third of America's largest companies conduct a board evaluation,[31] in which the board as a whole is benchmarked. Every director knows whether his board is strategic or not, regardless of whether the board is evaluated. The value of evaluation is specificity, accountability, clarity and communication. Governance charters, detailing specific goals and objectives, policies, and procedures for the board, are the logical foundation for evaluations. If they include measurable benchmarks, so much the better. (See Appendixes 3, and 4 for sample governance guidelines.) Sixty-four percent of Fortune 500 boards have written guidelines on corporate governance.[32] Ironically, many of them keep the documents secret. Almost all evaluations are confined to the input of the board members. Few boards, if any, ask for feedback from other constituencies and stakeholders. If they did, it would accomplish two things. First, the board would gain valuable information. And two, it would validate the board and the process to those constituencies and shareholders.

Board evaluations generally consider most of the following questions:

- Are there regularly scheduled meetings?
- What is the process by which the board evaluates its own activities?
- What is the level of attendance? The SEC requires directors to attend a minimum of 75 percent of the meetings.
- Are the directors getting the information they need when they need it?
- Are there the right committees?
- How are the committee chairs appointed?
- Is the board getting the job done?
- Are the right processes in place?
- Is the CEO effectively evaluated?
- Is the board seeing the next generation of leadership? Is there a succession plan?
- Are the heads of the business sectors coming before the board on a regular basis?
- Is there enough time allocated to the strategic issues?
- Is there a system in place for evaluating directors?
- Is there a strategic, proactive, ongoing system in place for recruiting new board members?
- Is there a system in place for rotating directors off the board?
- Is there unstructured time available for discussion?
- When do the independent board members meet privately without management?
- What are the board's objectives?
- How does the board add value to the company?
- Is the board the best it can be?

If you don't know how you are doing and what the measures are, how can you improve? And, how can you know if you need to improve?

At Phelps Dodge, the board is evaluated annually; individual directors are not. Directors are surveyed in a questionnaire detailing key board responsibilities. At Motorola, the nominating committee oversees the distribution and consolidation of a questionnaire that is presented to the full board. One outcome is that the board increased its emphasis on strategy and longer term issues.

In the process of Campbell Soup's evaluation, former CEO David Johnson talked to each director. "Are we doing the right thing? How do you like your committee chairman? Do we need new blood?" Also, says Bennett Dorrance, "The strategic plan is such an important part of our discussion. Because of the evaluation, the directors are more aware of the strategic plan and our financial goals. I don't think there is anyone in the company who doesn't know our financial goals and where we are going. We focus on the four most important things— evaluating the CEO, the strategic plan, the operating plan, and the succession process. Do we do a good job of those?" That is the crux of the evaluation.

Bethlehem Steel conducts a comprehensive evaluation. "One issue is whether we have enough time and too busy an agenda," Curtis Barnette says. "Do we have the right types of presentations in form and substance that are supplementary to materials that are sent out? The informal communications are paramount."

Each year, Barnette meets with each director individually. He goes to their home and their city and reviews about twelve subjects in depth. " 'How are we doing as a board? How are you doing as a director? What advice do you have to give me as chairman? What are our greatest problems as a company?' They will have questions of me in the process. Directors appreciate the freedom of a one on one conversation.

"I summarize these discussions for the whole board, and we will have a session and go through the very same points. I'll say, 'this is what I believe you are saying.' I've learned how important that process is," Barnette says. "And, I've learned how important it is to match your conduct with your plans—to do what you say you are going to do." With the steel industry going through an "enormous restructuring," Barnette says the board has reaffirmed Bethlehem's strategy and community commitment.

DIRECTOR EVALUATION

Seventy-three percent of the respondents in a Korn/Ferry survey think directors should be evaluated on an individual basis. (See Appendix 6 for a sample director evaluation.) Further, directors rate their boards' effectiveness much more positively at companies where individual board members are evaluated. Yet, only 20 percent of Fortune 500 companies evaluate individual directors.[33] The overwhelming majority of those are self-evaluations that are usually kept private and, if it is shared at all, it's with the full board only in very general terms. Director review is a sensitive subject.

Although Campbell's Soup, under David Johnson, has been out front in great governance, it only began evaluating board members on an individual basis in a structured manner in 1999. "There are some directors who don't say very much," Bennett Dorrance says. "It gave us an opportunity to encourage them to give more input and be sure they read the materials and come prepared. Our objective was not to clean out directors who are a little sleepy. It was a self-evaluation. Why encourage directors to point fingers?" asks Dorrance. One result of recent evaluations was that committee assignments were realigned.

Gary Tooker of Motorola says that all directors should be asking themselves if they are adding value. "Or are they taking up a seat. Do they take time to understand the company? Are they interested in the industry? Do they bring a business expertise? Are they thinking about the strategy? Board members lose interest. Interests change." Tooker does not oppose individual self-evaluation, and knows of at least one instance in which a director self-selected himself out, saying he was not satisfied with his own performance. However, he has "mixed feelings about peer review. It would get in the way of collegiality. But, I do think the board and board member should be able to answer specifically about their performance to the shareholders and respond to any challenges about the quality of governance."

At Bethlehem Steel, the directors complete an annual self-evaluation, going through a comprehensive checklist. "That discipline, " says CEO Hank Barnette, "has been very important." Evaluating directors, another CEO reminds us, "is a very difficult proposition." At his board, "I became de facto a senior member because of my knowledge

Value Added

Leadership
Value Added
Information
Diversity
The Money
Cronyism
Family
Conflicts
Insiders
Recruit
Strategically

0
Captive Board

10
Strategic Board

of the industry and my willingness to speak up and out. If you evaluated my performance, it would be one mark. At another board I'm part of, there are lots of older CEOs, and I've not had a major impact. I'm still a junior member of that board. I'd get different marks and yet I'm the same director."

At Wolverine, directors stand for reelection every three years, so three directors of the nine-member board come up for review each year. Directors being reviewed spend about twenty minutes with the nominating committee to discuss how they feel about their progress against the objectives they set for themselves.

"It is amazing," says chair Phil Matthews. "People know they have problems, and they put them on the table. People who talk too much at board meetings. People who don't talk enough." It is obvious from questions asked at board meetings that directors have not read the materials, for example. They get feedback from their peers.

Any individual director review is valuable, but the most productive are those that go beyond self-evaluation. According to investor relations advisor Carl Hagberg, "I don't know any director who would not welcome candid feedback with the goal of doing better. They didn't get as far as they did without making candid assessments of their own mistakes."

"The purpose isn't to punish or humiliate," Robert Lear reminds us. "The purpose is to show how to be a better board member. I see director resistance as proof positive there are skeletons. Otherwise, if there are problems not being addressed, they would welcome a formal evaluation process." One approach is to have all directors complete evaluation forms for each director, have a trusted individual tally them, and then share the combined results with the board annually. For any director needing improvement, you "have a one-year self-cure built in" before the next annual evaluation. "People get religion and fix up their low scores or they gracefully leave."

Individual evaluation is a critical element in good governance. The best directors welcome it, because it improves their total board experience. The worst directors shun evaluation, because with it or without it, they know. Considering the tremendous responsibilities and the thousands of individual shareholders whose interests are on the line, considering too that the business of governance is done behind closed doors, is it unreasonable to ask for gentle accountability?

Great boards ask the right questions and challenge, select, and support the best people. *Key questions*: Do the directors govern well in crises? Is the audit committee informed and independent? Are your board members engaged in succession, CEO evaluation, and board practices, including issues of tenure? Do you evaluate your board, and your directors, individually? Do you harbor entrenched directors? Is there a thorough evaluation of board practices and effectiveness each year? Is there any input from outside the board? Is there evaluation of individual directors? Is there peer feedback?

If your directors are proactive, independent, and strategic, rather than passive and entrenched, add one point to your strategic board continuum quotient. You now have a possible total of nine points, if you have avoided making the nine mistakes discussed so far.

NOTES

1. John Bryne, "The Best and Worst Boards," *Business Week*, 25 November 1996.
2. Robert Townsend, "Further Up the Organization," *Directors & Boards*, Winter 1998.
3. Ann McLaughlin, speech to General Motors corporate legal staff, "View of a General Motors Director on Integrity Issues: Role and Responsibility of Corporate Legal Staff," Detroit, April 1997.
4. John Byrne, "The Best and Worst Boards," *Business Week*, 25 November 1996.
5. Ann McLaughlin, "The Demand on Directors to Be Independent," *SpencerStuart Governance Letter*, Winter 1996.
6. Chris Augur, Snell & Wilmer, Arthur Andersen Board Roundtable, November 1998.
7. James D. Westphal, "Collaboration in the Boardroom: Behavioral and Performance Consequences of CEO Board Social Ties," *Academy of Management Journal*, February 1999.
8. Chris Augur, Snell & Wilmer, Arthur Anderson Board Roundtable, November 1998.
9. John A. Byrne, "Listen Up," *Business Week*, 25 November 1996.
10. Lawrence A. Cunningham, "Warren Buffet on the Role of the Board," *Corporate Board*, July/August 1998.
11. Bart A. Brown, Snell & Wilmer, Arthur Andersen Board Roundtable, November 1998.
12. Ibid.
13. Carter Pate, "The Denial Trap," *Directors & Boards*, Spring 1998.
14. John Furman, Snell & Wilmer, Arthur Andersen Board Roundtable, November 1998.
15. Arthur Levitt Jr., "The SEC Looks at Governance," *Corporate Board*, July–August 1998.
16. "SEC Announces Crackdown on Earnings Management," *Public Company Adviser*, Winter 1999.
17. "SEC Bullies Boards on Merger Accounting," *Director's Alert*, February 1999.

18. Mark S. Beasley, Joseph V. Carcello, and Dana R. Hermanson, "Fraudulent Financial Reporting: Implications for Corporate Directors," research commissioned by the Committee of Sponsoring Organizations of the Treadway Commission.
19. Ibid.
20. Excerpted from "Report and Recommendations of the Blue Ribbon Committee on Improving the Effectiveness of Corporate Audit Committees," December 1999.
21. John F. Olson, Esq., "How to Really Make Audit Committees More Effective," March 1999.
22. Arthur Levitt Jr., speech at Stanford Law School, *Investor Relations Business*, 12 April 1999.
23. Korn/Ferry International, *26th Annual Board of Directors Study*, 1999.
24. John L. Vogelstein, "As I, an Owner-Director, See It," *Directors & Boards*, Summer 1998.
25. Ibid.
26. Kenneth A. Brookhovish, Robert Parrino, and Teresa Trapani, "Outside Directors and CEO Selection," *www.lens-library.com*, April 1996.
27. Joann S. Lublin and Daniel Machalaba, "How Companies Deal with a CEO Who Drinks," *The Wall Street Journal*, 1 November, 1994.
28. Eugene Jennings, "How to Succeed at Succession Planning," *Corporate Board Member*, Winter 1999.
29. Del Jones, "Job Demands Overwhelming Many CEOs," *The Arizona Republic*, 6 March 2000.
30. "MGM Grand Bids for Mirage," *The Arizona Republic*, 24 February 2000, D.
31. Korn/Ferry International, "Evaluating the Board of Directors," pamphlet, 1998.
32. Korn/Ferry International, *26th Annual Board of Directors Study*, 1999.
33. Korn/Ferry International, "Evaluating the Board of Directors," pamphlet, 1998.

Chapter 11

◆━━━━━━◆

Empowering the Board—Board Leadership

✦ THE TENTH MISTAKE: FAILED LEADERSHIP ✦

Despite the brilliance of a board, despite the fact that a board charter exists, that directors are recruited strategically and are independent and diverse, that there is clarity in their mission, and that there is commitment to independent thinking, it's still the CEO who imprints the board and shapes its culture. Except in times of extreme crisis, when his job is on the line, it's the CEO who makes the difference.

THE ROLE OF THE CEO

As Bennett Dorrance says, "Campbell's is really a story of the CEO, one of the very best. He produced incredible results," says Dorrance of David Johnson, who retired in June 1999. "He was thoughtful about where the company needed to go. He was responsible for adding top directors, George Sherman, Harvey Golub, Charles Perrin, outgoing CEO of Avon, Kent Foster, COO of GTE. These people are much more than names. Our board is one where you don't just sit and listen."

On the other hand, as Craig Weatherup emphasizes, "a bad CEO is a bad CEO. No board is going to help very much." Unfortunately, too many CEOs believe the boards of their companies exist to serve their needs and not those of their shareholders. They see the board as their personal perk. How many CEOs talk about "my board" and "my directors"—and mean it? Symptoms of a captive board and failed leadership are restricted information; monotonous, one-way meetings that are controlled and orchestrated by management; the absence of engaged dialogue; and no opportunity for independent directors to meet apart from management. In other words, captive boards are riddled with the ten critical mistakes.

The best CEOs prioritize strategic boards. Gary Lutin, consultant to the NYSE Security Analysts, believes that the only thing that matters is whether a company adapts. This ability is driven by an effective executive with the "board as the most critical element. As long as a company like Disney has a capable CEO managing competition, the company will perform well." But, insists Lutin, "long-term adaptation to change is entirely dependent on the board," because the CEO tends to be too involved in the operations to have the needed objectivity over the long term. His function is the definition of strategies and their execution. You need an independent board, people with objectivity and detachment with broader perspectives. Even if the CEO can continue to adapt the company, you still need independent oversight to validate his ability and to ensure effective long-term adaptation.

"No one criticizes Berkshire Hathaway, which has a dysfunctional board. I'm not sure you would want to sacrifice Buffett's leadership by imposing objectivity on it," Lutin continues. But you still need oversight to know when the leader is no longer good. As Pat McGurn says, "Microsoft fails every test, but no one ever put it on a worst company list. There is no nominating committee, and inside directors are on the key committees. But when you perform that well, it's not an issue." But, is there life after Gates?

"I would look hard at any board, if one individual has control," says Steve McConnell, "you have to ask yourself, 'why is the board there?' " The worst of all possible worlds can occur when a company is headed by a CEO who is highly intelligent, a charismatic leader, a dynamic personality, and a great communicator—and yet somehow has it wrong.

"When you talk about governance, there are three very different parts," Curtis Barnette believes. "One is the individual director, what he or she brings to the board as an individual. It is usually one on one, perhaps as a mentor or to brainstorm in a particular area of expertise, such as legal or accounting or personnel. For example, Bethlehem's audit chairs have directly counseled with Bethlehem's controller or CFO on changes in accounting or tax approaches mandated by the SEC."

The second part is the committee structure, with several directors working together as a group, to address a specific issue, such as the environment or growth. The third aspect is the board as a whole, which, according to Barnette, is a deliberative body that works through a process of problem identification, debate, and resolution. A strategic CEO will take advantage of each.

THE CEO's ATTITUDE

"The board is my boss," says former Avon CEO Charles Perrin. A lot of CEOs give that concept lip service—and little more. But it is fact. And the best CEOs understand its importance. The board must "function for all the stockholders and all of the constituents," according to Curtis Barnette. Those two focuses, he insists, are interdependent and synergistic and what he believes will allow Bethlehem to be the premier steel company. The board plays a critical role in helping set core values of the company. "The strategy can change," he says, "but vision and values don't change." Barnette involves the Bethlehem board in planning, in development of the yearly business plan, the long-range strategic plans, and in allocation of capital.

One of our objectives, explains Barnette, "is to be a good citizen. If you mean that, the governance must be the very best. To do the right thing is very important. It's also very good business. Being recognized as the employer of choice in your community, and the supplier of choice, has a lot to do with the way you conduct yourself," he believes. "And, it must come from the top."

It is a luxury for a CEO to have the opportunity to form a strategic board from scratch. A CEO more typically inherits a board, which can include family, gray directors, directors with allegiances to his predecessor, investors with different allegiances, and directors with strong opinions on the direction of the company that may differ from yours.

But, a CEO can set the stage to engage the directors by:

- Providing enough information for board members to be effective and timely in their input.
- Staying in touch.
- Fostering honesty and openness in communication.
- Responding to the board's advice. If the CEO and board agree on something to be done, make sure that it happens.
- Being willing to be held accountable.
- Ensuring that the directors participate in the rewards.

The challenge is keeping the board engaged and employed at their highest and best possible use. Bob Hartman sees UTI board members for lunch in between meetings, talks to them often on the phone. He tries to follow up on their advice and "prove that we are listening and responsive." Doug Yearley at Phelps Dodge says every board he is on has a statement of governance policy and a formal statement of director qualifications. The key ingredients to an effective board, according to Yearley, are 1) acknowledging that it is important, 2) understanding the separation of powers between the CEO and the independent directors, and 3) the establishment of a Committee on Governance with independent directors.

The board at E. W. Scripps, the publishing company, is a unique combination of family and independent directors. "The greatest frustration is getting us all on the same page," admits William Burleigh. "Sometimes I wonder if I expect directors to be more engaged and educated in our businesses, than I have a right to. We've made wonderful progress. I work hard at providing information to our board members and challenging them—in a nice way. After all, I work for them."

When America West went through Chapter 11 proceedings, CEO Bill Franke inherited a new, 15-member board of creditors and shareholders appointed by a Federal bankruptcy judge. There was no existing board to shape their personality. Franke told them, "You no longer represent creditors or stockholders. You represent all of us." It took about two years to "get this group with disparate points of view" to fully work together, without regard to their original constituencies, Franke said.

In 1998, the court-appointed directors' terms expired, and the board was pared down to nine members. There were performance reviews, and Franke offered directors "an opportunity to step down." He has added two internal board members along with several outsiders, including two women. Franke likes the example of Phelps Dodge, on whose board he sits. "A great deal of care goes into the selection process and the education of directors. They are very thoughtful, very careful about the management of new directors," Franke says. "This is serious business," Franke says about governance. "You can't have your twelve best friends. Those days are gone. Directors need to be carefully selected and be partners with an independent point of view."

There are many opportunities for CEOs to veer off course. The greatest tempter is the market. "I see a lot of my peer companies out there in the software industry," observes Steve Whiteman, CEO and chairman of Viasoft. "Historically, they get caught up. Each quarter gets a little tighter, a little tougher. And, they get more focused on the ninety-day window. After several years of being public, that's all there is."

"There is no long-term plan. Everything is focused on the ninety-day window. You can only do that so long," he says, "and you get caught and then you have problems. Some companies come out of it. They reset the stage, and they move ahead. Others fail, and they get sold or other things happen to them. We need to remember what we've agreed upon as a board—that we have to balance." Beware of CEOs who undermine the process and set the board up for failure. If there is a bad event, CEOs may be tempted to postpone meetings, instead of bringing the board in to help.

"Every once in a while, I find management who is not accustomed to being publicly owned," says Walter Auch. "It requires a substantial change in mindset to think of the faceless people out there who own part of their company." In one case, on a NYSE company board, he felt the CEO was being "overly generous with himself" and told him so privately. "All of a sudden, I became a dissident. I started thinking I've got too much responsibility here for the way I see things going." Auch resigned.

John Whiteman said, "When we erred [at Empire Machinery] and went perpendicular to common sense, we didn't have a strong board to right us around."[1] As the board began to mature, founder Jack Whiteman, John's father, fired the board—twice. Eventually, Jack Whiteman acquiesced to the board, but not without a lot of turmoil. "He was mad and we were mad," John Whiteman, his son, says. "A CEO has got to share the authority, and that is difficult for most entrepreneurial types to do. But it is crucial for an organization, if you want to get out of the adolescent stage. When the board is six to one against the chairman," John Whiteman says, "the chairman had damn well better listen." As Charles Perrin observes, "a lot of problems are not new problems to the board. They bring a wisdom and perspective that management doesn't bring, because we get so caught up in the issues."

Tom Higgins, senior vice president of Edison International, talks about a "real tension that is healthy between the CEO and the board." The question, Higgins says, "is how to make sure it's healthy." The CEO makes the call. When a tough issue comes up, Terry Lee brainstorms with his board. And, in the final analysis, "I take what they say and process it. It's the operating guy's decision, because he's the one who has ownership. He's the one who suffers the consequences."

THE BOARD CULTURE

The culture of the board, its cohesiveness, and its ability to independently engage issues as a team is what defines it. And, no checklist will guarantee the outcome. Recruiting well positions it for success. But, from there, every board evolves and creates a separate personality, a personality that is far more than the sum of its parts. Avoiding the ten mistakes is the platform for greatness. But, a board can soar to the top of the Strategic Board Continuum and still fail. It's the chemistry of the board and the tone set by the CEO. It has to do with attitude and expectations overlaid on capacity.

Phil Matthews describes a "team environment. The only time it gets tested," he says, "is when you are in crisis. Probably, in two out of eight boards that I am on, do we have a group of people who feel we are a team. If we are thrown into a room we will know how to work together. We can have a discussion and egos are not in the way. We are looking for the best solution. At the other six, it would be a struggle."

The best way to create that culture, Matthews proposes, is to work together. Retreats are valuable. Approve a board charter, needs matrix and governance guidelines. How do the other directors feel about tenure, retirement, compensation, nominations, access to information, independence, performance evaluation of directors. What is the mission? How can the board be improved? Where should the board be on the strategic board continuum? Learn how to work together on those things. When the crisis comes, the board will be ready.

Roz Ridgway says the way directors cohere into an effective board is "like a marriage. You don't know what makes a good one work." The culture derives from what she says is whether a board has manners. Directors know how to argue, ask the tough questions, how to give everybody time to talk. The board has a sense of humor. The directors have "a sense of their own humanity and weakness."

"The process and the level of communication with the board often sets the level of participation," says Curtis "Hank" Barnette. Bethlehem regularly forwards clippings and releases pertinent reports to directors, and Barnette is in touch with telephone calls and informal meetings. "There is an informal level of communication that's very important." William Burleigh insists that "the CEO has to be collegial with management and the board. It can be pretty humbling in both directions to admit you don't have all the answers, but it is much more valuable. The board should have a more interesting, yeasty process."

Integrating new board members into the culture of a board is a fine art. At ProLink, four new strategic board members were recruited to a board made up entirely of angel investors and the founder. "There has been a real mutual respect between the old and the new board," says CEO Doug Lecker, who attributes the success to "doing the due diligence and getting the right board members." The investor directors "have not felt that the new group has come in to take control. The board has been complementary to one another. The conversation is very constructive. We are talking strategy, what actions to take going forward and what we need to accomplish," says Lecker.

When Betsy Sanders went to her first Wal-Mart board meeting, the directors "had their jackets off and their sleeves rolled up and sweat on their brows." The directors didn't act as if "they had it made. It is an ongoing thought process. How do we keep doing this differently? We are becoming increasingly diverse, international and constantly re-attending to the customers."

Phil Matthews, who sits on eight boards, says "It's the kind of materials you get out and what you do in the meetings that really counts. It's creating the environment at the board meeting, insuring that two or three people don't dominate the discussion, including management. It's discussing the two, three, or four issues that are important, after the directors are steeped in what the issues really are," he says. "If you send financials in advance, there is no reason to discuss them in detail. I'd probably have an hour phone board meeting to discuss financials maybe six times a year, so everyone is up to speed. Numbers are easy to deal with on the phone." Discussion is better in person.

Well ahead of the meeting, information on expanding into Russia was sent to the directors of one board Matthews sits on. It allowed one director to consider the prospects and be prepared to explain that his company had been in Russia for three years and to detail the exposures they faced. He was prepared to add value. Acquisitions are another good example. If the directors get the company's thinking regarding criteria for acquisitions, their evaluation of management, the market, and the growth opportunities, including management's position on the proposal ahead of time, when "we come to the board for discussion, we will be able to deal with the real issues of whether it is a good fit," says Matthews. "If the board doesn't influence things, why have it?" Matthews asks.

Steve Whiteman, CEO of Viasoft, says that the Viasoft board and management agreed on three principles. The first is to focus on the business and not to worry about Wall Street. Wall Street will take care of itself. "Yes, you do have to go to New York and Boston and San Francisco and talk to the investors, but you really focus on the business." The second is to communicate realistic expectations. The third is to act above reproach with a high level of integrity.[2]

The best CEOs savor strategic boards. At Nuevo Energy, Doug Foshee wholeheartedly embraced strategic governance and transformed the board. "We began thinking independence and removed any hint of conflict. Next, we started talking about equity compensation and then writing governance guidelines (see sample guidelines in Appendixes 3, 4, and 5). The only thing left is to make changes regarding the poison pill. The momentum of our governance builds on itself," Foshee says. "The worst possible organizational structure leads to group think," Foshee claims. When a single person, usually the CEO, takes control of the meeting, the result of the group effort is that person's idea. "With nonindependent boards," Foshee believes, "that is the risk you run. Members are beholden. It's great if you are a CEO, because you are always right."

"But the way you are successful is having engaged debate. When you have board members not committed to me personally, with substantial equity, all uniquely qualified in different areas, it leads to constructive debate." Foshee talks of being challenged by the board with regard to Nuevo Energy's long-term capitalization and building the crude oil side of the business, when crude oil prices were going down.

There are trade-offs. When CEOs opt for a strategic board, more time is required, and the board often edges from policy to operations. "By design, we have an independent, free thinking board," says Lars Nyberg, CEO of NCR. "We wanted a board that was probing and challenging. It can be difficult to strike a balance, which shifts with the level of comfort a board has with the executive. I don't think the board should be involved in operations, but it needs to understand operational issues and what the executives are doing about it, so they can monitor the business. These directors are making decisions twenty-four hours a day," adds Nyberg, "and, all of a sudden, they come here and become board members. And, there's lots of work to be done. 'Hey Lars, why don't you do this? Why don't you do that?' And it is for one ambition only, and that is to help the company." Nyberg thinks the interplay is good for management and for him, although he admits that sometimes "it's not so pleasant to be challenged."

"The board has continuously raised the bar in every respect," Nyberg continues. If you want to understand, you need to get into some real detail, which means a greater time commitment. NCR has been in a turnaround phase, and now is focused on growth. "The board is challenging us on new businesses, how to expand. They have really helped us set the level of quality. We know not to come to the board unless we have done our thinking and know what we want to do."

"I want the directors more involved in the company," says Charles Perrin of Avon. But the focus must be on governance and strategy, not on running the business. At Avon, that is especially challenging, with the temptation of the board to say "I don't like that product. I don't like that package. That's the problem," Perrin adds. "It's a fine line with an activist board."

Home Depot has an unusual executive committee made up of the three founders of the company, which is used to hone major policy decisions before they go to the board. "We don't let the board micromanage," despite the requirement that they visit stores on a regular basis, says Stanley Marcus. "They are really there to help the CEO determine strategies. Our CEO knows our role is to make him more successful."

It is critical to engage the directors. Talk outside one-on-one with directors, either at dinners within their city or when they are in yours, suggests Terry Lee. "Make them feel their work is worthwhile rather than ignored. It's a style kind of thing. Some people need more attention. Some talk in shorthand to you. It's not a lot different than how you manage your team. Maintain an environment where people can speak out and not be shot. I need risk takers," Lee emphasizes. Knowing that the CEO is really listening is a powerful motivator to directors.

"I don't hesitate to use directors between board meetings," says Marcus of Home Depot. To keep the board educated, they meet a different officer of the company at every board meeting. Like Barnette of Scripps, Craig Weatherup at Pepsi Bottling has begun the practice of having dinner with each board member every six months. "It's very much in my interest and in theirs and therefore in the interest of the company." And it bolsters the culture.

David Tappan recommends giving board members an assignment outside of meetings. "They have years of good operating experience. They have been there, done that, fought for survival, and they are invaluable as a source of information." Ask for an introduction to a client, a supplier. Ask for help with financing, an introduction to Wall Street, advice on debt or restructuring. Ask a director to follow up on competitive information or to try to ascertain Wall Street's reaction to a specific course of action. "Most outside directors are flattered to be asked to do something specific," Tappan observes.

At early stage companies, a board can easily cross the line and become a venue for solving disputes among insiders. At Paraphonics, the founders asked a key marketing employee to assume a different role. The employee refused, took the issue to the board, and ultimately was fired. "The board is not the right place to resolve those kinds of things," says one of the directors. "It tends to be a shooting match." Three-time CEO Tom Emerson contends that "boards are rather blunt instruments. If a company needs heavy steering, a board may be able to provide that. Provided," he adds, "that there is strong leadership or strong consensus on the board." Where boards do more harm than good, Emerson continues, is in situations where there is "divisional polarization. Boards become instruments for warring factions within companies. Especially in early stage companies, the ability of a company to withstand bloodletting is fairly limited."

Because there is pressure on directors to be active, directors are becoming more outspoken. One Fortune 500 CEO laments that boards are less gentlemanly and less collegial. It is "Hi, how are you? Here's the problem. What are you doing to fix it?"

There is emphasis on focused topics, site visits, engagement and education of the directors. To do the exponentially expanded business of boards, to garner the best directors, and to use the time well—those are the mandates.

THE AGENDA

The agenda is at the epicenter of governance. A key measure of board independence is whether directors regularly have input into the agenda. The last item of every agenda should be recommendations for the next agenda. Ideally, the agenda reaches the board at least a week or two prior to the meeting with an open invitation to directors to add to or amend it.

At Ashland, whose board practices are highly rated, the CEO establishes the agenda and annually prepares a list of items to be on the agenda throughout the year, designating the meeting at which they will be addressed. In addition to financial reports, the agenda includes information on peer comparisons, market shares, customer satisfaction, relationships with suppliers, employee training, and employee safety and productivity. At the January meeting, the schedule for the year is presented and board members add any other items they think should be included.[3]

At the start of every fiscal year, Texaco's board defines its general areas of responsibility, such as succession planning, assuring adherence to corporate vision and values, performance review, and financial well being. At the end of the year, the nominating committee analyzes the meeting minutes to see how the board allocated its time relative to those priorities, a valuable tool for board assessment.

David Tappan organizes agendas along three lines: 1) items for reporting, 2) items for decision making, and 3) discussion where management wants the board's input.

Key Questions: Do directors have input into agenda content well prior to the meetings? Do directors receive a copy of the agenda at least one week prior to the board meeting? Are agenda items tracked for results?

Dinner meetings the night before board meetings can create the dynamic the board needs to do its job. A surprising number of directors and CEOs cite this as a must-have ingredient of strategic boards. It is an opportunity to sit informally with the CEO and talk confidentially about new business opportunities. It also allows directors to talk with people who are on the agenda the next day or to get to know business leaders who are in town from overseas. For companies with quarterly meetings, it reconnects management and the board and sets the stage for the board meeting the following day. It provides a key input for succession considerations.

The pre-meeting dinner sets the tone for the board meeting and feeds into the agenda in a critical way. At Pepsi Bottling, the agendas for the board meetings are proscribed well ahead with succession and strategic planning. "But the dinner agenda," says CEO Craig Weatherup, "is my opportunity to really use the board as a sounding board." In contrast to the studied informality of other pre-meeting dinners, Weatherup does set an agenda. After Weatherup initiated the director field trips, he used the dinner to glean feedback. Another pre-board dinner centered around how the directors would like to work as a board. At another dinner, Weatherup asked everyone how he or she came to be on the board and what motivated them to serve. "That was pretty basic. But I have found the dinners very constructive and helpful."

THE ART OF THE MEETING

George Aucott underlines the importance of keeping the meetings moving, being inclusive and ending soliloquies artfully. "When the point has been made, don't chop the speaker's legs off. Appreciate his input." If a vote is due, call for the vote. Usually someone on the board will help the chair if they see someone going on. If a director is not contributing, Aucott talks to him one on one. "Is there information I can get you? What are the issues here? You might find out the guy is uncomfortable or doesn't have the guts to say I can't contribute."

At Home Depot, Bernard Marcus fields unstructured board meetings, leaving "plenty of room for discussion on every subject. We use the board a lot. It's not like boards where you go through the financials, they hit you with the book, and you're gone. We lean on the board. We give them all the background. There are subjects where we need help. In many cases," Marcus says, "they have talked us into another direction. We used them in making our decision to go into Chile and Argentina. We had other plans and they persuaded us not to pursue them. Donald Keogh (retired president and chief operating officer, Coca-Cola) and John Clendenin, BellSouth CEO, were helpful in both targeting the markets and fashioning the right approach into those markets."

John Bryson, CEO of Edison International, describes a recent, off-site retreat where the board adopted a new corporate strategy. "The meeting was highly interactive with strategic discussion, and I thought an exceptionally good meeting. Every director present participated," Bryson says. "They asked questions, presented perspectives, and raised execution issues. We had a real dialogue and addressed tough issues. It was clear they were all ready for the discussion. It was a strong affirmation of our new strategy," says Bryson, whose industry is facing massive upheavals in relating to consumers, defining its core business and preparing for the future, which is unknowable.

Although the strategy was supported, "there was nothing routine about this meeting," Bryson explains. "We actively worked through alternative strategies, and it was not a foregone conclusion by any means." For example, Bryson said the directors "asked very important questions regarding the organizational structure for the execution of this strategy," which was not entirely in place. "Some of the points will affect our structure," he confides. "One of the worst things that can happen is a board that goes forward on a lukewarm basis, where the directors maintain private reservations. We put the alternatives in the materials. I invited open, candid review and indicated the meeting would not be a full success without it." Why was the meeting effective? "Some of it has to do with tone. Some of it has to do with providing sufficient time during which management is not presenting facts and proposing actions."

Charles Perrin believes that setting the stage for discussion is key to success in the boardroom. When he was Avon's CEO, he initiated dinners before the board meetings and changed the shape of the board table, where the officers had typically lined up on one side and the directors on the other. "It doesn't make for a very conversation friendly environment," says Perrin. He has also eliminated the podium at meetings, and makes informal presentations, as opposed to scripted ones. "I try to be conversational. I think that's clearly the way to go." Further, Perrin planned to establish strategic retreats, have the board visit other locations, and include the directors in the annual convention of the some 8500 Avon representatives.

Doug Lecker at ProLink, a technology golf company, which has a largely new board, has pre-meeting dinners where he includes four or five of his management people. Other than arranging seating, he tries to keep the dinners very informal. The board meetings begin with an independent director roundtable without management present. The entire meeting lasts about four hours, with much of the time reserved for input. Lecker reviews the strategy and outlines the issues impeding progress." Then there is a "huge discussion" on how to grow the company, how much funding to go after, what the correct approach is.

The marketing side at ProLink believes the best way is to get market share and get out there fast. The financing side is figuring out "how to feed this machine. The next big issue is what the value of the company is." At the end of each meeting, Lecker visits with each director. "Now that I have seven board members, I want to be sure I get all their input," he says. "I want to make sure we are using them. My job has evolved to be more of a strategic thinker, and I'm relying more on the management team to run the day-to-day operations. I'm really pleased how it's come together."

"I have a principle," explains Steve McConnell. "I want 100 percent of the votes all the time. I empower everybody around the table. There are times I didn't want to do something but others wanted to do it." At a recent board meeting, he argued in favor of paying down the debt instead of awarding an increased dividend, but was outvoted. To achieve unanimity, he conceded.

Terry Lee believes in taking solutions to the board, not problems. This does not mean eliminating discussion. He distinguishes between directors presenting their ideas to get the best thinking on the table—and destructive controversy, which can destroy board dynamics and immobilize decision-making.

STRATEGY

After making certain that a great team is in place, governance is increasingly about strategy. More companies are prioritizing it as an agenda item and holding strategic planning retreats at least on an annual basis.

When George Aucott was CEO at MCII, the Bus company, "the directors forced me to look at the fact that we had gone public at $13, but we were really a $10 stock. They forced me to look at the idea that we were drifting along and to think about what was best for the stockholders. A merger in Mexico turned out to be a disappointment. When you are the market leader and others are shooting at you, and there are no other products, you are going to have to merge. As chairman, I have to be able to take their advice."

At Phelps Dodge, Doug Yearley says he was always thinking how to maximize the role of the board. "We talk about new proposals and strategies and leave plenty of time for feedback. It's a great catalyst." Each year, the board devotes four hours to strategic review. "It's extremely helpful when you do it year after year, incrementally building on the knowledge base the directors already have. That's the place they can help you the most." Steve Whisler, the current CEO, believes the best value is as an independent sounding board. "Rarely are decisions black and white. We are looking for their judgment."

Phelps Dodge and Yearley have been through several cycles of market downturns. As a result, Yearley feels they went into the last downturn in good shape. "But, the board appropriately said, 'let's keep raising the bar—what if, what if.'" They pressed on worst case scenarios and kept pushing the numbers, to see where the breaking point is, where Phelps Dodge has to go in a worst case scenario. At every meeting, directors review the balance sheet and cash flow outlooks. And they study the world markets, trying to predict trouble spots and areas of opportunity.

"I wake up every morning," says Yearley, "and try to do something differently. We step back as a company and think what about the next ten years. We commission ten of the best and brightest in our company to look at the future," says Yearley, who was so annointed fifteen years ago. "We are always looking for change."

At Ashland Oil, corporate strategy is discussed and approved by the full board. No committee is granted exclusive responsibility for the subject. At Delphi Automotive Systems, the new spin-off of GM, the board will spend most of its time focusing on strategy, and over half of every meeting will be unplanned.[4]

Campbell Soup has a two-day retreat focusing on strategic planning. The plan is presented the entire first day. Evaluation is a critical part of the discussions, and a three-year incentive plan is crafted every two years. The board is concerned about how to support the CEO and be certain that the CEO is not insulated when things go bad. "Board members are innovative leaders in their own fields, " says Bennett Dorrance, "and they have made a real difference for Campbell Soup. Things don't go breezing through the board," explains Dorrance, who says directors make substantive contributions to Campbell's strategy.

A typical meeting at Evolutionary Technology Inc., Austin, is 70 percent devoted to strategy. A recent board meeting focused on ETI's market space, another capitalization event, a manager let go, and quarterly results. The board discussion at dinner the night before was almost entirely devoted to strategy. Motorola is spending more time on strategy at board meetings, moving from about 25 percent up to near 45 percent. At a typical meeting at Edison International, CEO John Bryson expects the board to absorb the written information and covers six or seven items in one or two minutes each. He devotes the balance of Edison's board meetings to two or three "very important items." The agenda is a composite of topics from heads of Edison's businesses and the directors' areas of interest.

E. W. Scripps recently instituted an annual strategy retreat. William Burleigh says "It's been very valuable getting us on the same page. It became more a question of which breezes we hope to catch and how to trim our sails. And, there were alternatives we decided not to pursue. Maybe two or three times in a century will a company have an opportunity to deal with something new," which is certainly the case for the media giant. "It makes me sorry not to be around," says the CEO, who retired in mid-2000.

UTI devotes at least 75 percent of the advisory board meetings to strategy. A month before the quarterly board meeting, CEO Bob Hartman asks management to define their key issues. They then prioritize three to five items and bring two to the board with an extra to fall back on. The board announcement goes out three weeks in advance of the meeting (meetings are always scheduled a year out). The agenda is circulated at least two weeks prior with each of the managers' issues summarized on a single page.

Contingency planning is a major focus of strategic discussions. "If everything goes off the trolley, what do we do then?" David Tappan always wants to know. At Fluor, Tappan asked managers, "What are the worst three things that could happen to your operation? I'll bet you ten to one that somebody is doing one of those things right now, and it just hasn't surfaced yet." When everything is going well, there is always something that will fail, Tappan says. The strategizing proved invaluable when an employee was taken hostage in South America. Fluor had done extensive contingency planning in anticipation of just such a crisis. It took about nine months to retrieve the hostage, but he returned alive and well and with enormous esteem for Fluor. The outcome was not successful for Fluor's joint venture partner, who failed to plan. Their hostage was killed.

One frustration, according to Roy Herberger, is when the CEO "troops out others from management to sing the song [in a long winded presentation] and, lo and behold, the board discovers the strategy at the end." Instead, the CEO should get to the point and share his strategy up front, Herberger says. "These are my thoughts, these are the issues I want you to consider. These are the conclusions I've drawn." Then a director can respond in a meaningful way.

With time and geographic constraints and increasingly abundant technology, there is a trend to tele- or video-conferencing. David Tappan believes the value of such meetings is limited to addressing routine matters and to when time is critical. "It never works where you need debate and real discussion," he says. "Once someone takes a stance in a teleconference, it is easy for one individual to grab the ball and dominate the conference," deflecting the give and take essential for discussion.

Key questions: Do board meetings focus 40 percent or more on strategy? Are contingency plans discussed? Is there enough unstructured time to allow for discussion of nonagenda items?

THE COMMITTEES

Many companies, such as Chevron and Phelps Dodge, rotate committee assignments, including chairmanships, so that members don't get stale. Directors are more valuable with the perspective of different committees. Entrenched committee members can block change, knowingly or not, by perpetuating old ways. Captive boards often have committee chairs who echo the will of the CEO. Executive committees used to make all the real decisions, with the board as a rubber stamp. As the size of boards shrink, executive committees are evaporating. And the board as a whole is filling that role.

Pepsi Bottling has three committees with rotating committee chairs. It makes for a more engaged board, says Craig Weatherup. "I applaud the trend to less committees and fewer board members," says Weatherup, who believes the smaller number of committees and reduced board size has "generated more dialogue and more debate. I challenge you to [go to a board meeting and first thing] listen to six committee reports, two of which you are on, with any degree of interest. It's not the best way to run a board." As Doug Yearley sees it, committees are the "nuts and bolts. You don't want to spend a whole board meeting talking about last month's results." (See also a brief discussion on committees in Chapter 2.)

Key Questions: Does the board have a voice in the selection of committee chairs? Who sits on the committees? Who creates the committee agendas? Do the independent directors take the lead in these areas? Are there committee charters? Are the committees made up exclusively of independent directors?

LEAD DIRECTORS

About 30 percent of Fortune 500 boards have lead directors or independent chairs. Lead directors are often looked at as a means of facilitating the governance process and catalyzing the interests of the independent directors—and as a way to balance a domineering CEO. If a board's primary responsibility is monitoring and evaluating management, and if the chairman of the board IS management, isn't this incestuous?

The major argument against lead directors is that it feeds divisiveness and adds a layer of bureaucracy. Maurice Myers, Chairman and CEO, Yellow Corporation, says "it's just one more domineering person getting in the way of the board functioning like it should."[5] Clayton Yeutter, who sits on the Caterpillar, FMC and Texas Instrument boards, probably speaks for many directors when he says that a lead director is "a dumb idea. You don't want classes of directors. You don't want a caste system. There is no sense at all in it. All the directors I know would resist that proposal enormously. I think," he adds, "that there would be a whole lot of resignations, including mine."

A leader arises naturally, depending on the situation. There is a member to whom other directors turn, who takes messages back to the CEO, often the most senior director or the chair of the relevant committee. There is a question, too, whether additional D&O liability is incurred by a lead director, the same question that is being raised with audit committee members. A lead director adds another issue for the board to deal with, many say. One long-time Fortune 500 director is emphatically opposed. "Don't get in the pattern of choosing among peers in a popularity contest," she protests. "Frankly, I don't have time to be a junior board member."

Edison International's John Bryson says a lead director can "work in some cases and not others. It can set up a competing super management and lead to uncertainties. The important thing is to select the right directors and the right management."

Carl Hagberg, investor relations advisor, opposes lead directors because "when vigorous action is necessary, almost 100 percent of the time it's a newer director who causes change. The lead director tends to be the oldest and most senior person on the board; the least likely person to start a palace revolt. He is like an associate king. Why would he be the one to say the king has no clothes?" asks Hagberg.

But there are compelling arguments in favor of a lead director. Advocates point to the success of lead directors in Great Britain. Robert Monks believes that one is "inevitably forced to the conclusion that the role of chair is not an independent function, but only one of a hierarchy of tasks the CEO has." Thus, the CEO is, by definition, conflicted in that role, because he is not independent. Roy Herberger thinks that lead directors are "really the key to making boards work." Lead directors can talk to a director who oversteps bounds in a way the CEO cannot. He can facilitate the meeting flow. James Kristie, editor of *Directors & Boards*, wonders if it is "just getting too much for one person at the top to do it all? Maybe it makes sense for a CEO to say, 'Why not have a separate chairman and let him take on some of these governance issues for me. Let me run the company and let him or her call the board together, run the board and handle some communications with shareholders.' " [6]

Phil Matthews talks about a facilitator as opposed to a leader who imprints his own ideas. "You kind of lose your own identity. If you do the job right, you bring out others. There has to be board leadership, and it can't just be the CEO. A board needs to have, even if it's informal, its own way of funneling things that are sensitive to the senior executive."

Ben Rosen, director at Compaq, is probably the country's most visible leading director and thus, not surprisingly, a strong proponent of the practice. "This is the single most important factor in creating the right balance of power needed for effective governance. Our country has this separation of powers. Why shouldn't companies?" he asks.[7] Compaq is a fascinating case, because the line is demonstrably fragile.

In 1982, when Compaq was conceived on a napkin, venture capitalist Benjamin Rosen insisted on separating the CEO role from the chairman and also mandated a board of outsiders with the CEO as the only insider. About nine years ago, Rosen, who has been chairman of Compaq since its inception, led the ouster of "Rod" Canion after a $70 million quarterly loss. Eight years later, Rosen spearheaded the removal of CEO Eckhard Pfeiffer. Was it easier to oust Pfeiffer because he was one insider versus eleven outsiders? Was it easier to do it a second time, because it was so successful the first time? And, has Rosen, who stepped in as part of a director triumvirate to run Compaq while the fairly sloppy search was on for a successor, crossed the line from policy to operations?[8]

Advisory board member Bill Hawfield believes it is important to have a lead director. "The owner should not facilitate his own meeting," he insists. "Let the CEO watch and observe" and not worry about whether it's time for lunch—or how to move the meeting along. The CEO should be focused on the substance, not the form. Management at Campbell Soup believes that, if the CEO is also the chairman, then a lead director is needed. Campbell's has regular executive sessions of independent directors. "There should be a central clearing house," says Bennett Dorrance, "someone any director can go to."

David Tappan also is "absolutely in favor" of a lead director, who should not be appointed by the CEO. "The general consensus is that nobody wants to assume it because they feel they are being pushy. But, everyone is aware someone must step up to bat when the board needs to meet separately from the CEO. In the absence of someone being nominated," Tappan adds, "it is left up for grabs. And, it can be a disaster. Most independent directors are reluctant to volunteer, but a process should be in place to make it happen."

Bundling the three megatitles—president, CEO, and chairman—confers tremendous status. And, our society reinforces it. For instance, *Fortune Magazine* hosts a chief executive conference and restricts attendance to only those individuals who hold all three titles. Does that mean the CEOs of Campbell Soup or Compaq would not be welcome? Tom Higgins, Edison International, sits on the board of two companies. At one of them, the long time CEO is agitating to add chairman of the board to his titles. The nonexecutive chairman facilitated a compromise among the six outside directors that, in a year's time, if the company is meeting goals, the CEO will be designated as chairman elect for a two-year term. Jonathan Ornstein, CEO of Mesa Airlines, recently reclaimed the chairmanship from attorney Paul Madden.

Regardless, there is growing support for separating the chair and the CEO roles and using the chair to facilitate and infuse the process with objectivity, troubleshooting, evaluating, optimizing board process, and freeing up the CEO to do what he does best—manage and grow the business. The argument in favor of nonexecutive chairs at private companies is especially powerful, because of the limited disclosure requirements and the extent of corporate power and discretion invested in a single person. In practice, a shadow lead director often exists de facto. Committee chairs, directors with longevity, with special expertise or credentials tend to take the lead. Almost every board has a non-CEO leader, whether he or she is formalized in that role or not.

MEETINGS OF INDEPENDENT DIRECTORS

Regularly scheduled meetings of independent directors is a best boards practice. Yet there are extraordinary examples of controlling or insecure CEOs who carefully quarantine directors from one another. The key is to schedule regular meetings of independent directors. Some boards set aside time at every meeting. At other boards, independent directors meet annually. Too frequent meetings can be repetitive. If meetings are too infrequent, critical issues can be ignored.

Sixty-nine percent of companies report that their outside directors meet in executive session, other than for discussion of compensation issues. Only about one fourth of the meetings are scheduled regularly.[9] As David Tappan points out, "you'd be amazed how directors open up. They start thinking in a different context. You think they haven't a thought [until the independent directors' meetings are held]." Directors need a vehicle to critique the CEO in a constructive way.

ANNUAL MEETINGS

Many directors disdain the contrivances and formality of the legally mandated annual shareholder meetings of public companies, which often are reactive and detractive because of strident, single issue activists. "It's the only part of serving as a director that I have questions about," says Bobby Inman. "I have not been to very many where I have found an intense interest in strategic issues." Too often, the questions are usually narrow and short-term. "I have never been to a board meeting of a company in a downturn where the questions asked related to what are you doing for the long term," exclaims Inman. A Texan finance company on whose board he served once held its annual meeting in a hotel room. The company, he muses, "was not less well off because of it."

At Firestone, when George Aucott was CEO, a shareholder stood up at the annual meeting and questioned an $8 item on an expense account for laundering shirts. "The whole crowd focused on that," says Aucott. "What does that have to do with running a $5 billion business? It is the directors' responsibility to keep the CEO focused, and this is totally disruptive to the entire process."

Key Questions: Are committees independent and well run? Is there a lead director or separate chair? Are there regularly held meetings of the independent directors?

TRANSPARENCY

The best boards are available to shareholders in a meaningful way. At a strategic board, there is a commitment to full disclosure. Governance policies and procedures are a matter of public record. Directors are visible and accessible. "It's mind boggling that most companies don't publish their corporate governance procedures," exclaims Pat McGurn of Institutional Shareholder Services.

As shareholders gain a greater voice, not only will governance procedures be available publicly, so will evaluation forms, more in-depth information on directors, and other important ingredients of the governance process. Voting will increasingly be via the internet, and comprehensive information will be available in real time.

Annual Reports

A recent three-year survey of annual reports of Fortune 100 companies by Addison, a branding company, revealed that more than two thirds of the largest public companies list no more than the names and primary affiliations of the directors."[10] This is the capstone written link to your shareholders. Shouldn't they know who their representatives are? Since they can do no more than vote them in or out of office, shouldn't the shareholders know something about the people who oversee their investment? Anecdotal evidence tells us the information given to shareholders at smaller companies is no better. Actually, most annual reports are antiquated, relatively outdated documents that are cumbersome, tedious, and hard to read. As they go on line and become interactive, there will be a dramatic revolution in transparency.

Here is the type of information that should be available on both the directors and the board:

Director information

- Current title, organization and industry.
- Length of time on board.
- Age.
- A photograph.
- Other board memberships, both for profit and nonprofit.
- A biography, which includes prior board experience and which details work history, including titles, organizations, and dates.
- Special qualifications or expertise.
- Committee memberships. Any leadership roles, past or present.
- Share ownership.
- Attendance. If poor, the reason.
- Personal information.

Board information

- Governance information.
- Any special board recognition, such as a best board award.
- Corporate governance guidelines.
- Board matrix.
- Number of directors. Anticipated vacancies.
- Key initiatives undertaken, including evaluations, strategic planning retreats, succession planning.
- Issues addressed. The Bell South report lists four major issues

Leadership

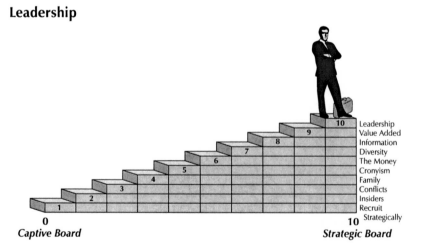

before the board that year and includes a list of upcoming issues.

This information should be included on the Web site under a corporate governance section.

Robert Lear believes you will have a good board if you have three things: 1) Independence—"the sine qua non," 2) the air of participative involvement by the board, and 3) the ability to rate the performance of the CEO, the board, and the individual directors.

Key questions: Do we have the best possible people for this company at this time? Do we have open communications with our shareholders?

If your board is empowered by strategic leadership, a positive culture, independence, effective meetings, member rotation, and transparency, step up to the final stair step and score an additional point on the strategic board continuum quotient. Congratulations!

NOTES

1. John O. Whiteman, Snell & Wilmer, Arthur Andersen Board Roundtable, November 1998.
2. Steve D. Whiteman, Snell & Wilmer, Arthur Andersen Board Roundtable, November 1998.
3. Robert Stobaugh, "The Ashland Inc. Board Guidelines," *Director's Monthly*, April 1997.
4. "How is the New Delphi Board Being Built?" *Director's Alert*, September 1998.
5. Robert L. Heidrick, "How Do Boards Add Value?" *Directors & Boards*, Winter 1999.
6. "A Leading Observer Talks About Corporate Governance and Board/Management/Investor Relationships in the New Millennium," *Equity Market Insight*, March 1999.
7. "Appraising Boardroom Performance," *Harvard Business Review*, January–February 1998.
8. Scott Herhold, "Compaq Chairman Has Never Been a Figurehead," *San Jose Mercury News*, 20 April 1999.
9. Korn/Ferry International, *25th Annual Board of Directors Study*, 1998.
10. Leslie A. Segel, "Presenting the Board in an Annual Report," *Directors & Boards*, Fall 1998.

Part IV

Legal Issues and the Future

Chapter 12

Director Liability

U nderlying every director's decision to join a board lurks the fear of being sued. As always, the key is the people. There must be trust—confidence in the ethics and the abilities of management and the directors. As Betsy Sanders says "you have to trust that the people are the best, or you can't do your job as a director."

Those with large personal fortunes at risk are understandably reluctant to serve on high-risk boards. In times of crisis, when objectivity is most needed, the very wealthy can be distracted by liability worries and compromise the long-term interests of shareholders.

When Texas Eastern was subject to a hostile takeover, famed governance lawyer Marty Lipton was advising the board. Concern about liability exposure tipped the balance in favor of the sale, and Bobby Inman was the only director who voted against it. Yet, unless it is a case of fraud or malfeasance, it is difficult to find instances of directors who have had to pay out of their own pocket in suits brought against directors. For instance, in an informal conversation, Judge William Allen, former head of the Delaware Circuit Courts, Peter Clapman, Chief Counsel, TIAA-CREF, and Philip Lochner, consultant in corporate governance, corporate and securities law, could not name a single instance of an individual director who personally paid a litigant.

Despite the somewhat dimmed spotlight on litigation, both the actual number of Federal cases and the average settlement costs have risen. The number of class-action cases reaching federal courts more than doubled in two years, from 126 in 1996 to 265 in 1998, according to National Economic Research Associates. More portentous is the new mix of cases. In 1995, 75 percent of class action cases were nonaccounting related. Now the number is up to 59 percent and rising. The message to audit committee members, especially, is intimidating. Red flags to the so-called suing machines are a steep drop in stock prices, insider trading, and restatements of earnings—all matters that embroil audit committee members.

The Federal Litigation Box Score for December 1995 to August 1999, tallied by the Stanford University School of Law, is revealing:

Companies sued in federal court	656
Federal complaints on line	351
Most frequently sued industry	High technology
Most active district court	Northern District of California
Percentage alleging accounting fraud	59 percent
Percentage alleging insider sales	55 percent[1]

Most vulnerable are the fast-growth and volatile technology companies, which are hit by almost 30 percent of the lawsuits. The fallout is expensive, no matter how it is measured—in time, resources, or money. According to National Economic Research Associates, some 83 percent of the suits are settled, typically within a year of being filed. Settlements average 14 percent of the alleged damages with the average payout per company in the first six months of 1998 adding up to $10.4 million.[2] That's a lot of shareholder money. And, it often feels like blackmail by the more aggressive firms, usually small, internetted operations which generate suits triggered by the red flag formulas inputted in their computers. It often isn't a question of right or wrong. Often, on a cost basis, shareholder interests are served by settling lawsuits, regardless of their merit.

The painful alternative is typified by T. J. Rodgers, CEO of Cypress Semiconductor, who dug in his heels. When fourth quarter earnings in 1991 slid 20 percent, attorneys Weiss & Yourman sued Rodgers and five other directors and officers for $120 million. Three years later, the case went to trial and was thrown out. The plaintiffs appealed twice and lost each time. Fees mounted to $5 million, so Cypress countersued for malicious prosecution. Eight years later, Rodgers' case was thrown out, and he is now appealing that verdict. Rodgers, whose attack on diversity ended up on the front page of *The Wall Street Journal*, says "I won't stop until the California Supreme Court tells me I have to."[3]

The most notorious of the plaintiff firms that aggressively pursue class action suits is Milberg, Weiss, Bershad Hynes & Lerach, which is involved in some 40 percent of all state and federal cases and boasts $2 billion in settlements of securities suits. Whichever firm assembles the largest stable of aggrieved shareholders to join the class in a particular suit, and thus piles up the greatest aggregate damages, becomes the lead plaintiff. And the group appointed lead plaintiff gets to appoint the law firm that will control the case and earn the biggest fees. Thus, to grow their groups and earn the fees, Milberg Weiss' Web site invites browsers to "Join a Class Action" and choose from among a list of some 57 companies being sued. If shareholders or antagonists don't want to join up, they can use the Web site www.milberg.com. to register complaints about corporate practices or stock performance to generate new lawsuits—and they can do so anonymously. "Report Fraud" is the button to hit.

It is no surprise there was great cheering when the tables were turned against Milberg, Weiss, who agreed to pay $50 million to settle allegations that it used the legal process to drive a hostile witness out of business. According to *The Wall Street Journal*, "many companies, especially in the high tech industries, who have been a prime target of Milberg Weiss in recent years, have come to view its law practice as a kind of legalized extortion."[4]

Steve McConnell tells of a Resolution Trust Corporation suit against the real estate company he was CEO of, which dragged on for years. "It was absolute blackmail that I'd have fought to the Supreme Court. But how do you fight the government?" he asks. Ultimately they settled for several hundred thousand dollars.

GENERAL LEGAL GUIDELINES FOR DIRECTORS

What drives the real liability of the board is the quality of the directors and the management. The willingness and ability of directors to assume the tremendous obligations inherent in a board membership is what enables the system of corporate governance. No checklist can ever ensure good governance. Only good people can.

"Remember," says Arthur Levitt Jr., "that every time directors sit down at the boardroom table, thousands of shareholders sit down alongside them."[5] All directors have a fiduciary responsibility to the shareholders. Remember that shareholders cannot force directors, once elected, to take any particular action. As governance guru Keith Louden so aptly says, directors can delegate authority and responsibility, but they cannot delegate accountability.[6] In return for exercising "reasonable business judgment," directors are insulated from personal liability.

But the burdens are heavy. Directors must review and approve mergers, acquisitions and combinations that are increasingly intricate. They must answer the demands of institutional investors, hire and fire managers and set their compensation based on targets that constantly change and that are being challenged in ever more strident ways. Board members must advise on strategic plans geared toward markets that can shift or evaporate overnight. Directors must act to prevent management wrongdoing. There is a tendency to compare the role of corporate directors with legislators. However, for directors, the mandate is more cohesive and focused, the accountability is more immediate and precise, and there is a greater commonality of purpose than is the case with legislators who are obligated to represent divergent interests in an increasingly tumultuous and cacophonous environment.

Corporate governance is evolving in remarkable testimony to the success of our free enterprise system. J. Sinclair Armstrong, past chairman of the Securities and Exchange Commission, reminds us that the virtue of American securities regulation is that it has "facilitated the development of the greatest capital markets of the world, by giving the public confidence in open and fair operation of the markets. No other system has done it so well. Directors have an awesome responsibility to keep the corporate ship sailing in the free-enterprise national and global economies."[7] But, as corporate governance moves to center stage and gathers a broader set of vocal, vested constituencies, heightened regulation looms.

BASIC DUTIES

The law sets the rules. The people set the standard. If ethics are absent, no law, no matter how meticulously prescribed, can prevent abuse. However, a high standard of duty has been prescribed that binds all directors under the law. The vast majority of directors carry out their responsibility with respect for the law and with integrity and commitment to their company.

Duty of Care

Directors and officers generally must act with the care that a reasonably prudent person in a similar position would use under similar circumstances. You must perform your duties in good faith and in a manner you reasonably believe to be in the best interest of the organization. The duty of care requires that directors act diligently and reasonably. It requires you to pay attention and attend regular meetings.

You are responsible for decisions taken by the board, whether you are in attendance at the time the decision is made or not. You have a right to rely on others to uphold the same standard. Being absent when a key decision is made does not absolve you of responsibility. One Fortune 500 CEO went on the board of his friend's microbrewery in the Midwest. The company went under, leaving sizable debt and a stream of unaudited statements. A couple of investors sued the board members. When the CEO took it to his lawyer, he said, "Don't worry. I've got the perfect case. I didn't go to one meeting."

Duty of Loyalty

Although other constituencies are clamoring for representation, it is generally agreed that board members have a duty of loyalty, the "sole purpose" doctrine, by which they must focus on enhanced shareholder returns. This is the duty that prescribes against conflict of interest. The best interest of the corporation and its shareholders must take precedence over any interest possessed by a director. Directors and officers are required to refrain from engaging in personal activities that would injure or take advantage of the organization. You are prohibited from using your position of trust and confidence to further your private interests.

Duty of Obedience

Directors and officers are required to perform their duties in accordance with applicable statutes and the terms of the organization's charter.

Duty of Oversight

The board must be proactive in ensuring that it has full and necessary information. This includes the responsibility to see that the corporation has a reasonable system of internal controls in place. The courts have ruled that being passively informed may not be adequate. If you have good reason for concern, you are expected to be proactive and make appropriate inquiries.

The former chairman and CEO of W. R. Grace negotiated a retirement package that includes perks valued at $3.6 million, including the use of a corporate jet and a company owned apartment. The company was also negotiating to sell a small subsidiary to the ex-chairman's son. One member of the board led the negotiations for the perks. Another was aware of the negotiations for the sale. The transactions were not fully disclosed or described to the shareholders, as required by law.

In deciding this case brought by the SEC in late 1997, the Commission determined that not only the company, but several W. R. Grace directors, bore responsibility. Each could have brought these matters to the attention of the lawyers preparing the disclosure and asked why they had not been fully disclosed. Says Arthur Levitt Jr., "we just felt that if the board knows something is not being disclosed, it should ask 'why not?' A director cannot rely on counsel's advice if he or she has reason to know that the counsel is not fully informed."

THE BUSINESS JUDGMENT RULE

This is the guiding principle and protection for all directors. The business judgment rule presumes that board decisions are made by disinterested directors acting on an informed basis, in good faith and in the honest belief that their actions serve the corporation's best interests. The rule recognizes that not every decision will benefit the organization.

If a plaintiff can plead facts demonstrating that some conflict of interest tainted the board's decision-making process, the business judgment rule may not apply.[8] Further, the rule protects directors from claims for wrongful acts, but not against claims for failure to act. Inaction by directors is protected by the rule only if it is the result of a conscious decision not to act. If a decision proves unwise, directors are free from liability—as long as they acted in good faith. They must be reasonably informed and rationally believe that a decision was taken in the best interests of the corporation.

A landmark case underlines the ability of the business judgement rule to shield directors from lawsuits. When the Armand Hammer Museum of Art and Cultural Center came to the Occidental Petroleum board for support, where Armand Hammer presided over, a special committee that approved spending $50 million for construction, granting a thirty-year rent-free lease, funding a $24 million annuity, and granting an option to purchase the museum complex.

Although the Delaware courts did say that the court's role is "severely limited," they ruled that the gift was "within the range of reasonableness." The principle drawn is that the rule prevents courts from second-guessing directors who have acted rationally. The courts have ruled that directors can be liable only if a decision is made on an "uninformed basis." This is the ruling that has spurred directors to call on third party advisors to provide expert opinions and which drives elaborate decision making procedures. This is the ruling that elevated process as protection.

The concern now is that clear, lucid decision making will be overwhelmed by paper and process. Hoffer Kaback, president of Gloucester Capital Corporation, says, "We ought to move away from glorifying form and process. A board should be held accountable for wasting corporate assets even if its choreographed process is cosmetically pristine."[9] According to director and governance expert Charles Elson, the ruling created a "process that was primarily designed to produce a liability-precluding paper trail rather than a truly informed and deliberated business decision. Nothing is gained by such a charade."[10]

One other point, although an individual director is responsible under the law, an individual director has no authority to act on behalf of the corporation outside of the board.

Conflict of Interest

All states address conflict and relax the common law rule that automatically voids all conflict of interest transactions. In Delaware, a conflict of interest transaction can be saved if the interested director fully discloses his or her interest in the transaction, and the transaction is then approved by a majority of the disinterested directors or shareholders. Otherwise, the board must prove that the transaction was entirely fair to the corporation.[11]

Causation

Inattentive directors cannot be held liable for a corporate loss, if attentiveness would not have prevented the loss. There must be a direct causal relationship proven for a director to be held liable for bad behavior.

Shareholder Resolutions

Shareholders may express their views on corporate affairs to the board through shareholder resolutions. Thus, governance oriented resolutions cannot be excluded from a company's proxy.

Takeovers

Once a board concludes that a sale of the company is inevitable, it must abandon its role as an active participant in the contest for control and instead act as a neutral arbiter to ensure that the shareholders get the best possible price for their shares.

Insider Trading

Any individual with access to material, nonpublic corporate information must disclose that information prior to trading in the corporation's securities or abstain from trading completely.[12] Avoid trading before or after a company announces restated earnings, a merger, or the settlement of a lawsuit. It's a wise practice for directors and officers to check with a gatekeeper, usually the chief financial officer, before exercising options and to sell small amounts of your holdings, less than 10 percent, at any one time.

OTHER LEGAL FLASHPOINTS

- *Hostile work environments.* Directors who are aware of problems are at risk if they take no action.
- *The Millennium bug.* Companies were required to fully disclose their preparedness. Experts estimate that the cost of year 2000 litigation could run as high as $1 trillion dollars and will carry forward for decades.[13]
- *Environmental issues.* In addition to direct liability issues, parent companies whose subsidiaries owned or operated a polluting facility are frequent targets in environmental lawsuits. A parent company may engage in general corporate activities with its subsidiary without subjecting itself to direct liability.[14]
- *High turnover of financial people.*
- *Overstating revenues.* Most fraud stems from overstating revenues and fourth quarter bonanzas.
- *Failure to police or prevent copyright infringement.*
- *Bribery.* There is increased attention to the Foreign Corrupt Practices Act forbidding U.S. companies from giving or accepting bribes overseas. For years, Motorola has had a flat policy against this.
- *Big sales shipments in the last week of the quarter.*
- *Accounting adjustments.*
- *Requests for changes in public accountants.*
- *Growth in inventory levels and receivables.*
- *Significant changes in income tax rates.*
- *General concerns.* To protect yourself, note your concerns in the minutes. As a director you can't be held liable for a decision judged to be improper, if you are on record as voting against it.

Be particularly careful if you join a board in the midst of a major transaction for which you may have legal responsibility, but in which you have had no influence in the decision making. For example, if a big merger is pending, avoid going on the board just as it is brought to a vote. If a lawsuit is imminent, be certain there is full disclosure. If the company is going public, if someone brings a shareholder suit, will you have helped insure it was done properly or will you just be coming on board for the vote? According to attorney Quinn Williams, if you are a director at the time of the vote, you are liable, regardless of your prior involvement.

INSURANCE AND INDEMNIFICATION

Despite the surge of litigation, and probably because of the cost, the percentage of companies providing liability insurance for their directors has dropped from 85 percent in 1988 to 74 percent in 1998.[15]

According to attorney Stephen Weiss, "director protection is like a three legged stool":

- Indemnification
- Exculpation
- Insurance

Broad indemnification is provided in a company's bylaws or by an individual indemnification agreement and indemnifies a director beyond the insurance coverages, so you won't have out-of-pocket costs. Exculpation limits liability of directors to shareholder suits either automatically as in Florida or by state statute as in Delaware. Generally, minimum coverage for smaller companies should be for at least $3 million and preferably $5 million, assuming it is not a high risk company or industry. For larger companies, the recommended minimum is $10 million.

Most directors don't go any further than asking whether there is directors' and officers' liability (D&O) insurance, the third protective leg on Weiss' stool. The tendency is to focus on premium levels rather than breadth of coverage. So, if you ask directors what's in their policy, what its limits are, or what the exclusions are, the odds are they won't know. Yet, there are some eighty different D&O forms, and they vary greatly, because it is the exclusions that dictate the true coverage. It's the exclusions that count.

D&O Liability Insurance Tips

- Make sure that *wrongful act coverage* is adequate for the specific types of risks faced by your company.
- Verify that the company's *bylaws* allow indemnification for D&O.

- Does the *carrier* write a lot of D&O policies? Is it an A-rated carrier?
- What is the financial size category of the insurer? D&O policy expert Duke Schwartz of Brown and Brown Insurance recommends at least a 7 out of a 15 rating.
- Be certain that acts of directors and officers for *subsidiary or affiliated companies* are covered.
- Be sure your policy covers *mergers, consolidations, and acquisitions*. Acquiring organizations are usually expected to provide D&O coverage, yet policies often cover only subsidiaries in existence at the inception of the policy.
- *IPO coverages*. If insiders are selling shares to raise money, it could increase the premium. Lawsuits loom if the stock dives, if the information in the funding document is not accurate, or if market expectations are unrealized.
- If the company is doing a private placement, be sure there is *no SEC exclusion*. If there is, any instrument you offer to the public to raise funds is excluded from coverage.[16]
- Beware of a provision that permits *policy cancellation* based on an inaccurate or incomplete insurance application. After one company and its directors and officers had been sued in a securities class action, the insurance company voided the policy to all insureds because the information in the application was inaccurate.[17]
- Look for an *application-severability provision* to protect innocent directors and officers against cancellation.[18]
- Beware of policies that do not *cover criminal proceedings*, especially in light of the movement to criminalize securities violations.
- Be aware of the timing as to *when a claim begins*. As a director, you want the policy to kick in as early as possible, ideally when there is a formal order of investigation. Also, some policies don't pay defense costs until the end of the proceedings. The argument is that they don't know the outcome. Directors and officers should not have to front any costs.
- Be certain that *tail coverage* or *run-off coverage* is in place to cover a director after you leave the board. In smaller companies or in situations in which a director has left because of concerns about the viability of the company, it can be critical. Snell & Wilmer attorney Quinn Williams advised setting up a "sinking fund

pool" to anticipate a legal defense fund for D&O, to survive three years after the corporation is sold.

- Separate *employment practices liability* (EPL) coverages. A perfectly adequate policy limit can be gutted by adding an EPL endorsement to a D&O policy. A particularly serious claim against one or more covered employees conceivably could burn through the entire D&O policy limit—leaving no coverage at all for directors and officers defending a lawsuit.[19]
- A "throw-on" (free) coverage covers you as a director of *nonprofit boards* that the company asks you to sit on. You may need to ask the insurer for this coverage. It won't be automatic. But, it could be critical.
- Obtain "throw-on" coverage for *advisory board* members as well.
- Before joining a board, it is prudent to obtain a D&O *audit* from an expert.

As Duke Schwartz, senior vice president at Brown and Brown Insurance, points out, "You can be sued for anything. Who knows how they are getting valuations for companies today? Price earnings ratios used to be around 15. All ratios are out of whack today. There are valuations strictly based on ideas. Today, you need protection," he warns. "That stock can go down as fast as it goes up."

The best way to avoid lawsuits is to do your due diligence and not count on insurance and indemnification. (See Chapter 2, "The Director's Checklist.") Directors are often too casually recruited and, equally casually, they accept basically on the word of the founder or CEO without looking carefully at the company. After joining the board of Employee Solutions, one board member lamented not researching the company relative to lawsuits and legal issues. "We can only do so much to turn the company around," the director said. "It is out of our control. It has really been a challenge for us spending cash and resources, with shareholder lawsuits, contracts with customers and employee issues. We could have had a much stronger year; if we had full information."

As Steve McConnell says, "there is no better protection than your own vigilance. What's nice is if you have other experienced directors." McConnell asks the chief financial officer to give him a signed letter at every board meeting stating that all employee wages and taxes have been paid, because the withholding taxes are the one thing the director can be personally responsible for if they go unpaid. In Canada, directors are responsible for the full amount of unpaid taxes.

Regardless of the merits or the outcome, even the threat of a suit can be consuming, expensive, and upsetting. McConnell was a director on a real estate company board which was sued for $80 million. The company settled under their D&O policy for $2 million. "You're on ice. You can't do deals. D&O is not the panacea people think," McConnell says. Shareholder litigation attorney Barbara Dawson of Snell & Wilmer says that whether or not you are named in a lawsuit, if you were a decision-maker on the issue in question, you will be involved. You will need to spend time with the lawyers. You'll be asked for all the related documents you have and will be required to go through depositions and hearings. There may be a trial.

If you are named and face potential personal exposure, what happens if you want to refinance your house, and you have to answer yes when asked if you are a party to any litigation? Further, Dawson says there is very real "mental fatigue from having a lawsuit hanging over your head. You made a decision that is being called into question."

About 50 percent of D&O claims are generated by stockholders. Private companies can therefore eliminate that category of claims, except for companies with many private shareholders. "If I have a company with one hundred or two hundred shareholders, it would be high risk and I would treat it like a public company," says corporate attorney Quinn Williams.

ADVISORY BOARDS—ARE YOU LIABLE?

As a rule, advisory boards carry no liability. However, self-dealing and fraud do subject advisory board members to legal action. "If there were some injury to the corporation and somebody used their position" as an advisory board member, says Quinn Williams, it is conceivable the director could be held responsible. For example, Williams postures, "if I knew the financial statements of the company, and if I knew they were doing business with a certain supplier, and if I could get business in return for a referral fee, a corporate shareholder could make a claim that I violated my fiduciary duty."

If an advisory board member is deemed to be a de facto director, by acting like a director and making decisions like a director, you could be vulnerable. Admittedly it would be "a high bar to cross over," says Williams, who together with his partner, Barbara Lawson, know of no such cases. "The concern is that an advisory board member is potentially put in harm's way of having a shareholder say they made decisions," such as approving disposition of an asset or a merger or helping negotiate a deal with a third party. "All of a sudden, the large issue is raised as to whether, in fact, the advisory board therefore has a duty to shareholders," Williams explains.

Williams suggests that advisory board members do the following:

- Review the D&O policy and make sure it covers advisory board members. Get it in writing.
- Ensure there is a supplemental, contractual indemnification by the company and get it in writing.
- Obtain a resolution by the statutory board making it clear that this is an advisory board and entitled to indemnification under the charter of the organization.
- It is best not to commingle the boards.
- Define the role and mission of the advisory board.
- Make it clear that the advisory board is not responsible for the business and affairs of the corporation.

NOT-FOR-PROFIT BOARDS—ARE YOU LIABLE?

Nonprofits are such an integral part of our country's social fabric, so critical to supplementing government and patching together a safety net for the needy and impoverished, that they are sheltered from the more rigorous standards we apply to business. Yet many of these enterprises are now enormous and have many of the same qualities and challenges as for profits. In Maryland, for instance, the nonprofit sector is bigger than manufacturing, and it accounted for 25 percent of all jobs created in the ten years ended in 1998. In addition, wages were largely on a par with for-profit workers.[20]

The key distinction is that nonprofits are accountable to stakeholders, not shareholders, and nonprofit directors are volunteers and typically focused on fundraising. However, both nonprofit and corporate boards are responsible for the business and the policy of the organizations they direct—the essence of governance. Because of the lower standards, the opportunities for abuse are prodigious. Good will does not automatically translate into good practices—or into good governance.

After the United Way of Santa Clara County depleted its reserves together with most of a $1 million line of credit, the organization laid off half the staff and handed out almost $1 million in severance pay. The latter came as a surprise to the United Way's board members, who read about the layoffs in the media.[21] Where was the board? One would expect more diligence in the wake of the 1994 United Way scandal four years earlier which resulted in the conviction of the agency's three top executives for conspiracy, money laundering, and filing false tax returns. That board of business leaders was utterly dormant.

A lot of abuse can be perpetrated in the name of charity. The Saint Francis Foundation, an instant, virtual charity claiming to bring $1 to $3 billion to world charity, boasted about having former Chrysler Corp. Chairman Lee Iacocca and newscaster Walter Cronkite on its board, former U.S. ambassador to the Soviet Union and attorney Robert Strauss as legal counsel, and Ernst and Young as its auditor. None of those claims were accurate. Now the foundation is embroiled in a multistate financial debacle in which a string of insurance companies is missing at least $335 million, and the foundation's existence is in question.[22]

The Bishop Estate trustees are an extreme case, but, nonetheless, exemplify the excesses that are possible with neglect. The Estate is bigger than any corporation in Hawaii. One million dollar salaries for the trustees was the norm. Monies were to be preserved for the education of Hawaiians, but abuses were rampant and trustees set up personal fiefdoms. For example, trustee Lokelani Lindsey regularly flew Estate employees in to work on her Maui home.

It wasn't until an IRS investigation threatened their tax exempt status that the trustees were removed in 1999. Four trustees refused to resign, two of whom were indicted by the state of Hawaii for receiving kickbacks on a land deal involving property owned by the charity. "We are big. We are massive. We are wealthy. We are proud of it," former Trustee Henry Peters told the *New York Times*, refusing to apologize for the trustees' abuses. Eventually, the four recalcitrant trustees were deposed. There will now be five trustees, with a CEO/chair who will receive no more than $120,000.

The Baptist Foundation of America (BFA) recently froze all new and existing accounts, including those of some 13,000 investors, and Arizona state regulators ordered a halt in securities sales. BFA listed total liabilities of $640 million, of which $590 million is owed to investors. Assets are approximated at about $180 million.[23] The Baptist Foundation brochure claimed the foundation had always been profitable, and it claimed the BFA was a "low cost operation." In truth, audited statements showed an operating loss in 1996 and "difficult years" from 1989 through 1992. The 1997 report showed that, despite taking in $91 million, salaries, wages and general administrative costs consumed $34 million, well over a third of the intake, and hardly "low cost."[24] The BFA is facing dissolution and a battery of lawsuits. The bankruptcy case cost about $1 million a month.[25] Where was the board?

Over two thirds of all CEOs and corporate directors sit on at least one not-for-profit board. The toughest issues are wrapped around the compensation of the chief executive and how she spends the nonprofit's money. Top executives at the largest philanthropic foundations saw their salaries balloon five times the rate of inflation in 1998, with the average salary hitting $363,000. So many abuses have surfaced that the Internal Revenue Service (IRS) has joined the fray.

The IRS now requires nonprofit board members to set compensation levels at fair market value and to determine the proper price for goods and services. How many directors of nonprofits know that they can be held personally responsible for excess compensation paid and that they must reimburse the organization for those portions deemed excessive? The IRS will impose a $10,000 fine on directors who are overpaying their not-for-profit CEOs.[26] And, how many directors realize they are liable for all board decisions taken while they are board members, regardless of whether they are in attendance or involved in the decision making process or not?

Generally, when board memberships are tallied, directors simply ignore their nonprofit directorships. They simply don't count. Yet, of course they do. Nonprofits require time and resources. As demands on directors swell, the number of board seats will be increasingly important. And nonprofits will be counted. The fear of nonprofits is that this new accountability could slash the number of high-powered directors willing to serve on their boards.

Nonprofit boards are discounted in other ways as well. Strategic boards are no less valuable for nonprofits, than for profits. Yet, according to Robert Kile and Michael Loscavio, executive search consultants who head a division that recruits senior executives for nonprofits, "the search for new members often involves well-intentioned volunteers with little or no recruiting experience contacting well-intentioned candidates with little or no board experience. They simply round up the usual suspects." Kile and Loscavio recommend a highly regarded eight-step process spearheaded by a "board development team charged with the broad responsibilities of recruiting, orienting and developing board members." The result, says Kile, "is that you will get the people you want for the board. You'll get cooperation from additional people who can't sit on the board. And you'll get better results."[27]

As success-oriented individuals increasingly funnel income to nonprofits, their expectations and the accountabilities demanded are revolutionizing the nonprofit world. The bottom line is that nonprofits and foundations are becoming more professional and embracing the tenets of best practices. The best are incorporating good governance as a policy priority. Great boards mean great nonprofits too.

MUTUAL FUNDS

Mutual funds, where ownership rights are nontransferable, are a special case. Their boards have been nearly invisible and thus virtually immune to lawsuits and other pressures of the marketplace. Now, accountability looms as their numbers multiply. By mid-1999, 66 million Americans had invested more than $5 trillion in mutual funds, according to the SEC. And only 40 percent of their directors were required to be independent. A collapse in stock prices could trigger a debacle. Already activists are aiming at these funds.

In March 1999, SEC Chairman Arthur Levitt Jr. launched a regulatory initiative. The new rules require fund boards to have a majority of independent directors and to disclose director compensation and the number of board seats held. Astonishingly, at Fidelity investment, for example, twelve board members (three insiders and nine outsiders) are responsible for all 259 of the firm's funds. Fiduciary responsibilities include negotiating and overseeing fund fees, monitoring performance, policing conflicts of interest, and insuring that good management is in place. How can twelve people do that?

A hot issue is the "soft dollar" rebates that money managers receive for channeling trades through certain brokerage houses. Pension fund manager Alan Bond, a regular on "Wall Street Week with Louis Rukeyser," was accused by federal prosecutors of taking more than $6 million in alleged kickbacks from brokerage firms. He allegedly used the money for some seventy-five cars and a decorator to spiff up the warehouse where they were stored.[28]

In 1998, the SEC successfully sued two outside directors of the Parnassus Fund, accusing them of aiding and abetting the fund manager in overstating the fund's net asset value. And, although mutual funds hold some 20 percent of all outstanding U.S. stock, they are not required to disclose how they vote proxies on those shares. Other areas that drag down performance are huge marketing outlays and portfolio turnover that is nearly 90 percent. Vanguard Group Founder John Bogle has called outside directors of mutual funds, "a bad joke."[29]

Because there is so much potential self-dealing, a whole panoply of regulation under the Investment Company Act exists. But who is watching? In September 1998, Deep Discount Advisors, which owned shares in the Clemente Global Growth Fund, won a proxy battle to capture three of nine board seats. No doubt this is just the beginning.

Key questions: Are your board members ethical? Do your directors understand their legal responsibilities? Are your compensation and audit committees made up exclusively of independent directors? Are you sure you are insured? How are the nonprofits governed? Who is governing the mutual funds?

NOTES

1. *Stanford Securities Class Action Clearinghouse*, Robert Crown Law Library, Stanford University School of Law, August 1999.
2. "Bill Lerach Is Watching Your Stock," *Corporate Board Member*, Autumn 1999, 43.
3. Ibid.

4. Richard Schmitt, "Milberg Weiss Agrees to Settle Lexecon Case," *The Wall Street Journal*, 14 April 1999.
5. Arthur Levitt Jr., "The SEC Looks at Governance," *Corporate Board*, July–August 1998.
6. J. Keith Louden, *The Effective Director in Action* (New York: AMACOM, 1974).
7. J. Sinclair Armstrong, "Forays on the Governance Frontier," *Directors & Boards*, September 1997.
8. Barbara J. Dawson and Patrick J. Barrett, "Director Conflicts," *The National Law Journal*, 7 September 1998.
9. Hoffer Kaback, "Waste Not," *Directors & Boards*, Winter 1999.
10. Charles M. Elson, "Courts and Boards: The Top 10 Cases," *Directors & Boards*, September 1997.
11. Barbara J. Dawson and Patrick J. Barrett, "Director Conflicts," *The National Law Journal*, 7 September 1998.
12. Ibid.
13. "Boards Brace for Y2K Wars," *Director's Alert*, January 1999.
14. Stuart Hammer, "Welcome News on the Environmental Front," *Directors & Boards*, Fall 1998.
15. Korn/Ferry International, *25th Annual Board of Directors Study*, 1998
16. Data from Brown & Brown Insurance, Phoenix, Arizona.
17. Stephen J. Weiss, "Protecting Against Cancellation," *Directors & Boards*, Winter 1999.
18. Ibid.
19. Stephen J. Weiss, "Will Your D&O Coverage Be There When You Need It?" *Directors & Officers*, Fall 1998.
20. "Business Bulletin," *The Wall Street Journal*, 2 March 2000, 1.
21. "Crisis at Santa Clara United Way," *Board Member*, June 1999.
22. Mitchell Pacelle and Deborah Lohse, " 'Saint Francis' Foundation Becomes Focus of Questions," *The Wall Street Journal*, 22 June 1999, C1.
23. Max Jarman, "Baptist Foundation Files Chapter 11," *The Arizona Republic*, 11 November 1999, E1.
24. Jolyn Okimoto, "Probe of Baptist Group Expected to Find Losses," *The Arizona Republic*, 4 September 1999, E1.
25. "Baptist Foundation to Sell Properties," *The Arizona Republic*, 16 February 2000, D1.
26. *Director's Alert*, January 1999.
27. Robert W. Kile and J. Michael Loscavio, "Building a Better Board: Get the Board Members You Need Through Strategic Recruitment," *The Non-Profit Times*, November 1994.
28. Michael Schroeder, "A Popular Fund Manager Allegedly Took Kickbacks," *The Wall Street Journal*, 17 December 1999, C1.
29. "The SEC Takes Aim at Mutual Fund Directors," *Corporate Board*, Summer 1999.

Chapter 13

---◆---

The Future of the Strategic Board

◆ "Boldness Has Genius, Power and Magic in It. Begin It Now."[1] ◆

T he stakes are soaring—the power, the responsibilities, the risks. No longer are boards afforded the luxury of secrecy, gentle time-lines, and soft decisions. No longer are companies afforded the luxury of trial and error, of peaceful growth, stagnation even, of compliant indifference, of casual governance. The doors of the boardrooms are being pried open by the huge number of shareholders and stakehold-ers who see governance as their voice in the system, the safeguard for their interests. No smaller result than success is mandated, and the board is now assigned real responsibility for that success.

GOVERNANCE DRIVES SHAREHOLDER VALUE

The most pragmatic reason to have strategic boards is increased share-holder value. There is, indeed, a correlation between successful compa-nies, their value either privately or publicly, and strategic boards. It's not a science, but it's there. If you want a better company, look for a better board.

Warren Buffett believes how the board does its job and its relation-ship with management provide crucial clues for investors. Managers are the stewards of shareholder capital.[2] And the board is there to ensure that is the case. Many large private money managers are willing to pay a higher stock price for companies with strategic boards. In one survey representing $850 billion in assets, the managers were willing to pay an average premium of 11 percent for companies with good boards.[3] And, a study of small companies "found a significant positive correlation between the board's contribution to strategic planning and the growth of the firm. . . . Entrepreneurs' resistance to establishing boards of directors plays an important role in constraining their firms' growth."[4]

"Better governance leads to better share price," says Doug Foshee. "Over long cycles, companies with better governance show better returns to their shareholders. Most of my personal net worth is now in the form of equity in Nuevo Energy, so the pure economics of good governance accrue to my benefit as a shareholder. The results are irrefutable. Even if I were totally mercenary in my approach, it would be the right thing. At the end of the day, it's really hard to prove," Foshee continues. "If you think from the 30,000 foot level, however, the logic is inescapable. I'm not sure I care if McKinsey can prove it. Common sense and your gut tell you it's true." More than 84 percent of the directors Korn/Ferry surveyed in 1999 agree there is a direct correlation between the quality of the board and stockholder value.

According to a report in *The McKinsey Quarterly*, there are three main reasons investors will pay a premium for good governance. One, some investors believe a company with good governance will perform better over time. Two, others see good governance as a way of reducing risk, because it decreases the likelihood of bad things happening to a company. Further, when bad things do happen, well-governed companies will recover more quickly. Third, a well-governed company will be worth more because governance is trendy and thus adds value on that basis alone.[5]

Christensen & Associates regularly polls some 1600 security analysts and portfolio managers. "We have never had a single person ever say the board is a part of the evaluative criteria used when purchasing a stock," says CEO Howard Christensen. However, when asked on an "aided" basis to rate the importance of the board in the decision making process, investors ranked the board as very important. In other words, governance is not yet on the general radar screen of the analyst community, except as it may be implicit in general management. It is "unfortunate that the financial community has no understanding of how intimately involved the board is in planning the company's growth," says Patty Bruner, vice president of market research at Christensen. "There doesn't seem to be enough emphasis by management on creation of share value and how boards' decisions impact share value," Christensen adds.

That will change. The New York Society of Security Analysts has taken the lead in prioritizing governance. And, other analysts and money managers will follow. But, until then, until governance is proactively considered and not just scapegoated when trouble hits, it's no wonder that analysts, and thus management, are driven by the numbers.

Of course, boards are no panacea. They face built-in limitations on what they can do. However, good boards are more influential, more effective, and more supportive than the public—and the skeptics—realize. A strong board has become a necessity, not window dressing. The days of regal anonymity are gone.

SHAREHOLDER ACTIVISM

As CalPERS, the largest public pension plan in the United States, reminds its shareholders, stock ownership is an ongoing event with ongoing oversight responsibilities. "The choice of a common stock is a single act. Its ownership is a continuing process. Certainly there is just as much reason to exercise care and judgement in being a shareholder as in becoming one."[6] There is a growing swell of willing activists waiting for an opportunity to install change.

Now that over 50 percent of all adult Americans own stock, as more constituencies realize how powerful governance can be, it is inevitable that the owners will agitate for a greater voice. And, as they become more educated and gain an appreciation of their potential power, they will clamor for reform, as is their right.

As corporate governance peels back its armor and corporations become more responsive to their constituencies, the cacophony will rise. Technology will be the enabler, adding substance to their message, and ease to its delivery. There is a soaring wave of shareholder democracy and all it implies. Instead of withdrawing—the "Wall Street Walk," whereby dissatisfied shareholders register their displeasure by selling their stock—shareholders now realize they can make a difference from the inside. This signals a tremendous upheaval in the way governance is viewed.

There are millions of individual shareholders who invest in good faith and who deserve to be fairly represented by the directors. Often, individual shareholders are dismissed as gadflies, misdirected and micro-focused. Some activists indeed are true irritants and buy one share of various stocks so they can harangue management about their cause. Some activists fix on incidents and turn them into issues.

However, two impediments to broader shareholder activism—mountainous paperwork and lack of information—have been obliterated by the Internet. CalPERS and Domini, for example, post their voting decisions on the Web. With the burgeoning numbers of educated investors, the profile of the individual investor is as varied as our population. And, the gadflies will be outnumbered.

INSTITUTIONAL INVESTORS

Investment funds represent thousands, sometimes millions, of shareholders, and they are investing billions. They know that great boards mean great companies and they are the real drivers of governance reform. The shareholder funds have begun a practice of listing key governance criteria and then targeting the most flagrant corporate abusers, and, if necessary, taking their complaints public.

When Nell Minow, of Corporate Library, looks at a board, she wants to know three things:

- How much stock do the directors own in terms of their own net worth?
- Do the outside directors meet alone and regularly in executive session?
- Do the independent directors control the board nomination process?

Sherwood "Woody" Small, senior partner at E. R. Taylor Investments, says their mutual fund examines the board of directors before purchasing a company of any size. "The board of directors is not a definitive criteria. But the more extreme a board is—either outstanding or very poor—the more it influences our decision."[7]

Institutional investors are becoming ever more effective, as they hone their skills, tamp down their aggressiveness and refine the nuances of working with target companies. Some complain the institutions are too driven by formulas, but most agree the formulas are derived from best practice models. No one can deny that institutional investors are a force in establishing the platform essential to good governance.

In 1999, for example, CalPERS, the $150 billion plus pension fund, alone succeeded in gaining tremendous advancements in independent governance at a number of the companies in which it is invested. CalPERS will need to pay out $30 billion each year to its beneficiaries by 2020, so it must perform.[8] Here is an example of CalPERS' influence:

- Cummins will adopt an independent audit committee, appoint a lead outside director, consider EVA as a performance measure, and add strong independent directors.

- National Semiconductor agreed to add independent directors.
- Pacific Century Financial agreed to adopt CalPERS' definition of independence and restructure its board so it has a majority of independent directors, to identify a lead independent director, and to diversify its board geographically.
- Pioneer Resources will have a majority of independent directors.
- Sierra Health will add two independent directors.
- St. Jude Medical will have a majority of independent directors and restructure so that the audit, compensation, nominating, and governance committees are exclusively composed of independent directors.[9]

Ken West, who leads corporate governance reform at TIAA-CREF, the $275 billion pension fund, keys in on the following:

- Independence.
- Unequal voting rights.
- Independent committees.
- Age. A board with an average age over 70 is a red flag.
- Compensation with high levels of stock dilution. "Alarms go off if it is more than 15 percent in ordinary companies, more than 25 percent in high technology companies."
- Option repricings.

TIAA-CREF generally writes a target company citing concerns and then calls on them. As is the case at most of the shareholder groups, they only publicize their concerns if a company refuses to respond and the issue is going to a shareholder vote. At first, companies resisted. Now they have learned compliance is in their best interest. In 1998, TIAA-CREF filed seven resolutions on independence and withdrew them all after the targeted companies agreed to take action. They filed ten resolutions against "dead hand poison pills," an oppressive takeover defense, and withdrew all but three, against Lubrizol, Bergen Brunswig Corporation, and Mylan Laboratories. Brunswig and Lubrizol rescinded their "dead hand poison pills," and Mylan's action is pending. "I've contacted over one hundred companies and never had one acrimonious conversation," says Ken West. "We seldom encounter disagreement on independence." Target companies "always say we are more independent than you think we are. If they say, 'give us a couple of years to get there,' we go away for a while."

In evaluating boards overall, "it almost gets down to sociological factors," says West. "You just want boards to be independent, to act in the company's best interest. We understand that boards make mistakes, just like everyone else." The hope is that board members will "use their best judgment without special or self-interest, without being lazy and uninformed. They are dealing with complex issues that take a tremendous amount of time."

According to Peter Clapman, Senior Vice President and Chief Counsel, TIAA-CREF has thirty-five to forty companies on the scope for 2000. It has taken time, says Clapman, for the shareholders' group to figure out how to get the information it needs to target companies. One outgrowth of shareholder activism will be increased transparency and communication. "We welcome companies," says Clapman, "that trumpet what they are doing."[10]

SECURITIES ANALYSTS

In contrast to most securities analysts who generally ignore governance, The New York Securities Analysts society has taken the lead among analysts in targeting governance issues. Gary Lutin said the purpose of the New York Securities Analysts is to make people more alert and put in a process to reward effective responsibility: The society wants to target "indifferent or lazy or irresponsible" directors. In particular, the analysts want to focus on directors who "ignored or rejected corporate bids at higher prices and used their ability to control assets that belong to shareholders to benefit deals that favor them."

Doug Foshee, CEO of Nuevo Energy, says that institutional investors are "very keen" on the subject of reform. "They like independence and they love the idea of directors—and management —having skin in the game. I don't think it's an accident that of twelve analysts who write on our industry, eleven have buy recommendations on us. But I don't think you get as much credit in the market [for strategic governance] generally as you are led to believe. You will in the long run, because you will outperform the competition," says Foshee. "It's not at the top of the list for people who follow our business. If it doesn't show up on the Bloomberg screen, then it doesn't count," Foshee observes. "As a rule, you find out if management and governance count when something really bad happens.

Gary Tooker of Motorola is concerned that sell-siders are too short term oriented. "It's tough to talk about long term strategy. The next quarterly results are very, very important. For a company like Motorola, you would never invest in a project like Iridium, the global satellite communications system, if you were responding to sell-siders."

"One of the dreadful things is that we've become a quarterly business environment," laments Betsy Sanders. "We are driven constantly by ninety-day timelines that are arbitrary determinants of decisions."

Wall Street analysts are young with huge turnover and burnout rates. As a rule, they know the numbers far better than the people or the companies. Doug Yearley at Phelps Dodge thinks that shareholder activism can be abused. They "insist on change or want to enhance value in ways they perceive are important, which may or may not be appropriate."

While most institutional shareholders are refining and tempering their approach, at least one investor group says this is merely veneer. Kurth Schacht, General Counsel for the State of Wisconsin Investment Board, believes the "corporate governance pendulum is swinging back toward the confrontation mode and away from the cooperation mode." According to Schacht, the only lever left for the shareholder groups that will work is orchestrating proxy fights to elect their own directors.[11]

As Pat McGurn of Institutional Shareholder Services observes, "we are at a crossroads. Now, we have the phenomenon of institutional investors going over the heads of management taking seats themselves, because they think their voices are ignored or not compelling enough. If boards don't do a better job in strategy, succession and compensation, leading edge activists have no choice but to offer their own representatives for board seats. Many of us are but a step away from that sort of activity, and that's a terrible outcome for everyone involved."

CalPERS for one says it will not take that route.[12] Instead, there will be more shareholder proposals. No doubt shareholder activism will multiply and the next battlefield could be the seats in the boardroom. However, already, there are fewer flagrant abuses at public companies, and the focus is turning from large to smaller companies.

REGULATION

The positioning of companies as corporate citizens is gaining tremendous currency. We rely on the corporation to play a role in training our workforce, addressing social issues, health care, charity, education, retirement security, equal opportunity, and diversity. To the extent corporations don't meet implicit and explicit expectations, regulation looms. As policy making becomes more diffused and transnational, and the power of centralized government erodes, the corporate sector is filling the gaps. And, our expectations and dependence surge.

"CEOs would be wise to embrace the idea of strongly independent boards," says Jennifer Hawkins in *The McKinsey Quarterly*. "For if investors can't get boards to work well, they may resort to other measures: sitting on boards themselves, lobbying for director government regulation, or supporting a return of corporate raiders."[13]

Government regulation should aid, not harm or hinder. Its role should be to define and enforce the ground rules that make the playing field level and keep the system open. When change is the barometer, government regulation, which looks backwards, instead of forward, can be stifling, if not crippling. It smothers the very creativity and innovation that has allowed business to flourish.

John Bryson, CEO of Edison International, is disturbed at the prospect of "legalistic approaches. There are a number of ideas," he suggests, "that strike me as a potentially enshrining process. Governance begins to sound like legal mandates that can stand in the way of best practices." The threat of regulation has a tremendous self-regulating effect. That threat is moving governance reform to center stage.

GOVERNANCE TRENDS

What does all this mean? What are the trends in governance? Boards are changing as rapidly as the companies they govern, and the trends seem to presage best practices. The major trends in governance include:

- *Ethics.* With change as the only constant and the swell of litigation and activism, ethics will take center stage as the key driver of best practices. Boards should be informed about the ethical and legal behavior of their company and set the stage for a values-based company. Directors will be more proactive if there are problems.
- *Community citizenship.* The role of the company in the community it serves will be increasingly important in defining corporate leadership.
- *Fewer inside directors.* We are moving toward having a single insider on the board. Retiring CEOs will leave the board.
- *Independent directors.* There will be an increasingly rigid standard for independence. Independent directors will meet regularly in executive session without management.
- *Fewer board memberships.* Active executives will hold one or two outside board memberships. For others, four or five directorships will be the limit.
- *Strategic boards.* There will be more engagement in director recruitment, evaluation, succession planning, and other key governance processes. Boards will be better informed and play a more active role in evaluating and tracking strategy and its im-

plementation. More time will be spent on strategy at board meetings.

- *Smaller boards.* This trend will escalate as boards become less ceremonial and more strategic. Small company boards will range from five to seven and larger companies eight to ten directors.
- *Family boards.* The family will become more widely used as a strategic resource, as governance becomes more important. Family owned companies will increasingly embrace independent boards as a means of validating their value to their constituencies.
- *Compensation.* There will be an increased percentage of pay in equity, although a balance of cash and equity will be achieved as the markets adjust. Market lurches will dim the trend to all equity pay packages. There will be higher compensation for directors to reflect increased obligations and liabilities.
- *Equity pay.* Equity pay for all employees will be trumpeted by boards. A looming issue is the disparity in pay between executives and workers. This issue could derail the entire free governance system, because it has the capacity to escalate tension and catalyze the division between the haves and have nots. There will be greater emphasis on aligning director and shareholder interests and ensuring directors have a meaningful financial stake in their company. And finally, hooking pay so tightly to stock price may be less effective than is currently thought. When the markets turn, the fallout will have profound repercussions. Directors of failed technology companies will find they have served for free.
- *Technology.* Technology will appear more regularly and vigorously on board agendas, and more board members will bring technology expertise and vision to the board. Directors will scramble to become techno-literate. Governance will increasingly be modeled on board practices at the successful rapid growth technology companies as a change paradigm.
- *Director recruitment.* The process will increasingly track our ninestep model of proactive, strategic recruitment of independent directors. The nominating committee will take the lead in proactively identifying and nominating directors. Directors will be selected for how they think, what they know, and how they deliver it as much as for who they know. Although the availabil-

ity of Fortune 500 CEOs will shrink, there will be an abundance of new leaders from a great breadth of disciplines, who will add value as directors.

- *Contested director elections.* Driven by shareholder activism and technology, CEO-anointed director candidates will no longer have a free ride into the boardroom. Shareholders will use this one lever to make an impact on governance and maximize their right to participate in the election process.
- *Diversity.* An increase in women and minority representation on boards is inevitable. There will be fewer available Fortune 500 CEOs, because of time, pressure, and the exigencies of technology and change. Directors will be younger and boards will seek those with financial, management, governance, and technology expertise. There will be more international representation on American boards, and more Americans will serve on non-U.S. multinational boards.
- *Evaluations.* CEO evaluations will be standard, with measurables and increased accountabilities. Board evaluations will gain currency and be the norm. More boards will evaluate individual director performance and go beyond closely held self-evaluations. Feedback will be solicited from shareholders, analysts, employees, and other constituencies.
- *Fewer meetings.* The average number will trend below eight meetings.
- *Committees.* There will be an average of three or four committees made up solely of independents. There will be sharply increased responsibility and accountability, especially in the areas of audit, nominating, succession and evaluation, and compensation.
- *Training.* Ongoing training and enrichment will be integrated into the governance process.
- *Board culture.* Boards will be more businesslike, more results oriented, more involved and productive, more efficient, more time driven—with less tolerance for laggards and groupies. The culture could be upended in the process.
- *Crisis management.* There will be escalating emphasis on anticipating—and preventing—potential crises as a measure of successful governance.
- *Mergers & acquisitions.* Mergers and acquisitions will produce more "Noah's Ark" boards, where boards are blended. New

approaches will be created, such as combining directors in an ad hoc transitional board with a limited life in order to have a vital board moving forward. Board composition will be an integral part of M & A planning.

- *Globalism*. This steamroller will not stop. To compete, every economy will be fostering better boards as a means to better companies. The hundred-member Japanese board is an antiquity. Thailand, Brazil, and Poland are evolving better board practices, symbolic of the breadth of the corporate governance revolution. Great Britain's reliance on independent chairs will wash ashore in the United States. Our equities markets will flow across borders.
- *Litigation*. There will be more shareholder suits, especially in the area of audit. Technology companies will continue to draw disproportionate fire because of their volatility. Boards of mutual funds will be spotlighted.
- *Increased responsiveness to shareholders*. There will be more transparency and greater interaction between shareholders and boards of directors. Boards will form shareholder relations committees and elevate the board's focus on creation of shareholder value. Some say this will rival the audit, nominating, and compensation committees in importance. In turn, shareholders will insist on more private audiences with directors to encourage governance reforms. Concurrently, directors will learn more about the critical ingredients that create shareholder wealth, and shareholders, analysts, and money managers will gain an appreciation of the impact directors have on corporate growth.
- *Succession planning*. There will be greater and more proactive board involvement, and the process will be continuous and integrated into strategic planning. Boards will be more willing to replace nonperforming CEOs.
- *Lead directors*. More boards will separate the CEO and board chair roles above the current 25 percent, and more will designate lead directors. The independent board chairs and lead directors will increasingly serve as facilitators and as catalysts for director productivity.
- *Transparency*. Shareholders will expect to be informed about governance and where their companies stand on the strategic board continuum. If shareholders are patronized, if best practices are hidden from those they purport to help, as is the case

with many governance guidelines and charters, shareholders will assume laxity and passivity. Instead, there will be increasing communication in annual reports, proxies, and online about board practices and activities. There will be more interaction between boards and all corporate constituencies.

- *Shareholder democracy.* Boards will provide real checks and balances on corporate mismanagement and excesses and will be increasingly seen as management watchdogs.
- *Financial analyst activism.* Analysts on both the buy and sell sides will recognize the role governance can play in creating shareholder value, and they will prioritize governance as a measure of corporate success.
- *Constituency engagement.* The importance of governance to all constituencies will become obvious. Employees, customers, suppliers, analysts, and communities will recognize the power of boards as a measure of the company.
- *Better board practices.* Better board practices will permeate all sizes of companies, public and private.
- *Advisory boards.* More advisory boards will be created strategically as a way for private and smaller companies to test drive a board. Larger companies will rely on advisory boards to strategically engage global leaders and expand their reach and to focus on critical issues.
- *Certification for directors.* This is a significant trend outside the United States. Some certifications in the United States will gain support, but it is unlikely there will be any form of national certification empowering "professional" directors.
- *Director empowerment.* This will occur as an inevitable corollary to strategic governance.
- *Popularity of being a director.* More people will want to serve. In addition to being trendy, governance will attract serious thinkers who see governance as a way to impact society and globalism. There will be a tremendous flow of best minds into corporate governance as the new frontier.

GREAT BOARDS MEAN GREAT COMPANIES

In truth, no one outside the board's inner circle really knows what directors do. And, they rarely tell. It is still a closed system upon which the very health of our country and its citizens depend—a system based on our trust and the good will of the participants. And, as Robert Monks points out, the "continuation of the status quo is perfectly acceptable to those who have continuing power." However, it's a system that is being pried open and becoming increasingly accountable to its broader constituencies.

Happily, good governance practices and the trends are converging. And, it is too late to close the door. Despite the naysayers and egregious abuses, we are moving toward empowerment and partnership. On the whole, boards are working, and they are adding value. There is a lot of proof of that across the spectrum of successful companies. When asked what he would do differently in recruiting a strategic board, CEO Doug Lecker of ProLink said he would have done it sooner. "I have no regrets. I am really excited about what we can do in the future."

"The big value is in the questions," says Craig Weatherup of Pepsi Bottling. In their recent strategic review, questions focused on margins, returns, and the growth model. "Things get framed in very different ways. It's very, very thought provoking. A board is a big, big win," says Weatherup. "No matter how much you try to step away from your own business, the directors can instantly provide a perspective outside your own within a few hours. It is confirmation to me of why you have boards."

"If you have the best brainpower," Harvey Mackay says, "look at how valuable a board is and what one idea can do. It is the cheapest thing in the world to a world class business person." Doug Yearley, who completed his eleventh year as CEO at Phelps Dodge, says that "You must first have the will, then the mechanics. I'm a believer."

James Kristie defines what he calls the "ultimate board trend—a board of directors with the intelligence, integrity, and courage to exercise dutiful overview of management and contribute meaningfully to the strategic affairs of the corporation." As Paul Stern wrote in Kristie's *Directors & Boards*, by law, "directors have always had all the power that they need to govern. What they have not had was the process."[14] Or the will.

The overwhelming majority of directors are serious and sure and not likely to abdicate their responsibilities. The best minds are increasingly attracted to corporate governance, and that intellectual capital will empower strategic boards. Robert Lear reads some 500 proxy statements each year. "All I know," he says, "is it's getting better. It is harder to find bad boards." Because the governance system free floats on our open economy, public confidence—fragile and vulnerable—can be eroded. The danger is that the public becomes mobilized against what is portrayed as a closed elite system. If trust is undercut—and compensation or audit abuses are easy prey—this can spill over into the entire governance pool. Once that trust is gone, it is irretrievable.

As more of our investments flow into the financial markets, we become increasingly dependent on those markets for our security. And therefore we become increasingly dependent on the success of the companies that make up those markets. That success is driven by better oversight—by better governance at the board level—all enabled by our free market economy. The American people are looking toward the private markets and away from government to sustain them. And that is why boards are so important.

You would not be reading this book if you did not appreciate the potentials of great governance. Great boards do mean great companies. I challenge you to make your corporate board a strategic force in your company's success. Everyone who has an interest in a company should care. Everyone who has an interest—shareholder, director, officer, employee, customer, supplier, analyst, and citizen—can make a difference in the integrity and the value of the system. You can make a difference, because, unlike politics where results can be tenuous, with companies, there are direct accountabilities and hard measures of success.

With the blurring of geographic boundaries and the ebbing of the hegemony of the nation state, as the old paradigms that derive from force and territory are diminished, the power is surging to economic forces. Free enterprise, which has the luxury to experiment limited only by the imagination of the most extreme entrepreneur, offers a phenomenal test market for the best. Values-based enterprises can produce the best choices—and the best outcomes. And, the companies embracing the future will be at the forefront. The companies with the courage to discard complacency and use a strategic board will win.

As we move from an autocratic, top-down model to a participative, knowledge-based model that draws its strength from the depth of the very diversity that it embraces, strategic, progressive governance is the logical outgrowth. To the degree that boards reflect the new paradigm in their diversity, their inclusiveness, their openness, their values, and their strategic vision—so will corporate America thrive.

Corporate governance is a wonderful outgrowth of our free enterprise system. If we don't govern well, government will do it for us. Those who resist may choose independence above all else—including survival.

Great boards mean great companies. Prepare to win.

MAKE A DIFFERENCE

Evaluate your company—public or private, large or small, regional, national or global—on the following strategic board continuum: as a

CEO, a founder, a director, a stockholder, an employee, a customer, analyst, a consultant, or a citizen of your company's community.

For each company, send your evaluation on the strategic board continuum (SBC) to us and to the company. Please share your board stories and ideas for corporate governance with us as well. We will tally the continuum totals and include the best stories and ideas, with your permission, in our next book.

Write us, fax us, call, e-mail, or visit our Web site:

>Susan F. Shultz
>SSA Executive Search International, Ltd.
>4350 East Camelback Road, Suite B200
>Phoenix, Arizona 85018
>480-998-1744; Fax: 480-998-1082; E-mail: *ssaexec@aol.com*
>Web sites: www.ssaexecsearch.com
>www.theboardbook.com

STRATEGIC BOARD CONTINUUM EVALUATION

Look again at the ten most damaging mistakes in board practices. If you know a board with the following characteristics, agitate for change. And, let us know.

TOXIC BOARDS = 0 points
1. Failure to recruit strategically. CEO anoints board members.
2. Too many insiders.
3. Too many paid consultants/conflicts of interest.
4. Too much family.
5. Cronyism/interlocking directorships.
6. Getting the money wrong.
7. Fear of diversity.
8. Information block.
9. Herd mentality/group think/complacency. Passive or entrenched directors.
10. Controlling or weak CEO. Failed board leadership.
STRATEGIC BOARDS = 10 points

Look at your company's board again with the following ten things in mind. Give your board a point for each yes answer. If your company scores a 9 or 10, the fundamentals—the platform for a great board—are in place. A score of 10 means your company is positioned to leverage this powerful resource to the maximum. It means the foundation is there for success. Congratulations!

Anything less than 8 points is reason for investigation. A total of less than 5 points is cause for alarm. Anything less than 3 points cries out for action. Use *The Board Book* as a workbook for success.

COMPANY NAME _____

Location: _____

1. Has your board been recruited strategically? See
    Chapter 2.   Yes ___ No ___
    a. Is there a board charter?
    b. Is there a needs matrix?
    c. Are board structure and procedures defined?
    d. Were measurable profiles developed for
        each director slot? Were expectations
        specified?
    e. Did you know why directors will want to
        serve?
    f. Did you recruit proactively to each profile?
    g. Did you interview and reference potential
        directors in the context of your board?
    h. Did you provide comprehensive orientation?
    i. Did you recruit in a continuum?
2. Does your board have no more than two
    insiders? See Chapter 3.   Yes ___ No ___
3. Do you have no paid consultants or no more
    than two venture capitalists on your board? See
    Chapter 4.   Yes ___ No ___
4. Are family members outnumbered by a ratio of
    at least three to one on your board? See Chapter
    5.   Yes ___ No ___
5. Do you have no conflicted directors? See
    Chapter 6.   Yes ___ No ___
6. Is compensation fair and performance based?
    See Chapter 7.   Yes ___ No ___
7. Is your board diverse? See Chapter 8.   Yes ___ No ___
8. Is there free and effective information flow? See
    Chapter 9.   Yes ___ No ___
    a. Do you provide free access to information,
        including all constituencies?
    b. Do you provide independent financial and
        legal advisors to outside directors?
    c. Do your directors meet with shareholders,
        analysts, employees, the community?

9.   Are your directors proactive, strategic, and
     independent? See Chapter 10.   Yes ___ No ___
     a.   Are your directors active in crises prevention
          and resolution?
     b.   Are your audit committee activities in
          compliance?
     c.   Are your directors responsible for director
          recruitment?
     d.   Are your directors responsible for hiring and
          firing the CEO?
     e.   Are your directors responsible for the
          evaluation of the CEO?
     f.   Are your directors responsible for succession
          planning as an ongoing process?
     g.   Are directors retained on merit? Is director
          turnover ensured?
     h.   Is there evaluation of the board and the
          individual directors?
10. Is there effective board leadership? See
     Chapter 11.
     a.   Does the CEO infuse culture of ethics,
          integrity, and independence?   Yes ___ No ___
     b.   Is considerable time devoted to debating
          strategic planning and direction?
     c.   Does management gain board input at front
          end of strategic decisions?
     d.   Are nominating, compensation, and audit
          committees entirely independent?
     e.   Are committee chairs elected by the board?
          Are committee assignments rotated?
     f.   Is there a separate, independent chair and/
          or a lead director?
     g.   Do independent directors meet without
          management on a regular basis?
     h.   Are internal and external communications
          open?   Yes ___ No ___
                                        TOTAL   _____

COMMENTS: _____

_____

_____

_____

Please attach additional comments.

(Optional)

Name _____ Title _____

Organization _____

Address _____

E-mail, fax, telephone _____

NOTES

1. The quote is from Goethe's *Faust*, written in 1808.
2. Lawrence A. Cunningham, "Warren Buffet on the Role of the Board," *Corporate Board*, July–August 1998.
3. Jennifer A. Hawkins, "Why Investors Push for Strong Corporate Boards," *The McKinsey Quarterly*, 22 June 1997.
4. Roger H. Ford and K. Matthew Gilley, "Board Building in Small Companies: What Are You Waiting For?" *Director's Monthly*, April 1999.
5. Robert F. Felton, Alex Hudnut, and Jennifer van Heeckeren, "Putting a Value on Corporate Governance," *The McKinsey Quarterly*, 1996, n. 4.
6. CalPERS Policy Statement, "Why Corporate Governance Today?" August 1995.
7. "Human Capital on Board: The Impact of Directors on Stock Value," *Director's Monthly*, August 1999, 8.
8. Jennifer A. Hawkins, "Why Investors Push for Strong Corporate Boards," *The McKinsey Quarterly*, 22 June 1997.
9. CalPERS, "List of Nine of Corporate America's Poorest Financial and Economic Performers," Press Release, 22 April 1999.
10. Peter Clapman, "The New Culture of the Corporate Board: Building and Restructuring for a Dynamic Future," American Management Executive Forum, September 1999.
11. "Shareholder Frustration Brings Up Confrontation," *Investor Relations Business*, 15 March 1999.
12. Ibid.
13. Jennifer A. Hawkins, "Why Investors Push for Strong Corporate Boards," *The McKinsey Quarterly*, 22 June 1997.
14. James Kristie, "Board Trends 1970s to the 1990s: 'The More Things Change . . . ,'" Presentation to the Institutional Shareholder Services Annual Client Conference, 26 February 1999.

Appendixes

Appendix 1

◆

Requirements of Statutory vs. Advisory Boards

Statutory	*Advisory*
1. Accountable for corporate conduct.	*Not accountable.*
2. Need directors' liability insurance.	*No such need.*
3. Required to make certain public disclosures.	*No such requirements.*
4. Hire and fire the CEO.	*No such power.*
5. Elected by stockholders for stated term.	*Owner-manager determines tenure.*
6. Nominated because of respected position, visibility, access, or to represent a constituency.	*Selected for prudence and diligence.*
7. Comply with legal requirements.	*No special requirements.*
8. Evaluate performance of CEO and key executives.	*Yes, evaluate performance.*

Statutory	Advisory
9. Review and approve major corporate objectives, policies, budgets, and strategies, as initiated by CEO.	*Yes, plus take some initiatives.*
10. Monitor the company's financial structure.	*Yes, monitor financial structure.*
11. Monitor the company's performance.	*Yes, monitor company's performance.*
12. Ensure company's compliance with all laws affecting the enterprise.	*No such function.*
13. Do not usually arbitrate quarrels.	*Arbitrate quarrels that threaten company's existence.*
14. Fiduciary responsibility.	*No fiduciary responsibility.*
15. Caught up in minutiae of regulatory requirements.	*Can concentrate on broad strategic issues.*

International Advisory Boards. A special form of advisory board. Global access. Brainstorm broad international issues. Often very senior multinational leaders who meet only twice a year.

Industry Boards. A way to enlist counsel and support of potentially conflicted directors, such as customers, suppliers, and even competitors.

Appendix 2

───────◆───────

Actions Requiring the Board of Directors' Approval*

Context: In the performance of their duties of care, diligence, and loyalty.

Resolved, that the prior approval by the Company's Board of Directors shall be required prior to taking any definitive action or entering into any agreement with respect to the following:

1. Reorganization
    1A.   Any matter pertaining to a merger, consolidation, acquisition, or reorganization involving the company or any subsidiary of the company.
    1B.   The sale, lease, or exchange of substantially all of the assets of the company or any subsidiary of the company.
    1C.   The organization, reorganization, or liquidation of any subsidiary of the company.

2. Changes to By-laws
    2A.   Amendment of the company's by-laws.

3. Committees of the Board
    3A.   Establishment of any committee of the board and appointment of members thereto.

*Sample document courtesy of Kenneth E. Olson.

4. Legally Mandated Board Actions
    4A.   Any action for which the Board of Directors is required by:
        - Federal or state law
        - Company by-laws
        - Commercial agreements which require board approval

5. Officers
    5A.   Election of an officer
    5B.   Removal of an officer
    5C.   The compensation of any officer, including any employee benefit not available to all employees.

6. Agreements and Revisions to Agreements with all Employees
    6A.   Programs such as stock options, stock purchase plans, general bonus plans, pension plans, and profit sharing plans.
    6B.   Any matter of personnel policy as it applies to any labor agreement or organization of a union, including any collective bargaining agreement or amendment thereto.
    6C.   Any commitment to compensate any employee or consultant in excess of $150,000 per year or to pay expenses greater than $10,000 associated with hiring.

7. Annual Plans and Changes to Annual Plans
    7A.   Adoption of the annual Business Plan (which shall include mission statement, market segments, technologies, targeted revenues and earnings, overview of staffing).
    7B.   Major changes to the Business Plan.
    7C.   Adoption of the annual Budget (which shall include revenues, direct costs, indirect expenses, earnings targets, capital expenditures, and cash flow), business plans, and amendments thereto.
    7D.   Any appropriation in excess of $50,000 for any group of capital items not included in the board-approved annual budget.

8. Commercial Banking
    8A.   Adoption of treasury policies and banking resolutions, including revisions thereto.

9. Agreements That Obligate the Company outside the Normal Course of Business
    9A.   Any agreement or amendment to an agreement, written or oral, in which the company may become obligated to:

      (1) Purchase goods or services of size or content outside the normal course of business.

      (2) New physical facilities (leased, rented, or purchased) involving commitments to expend more than $10,000 per year.

10. Investment of Cash
    10A. Investment of cash in other than short-term (one year or less)
    - Direct obligations of the United States of America
    - Obligations guaranteed by the United States of America
    - Money market mutual funds having assets of one billion dollars or more

11. Financing
    11A. Financing documents and events including:
    - short and long-term debt
    - private placements and corporate partnering
    - public offerings

12. Selection of Auditors and Legal Counsel
    - Selection of the company's and subsidiaries' independent auditors
    - Selection of the company's and subsidiaries' legal counsel
    - Selection of the company's and subsidiaries' property counsel

13. Litigation
    13A. The commencement of litigation (exclusive of collection efforts) in which the company or any subsidiary is the initiating party or plaintiff.
    13B. Strategy decisions in material litigation in which the company or any subsidiary is a defendant.

14. Monitoring of Insurance
    14A. The establishment of (or any material change to) insurance coverage on personnel or other key assets of the company.

15. Miscellaneous
    15A. Company involvement in community, political, or religious causes or programs.
    15B. The establishment or amendment of a code of business practices or ethics.
    15C. Any operating decision which, in the opinion of the Presi-

dent or CEO or CFO, should be presented to the Board, either before or after the decision is made.

15D. The setting of a record date and meeting date for an annual shareholders meeting.

15E. The selection of the board of directors for a subsidiary or joint venture.

15F. The establishment of or amendment to policies concerning the Foreign Corrupt Practices Act and anti-boycott laws, national controls over the export of technologies and products, and conflicts of interest.

Appendix 3

———◆———

Sample Corporate Governance Guidelines*

DIRECTORS

Personal Characteristics and Core Competencies of Directors

Passion—Directors should be passionate about the performance of the company, both in absolute terms and relative to its peers. That passion should manifest itself in engaged debate about the future of the company and an esprit de corps among the Board that both challenges and inspires the company's employees.

Core Competencies of the Board as a Whole

Accounting and Finance—Among the most important missions of the Board is ensuring that stockholder value is both enhanced through corporate performance and protected through adequate internal financial controls. The Board should have one or more directors with specific expertise in financial accounting and corporate finance, especially with respect to trends in debt and equity markets.

   Business Judgment—Stockholders rely on directors to make sensible choices on their behalf. The majority of directors should have a record of making good business decisions in the corporate sector.

   Management—To monitor corporate management, the Board needs

*Excerpted from Nuevo Energy Company *Corporate Governance Guidelines.*

to understand management trends in general and industry trends in particular. The Board should have one or more directors who understand and stay current on general management "best practices" and their application in complex, rapidly evolving business environments.

Crisis Response—Organizations inevitably experience both short- and long-term crises. The ability to deal with crises can minimize ramifications and limit the negative impact on firm performance. Boards should have one or more directors who have the ability and time to perform during periods of both short-term and prolonged crises.

Industry Knowledge—Companies continually face new opportunities and threats that are unique to their industries. The Board should have one or more members with appropriate and relevant industry-specific knowledge.

International Markets—To succeed in an increasingly global economy, the Board should have one or more directors who appreciate the importance of global business trends and who have first-hand knowledge of international business and have experience in those markets.

Leadership—Ultimately, a company's performance will be determined by the directors' and CEO's ability to attract, motivate, and energize a high-performance leadership team. The Board should have one or more directors who understand and possess empowerment skills and have a history of motivating high-performing talent.

Strategy and Vision—A key Board role is to approve and monitor company strategy to ensure the company's continued high performance. The Board should have one or more directors with the skills and capacity to provide strategic insight and direction by encouraging innovation, conceptualizing key trends, evaluating strategic decisions, and continuously challenging the organization to sharpen its vision.

IDENTIFICATION AND RECRUITMENT OF BOARD MEMBERS

One of the tasks of the Nominating and Governance Committee is to identify and recruit candidates to serve on the Board of Directors. A list of candidates shall be presented to the Board for nomination and to the stockholders for consideration. The committee may at its discretion seek third-party resources to assist in the process. The CEO will be included in the process on a nonvoting basis. The Nominating and Governance Committee will make the final recommendations to the Board.

OUTSIDE DIRECTORSHIPS

The CEO and senior management of Nuevo should limit outside directorships to one or two; non-employee directors who are employed on a full-time basis should limit other directorships to three or four; and retired executives should limit other directorships to five or six.

Direct Investment in the Company Stock by Directors

Since a significant ownership stake leads to a stronger alignment of interests between directors and stockholders, each director is required to personally invest at least $100,000 in company stock within three years of joining the Board. Exceptions to this requirement may only be made by the Board under compelling mitigating circumstances.

Service Limitations of Directors

In order to replenish the Board with fresh approaches to managing the company, the maximum Board tenure shall be 15 years.

A Board member may not stand for reelection after age 70, but need not resign until the end of his or her term.

In order to retain freshness in the process and to give new management the unfettered ability to provide new leadership, a retiring CEO shall not continue to serve on the Board.

BOARD OPERATIONS

Board Access to Senior Management

Board members have full access to senior management and to information about the corporation's operations. Except in unusual circumstances, the CEO should be advised of significant contacts with senior management.

Board Ability to Retain Advisors

The Board shall retain advisers as it believes to be appropriate. If management is retaining advisors to the Board, such decision must be ratified by the Board. Individual directors should not retain their own advisors except in exceptional circumstances.

Material in Advance of Meetings

The Board must be given sufficient information to fully exercise its governance functions. This information comes from a variety of sources, including management reports, a comparison of performance to plans, security analysts' reports, articles in various business publications, etc. Generally, Board members will receive information prior to Board meetings so they will have an opportunity to reflect properly on the items to be considered at the meeting.

The Board will ensure that adequate time is provided for full discussion of important items and that management presentations are scheduled in a manner that permits a substantial proportion of Board meeting time to be available for open discussion.

Executive Session

Time will be allotted at the end of each board meeting for an executive session involving only the independent directors.

Evaluation of CEO

The selection and evaluation of the chief executive officer and concurrence with the CEO's selection and evaluation of the corporation's top management team is the most important function of the Board. In its broader sense, "selection and evaluation" includes considering compensation, planning for succession and, when appropriate, replacing the CEO or other members of the top management team. The performance of the CEO will be reviewed at least annually without the presence of the CEO or other inside directors. The Board should have an understanding with the CEO with respect to criteria on which he or she will be evaluated, and the results of the evaluation will be communicated to the CEO.

Management Development

The CEO will report annually to the Board on the company's program for management development.

Succession Plan

CEO succession is a Board-driven, collaborative process. Although the current CEO has an important role to play, the Board must develop its own plan for succession while collaborating with the CEO in deciding the timing and the necessary qualifications for making a final decision.

Appendix 4

Sample Corporate Governance Guidelines*

PREAMBLE

The Board of Directors has adopted the following corporate governance guidelines specifically tailored to the needs of the company. These guidelines reflect the Board's commitment to monitor the effectiveness of policy and decision-making both at the Board and management level, with a view to enhancing shareholder value over the long term. The Board believes these guidelines should be an evolving set of corporate governance principles, subject to alteration as circumstances warrant.

I. SELECTION OF CHAIRMAN AND CHIEF EXECUTIVE OFFICER

The Board believes the positions of Chief Executive Officer and Chairman of the Board should be combined to provide unified leadership and direction. The Board reserves the right to adopt a different policy should circumstances change.

II. CHAIRMAN/CEO'S DEATH, RESIGNATION, OR INCAPACITY

In the event of the death, resignation or incapacity of the Chairman of the Board and/or the Chief Executive Officer, the Chairman of the

---

*Excerpted from Caterpillar, Inc., *Guidelines on Corporate Governance Issues*.

Nominating and Governance Committee will immediately call a meeting of that committee to recommend to the full Board the selection of a temporary or permanent replacement for either or both positions.

III. BOARD COMMITTEES

The Board currently has four standing committees: Audit, Compensation, Nominating and Governance, and Public Policy. There may be occasions when the Board will wish to form a new standing or ad hoc committee, or disband a current committee depending upon the circumstances.

Specific charters will be adopted by the Board for all standing committees.

The Board will approve committee assignments, including committee chairmanships. In so doing, the Board will consider the desires of individual directors and the recommendations of the Nominating and Governance Committee in consultation with the Chairman and Chief Executive Officer. The Board will rotate committee membership periodically, at about five-year intervals. Such rotation shall not be mandatory, however, since there may be persuasive reasons to maintain an individual director's committee membership for a longer period.

Committee chairmen will determine the frequency of meetings of their respective committees, and, in consultation with management, will set meeting times and develop committee agendas. Each committee will, at the beginning of the year, enumerate the subjects to be discussed within that committee during the year. This enumeration may be altered by the committee chairman, in consultation with management, should circumstances so warrant.

Only independent directors may serve on the Audit, Compensation, and Nominating and Governance Committees. Any director may attend and participate in discussions of any Board committee, although formal committee action will only be through the vote of appointed committee members.

Board committees shall have access to accountants, compensation consultants, investment bankers, or other independent consultants, whose expertise is deemed essential to carrying out the committees' respective missions.

IV. BOARD MEETINGS

The Board Chairman will establish the agenda for board meetings. Any Board member may, however, recommend the inclusion of specific agenda items. Such recommendations will be accommodated to the extent practicable.

Materials important to the Board's understanding of agenda items shall be distributed to the Board, in a timely manner, before it meets. These materials shall be informative but concise.

Members of the Executive Office who are not Board members may attend and participate in Board meetings at the invitation of the Chairman. Should the Chairman contemplate inviting any such person to attend and participate on a regular basis, Board concurrence will first be obtained.

V. BOARD ACCESS TO SENIOR MANAGEMENT AND AUDITORS

Board members shall have complete access to the Company's management and independent auditors. Board member contact with such individuals shall be handled in a manner that would not be disruptive to the company's business operations. Any non-routine written communications emanating from such contact should be copied to the Chief Executive Officer.

The Board encourages the Chief Executive Officer to bring into Board and committee meetings corporate executives: (a) to provide additional insight on items being discussed because of their personal involvement in such areas; and/or (b) to provide Board exposure to individuals with outstanding management potential.

VI. COMPENSATION FOR INDEPENDENT DIRECTORS

Compensation of independent directors shall be comparable to that offered by other companies of similar size and scope. Independent directors shall receive no additional remuneration, in the form of consulting fees or other special benefits, beyond that provided for service on the Board.

Directors who are officers of the company shall receive no additional remuneration for serving as a director.

Management will periodically review with the Compensation Committee the status of independent director compensation relative to comparable companies. Any changes to Board compensation shall arise from recommendations of the Compensation Committee, with full discussion and concurrence by the Board.

The Board is committed to fostering compensation programs and policies designed to encourage director and senior management stock ownership over the long-term. Such programs, in the view of the Board, will help align the interests of directors and top management with those of shareholders.

VII. BOARD COMPOSITION

The Board believes that it should generally have no less than 10 and no more than 18 directors. This range permits diversity of experience without hindering effective discussion or diminishing individual accountability. The Board is prepared, however, to increase its membership beyond 18 should that be necessary to accommodate an outstanding candidate.

To ensure Board independence, no more than three non-independent directors shall serve on the Board at any point in time. All other directors shall be independent. A director shall be considered independent if he or she: (1) is not currently employed by the Company; (2) has not been employed by the Company during the last five years; or (3) has not received significant remuneration from the Company in any capacity other than as a director during the last five years. This policy may be modified temporarily if, due to unforeseen circumstances, strict adherence would be detrimental to the Board's performance.

Any officer of the corporation, other than the Chief Executive Officer, serving as a director shall resign from the Board upon his resignation or retirement from the Company. When a Chief Executive Officer resigns or retires, he or she and all other former Chief Executive Officers then serving as directors will offer their resignations from the Board. Remaining Board members, in conjunction with the incoming Chief Executive Officer, will determine whether any conditions shall apply to the continuation of such directorships, and/or whether any of the resignations are to be accepted.

VIII. MEMBERSHIP CRITERIA

The Nominating and Governance Committee shall solicit and receive recommendations, and review qualifications of, potential Caterpillar director candidates. From its assembled list of qualified candidates, the Nominating and Governance Committee shall from time to time recommend to the full Board the election of new directors.

The Chief Executive Officer will periodically review with the Nominating and Governance Committee and, if he or she wishes, with the full Board, the particular attributes that would be most beneficial to the company in future Board nominees. This assessment will include, but not be limited to, issues such as integrity, competence, age and experience, commitment and dedication, collegiality, diversity, technical background, and international skills.

IX. TERMINATION OF BOARD MEMBERSHIP

The Board does not believe term limits are appropriate. While mandatory turnover would provide fresh viewpoints to the Board, term limits have the compelling disadvantage of losing the contribution of directors who have a unique insight into the Company's business and its operations. The Board believes it would be unwise to discard such value through the premature termination of a director.

The Board is presently satisfied with the current mandatory retirement age of 72.

Upon termination of his or her primary occupation or other significant change in business/professional circumstances, a Board member shall tender his or her resignation to the Board. The full Board shall decide whether or not to accept the resignation.

X. EVALUATION OF THE CHIEF EXECUTIVE OFFICER

The Chief Executive Officer will be expected to report annually to the Compensation Committee on his or her goals and objectives for the ensuing year, and also to report annually on the level of achievement of the preceding year's goals and objectives. All Board members shall be invited to those particular Compensation Committee meetings, and all shall have the opportunity to participate in any appropriate follow-up meetings or discussions.

The full Board shall participate in the evaluation of the Chief Executive Officer, since this is deemed to be one of the Board's most significant oversight functions. Both objective and subjective criteria will be used, including but not limited to: (a) the Company's financial performance; (b) accomplishment of the Company's long-term strategic objectives; and (c) the development of the firm's top management team. The Chief Executive Officer shall not attend full Board meetings discussing his or her evaluation.

XI. BOARD EVALUATION

The Board will engage in a self-evaluation annually. This evaluation will be of the Board as a collective body and not of directors on an individual basis. The evaluation process will be administered by the Nominating and Governance Committee and evaluation results shared with the full Board for their discussion and deliberation.

XII. BOARD MEMBER COMMITMENTS

We recognize that Board members benefit from service on the board of other companies. We encourage that service but also believe it is critical that directors have the opportunity to dedicate sufficient time to their service on our Board. To that end, the Chief Executive Officer and any other director who is a Company employee shall serve on no more than two public company boards in addition to our Board. It is recommended that directors other than the Chief Executive Officer or employees serve on no more than five public company boards in addition to our Board.

XIII. EXECUTIVE SESSIONS

The Board may meet periodically in executive session as circumstances warrant. Such executive sessions may be in one of three formats: (1) sessions involving only directors; (2) sessions involving only non-management directors and the Chief Executive Officer; and (3) sessions involving only non-management directors.

XIV. COMMUNICATIONS WITH SHAREHOLDERS AND OTHER CONSTITUENTS

The Board believes it would be useful to make its corporate governance guidelines available to stakeholders/constituents and requests that management do so in whatever manner is most feasible.

XV. EXECUTIVE SUCCESSION PLANNING

The Board deems as one of its most critical functions the selection of a Chief Executive Officer and Executive Office team that fits the Company's current culture, understands its business strategy and inspires others to follow their lead. To that end, the Board has an executive succession plan tailored to reflect the Company's current business strategy and vision. The executive succession plan involves creating profiles of ideal candidates based on the Board's understanding of the Company's strategy and vision, and selecting successors expected to fit the needs of the company over time. In implementing its executive succession plan, the Board believes that, at its core, succession planning: (1) is a board-driven, collaborative process; (2) is a continuous process; (3) should be driven by corporate strategy; and (4) involves building a talent-rich organization by attracting and developing the right people.

XVI. IMPLEMENTATION AND ALTERATION OF THE GUIDELINES

Implementation and alteration of these guidelines shall be the responsibility of the Nominating and Governance Committee, working in coordination with the Chairman and Chief Executive Officer.

Appendix 5

◆

Fortune 500 Companies without Women Directors*

Rank	Company	Rank	Company
50	Safeway	262	Gateway 2000
64	Atlantic Richfield	266	Bear Stearns
75	UAL	270	American Standard
133	Bergen Brunswig	281	El Paso Natural Gas
158	Coastal	285	Food 4 Less
170	Farmland Industries	293	Quantum
198	Amerisource Health	297	Wachovia Corp.
199	Best Buy	317	Stone Container
203	Tele-Communications	320	CHS Electronics
210	Worldcom	324	Owens-Illinois
216	Foundation Health Systems	331	Suntrust Banks
220	Unisource	333	MBNA
223	Apple Computer	339	Mutual of Omaha Insurance
224	Tech Data	342	Cinergy
237	PACCAR	349	Nucor
246	Tyco International	358	Universal
256	Navistar International	366	General Dynamics
260	Medpartners	368	Merisel

*1998 Catalyst Census.

Rank	Company	Rank	Company
370	American Financial Group	424	Pittston
374	Clark USA	431	Graybar Electric
376	Prosource	440	Jefferson Smurfit
384	Centex	445	AGCO
392	Supermarkets Genl.	446	Interstate Bakeries
	Holdings	449	York International
393	Solectron	455	3COM
395	Mapco	456	Mercantile Stores
398	Service Merchandise	464	Peter Kiewit Sons'
401	Turner Corp.	466	Kohl's
407	Shaw Industries	468	Millennium Chemicals
408	Echlin	473	IMC Global
413	Micron Technology	484	Lyondell Petrochemical
414	Borden	485	Fleetwood Enterprises
415	Rykoff-Sexton	491	U.S. Office Products
418	Williamette Industries	499	MAXXAM

Appendix 6

Sample Form for Director's Evaluation of CEO

Please provide your written assessment of the CEO's performance in the areas identified below, and rate his performance in each area in accordance with the following scale:

Well Below Expectations	Meets Expectations	Well Above Expectations	Qualified Response
1 → → → 2	→ → → 3	→ → → 4 → → 5	QR*

*Directors who feel they do not have sufficient information to provide fully considered ratings for those aspects of the CEO's performance may circle "QR" to signal that their ratings are qualified for this reason.

1. **STRATEGIC PLANNING.** Ensures the development of a long-term strategy. Establishes objectives and plans that meet the needs of shareowners, customers, employees and all other corporate stakeholders, and ensures consistent and timely progress toward strategic objectives. Obtains and allocates resources consistent with strategic objectives. Reports regularly to the Board on progress made toward strategic plan milestones.

    STRATEGIC PLANNING: 1→→→2→→→3→→→4→→5   QR

2. **LEADERSHIP.** Develops and communicates a clear and consistent vision of the Company's goals and values, and ensures that it is well understood, widely supported and effectively implemented within the organization. Fosters a corporate culture that encourages, recognizes and rewards leadership, excellence and innovation. Ensures a culture that promotes ethical practices, individual integrity, and cooperation to build shareowner value.

   LEADERSHIP: 1→ → →2→ → →3→ → →4→ →5   QR

3. **FINANCIAL RESULTS.** Establishes and achieves appropriate annual and longer-term financial performance goals. Ensures the development and maintenance of appropriate systems to protect the Company's assets and assure effective control of operations.

   FINANCIAL RESULTS: 1→ → →2→ → →3→ → →4→ →5   QR

4. **MANAGEMENT OF OPERATIONS.** Ensures high quality, cost-effective management of the day-to-day business affairs of the Company. Promotes continuous improvement of the quality, value and competitiveness of the Company's products and business systems. Encourages and rewards creative solutions to business and management challenges.

   MANAGEMENT OF
   OPERATIONS: 1→ → →2→ → →3→ → →4→ →5   QR

5. **MANAGEMENT DEVELOPMENT AND SUCCESSION PLANNING.** Develops, attracts, retains and motivates an effective and unified senior management team. Ensures that programs for management development and succession planning have the required resources and direction to grow the future leaders of the Company.

   MANAGEMENT DEVELOPMENT AND
   SUCCESSION PLANNING: 1→ → →2→ → →3→ → →4→ →5   QR

6. **HUMAN RESOURCES.** Ensures the development of effective programs for the recruitment, training, compensation, retention and motivation of personnel, and the availability of human resources necessary to achieve the Company's objectives. Establishes and monitors programs to promote workplace diversity. Provides for appropriate recognition of the achievements of individuals and groups.

   HUMAN RESOURCES: 1→ → →2→ → →3→ → →4→ →5   QR

7. **COMMUNICATIONS.** Serves as chief spokesperson for the Company, communicating effectively with shareowners, prospective investors, employees, customers, suppliers and consumers. Represents the Company effectively in relationships with industry, the government and the financial community.

COMMUNICATIONS: 1→→→2→→→3→→→4→→5   **QR**

8. **BOARD RELATIONS.** Works closely with the Board of Directors to keep directors informed on the state of the business, on crucial issues relating to the Company, and on the Company's progress toward the achievement of operating plan and strategic plan milestones.

BOARD RELATIONS: 1→→→2→→→3→→→4→→5   **QR**

Overall comments:

Key challenges in the year ahead:

Thoughts and concerns:

What key messages would you like the Board's representative to deliver in communicating the Board's evaluation to the CEO?

Appendix 7

◆

Sample Form for Board Evaluation

Rate the following statements in relation to our Board of Directors. Rank answers from 1—not performing to 5—outstanding performance.

1. The Board knows and understands the Company's beliefs, values, philosophy, mission, strategic plan, and business plan, and reflects this understanding on key issues throughout the year.   1 2 3 4 5

2. The Board has and follows procedures for effective meetings.   1 2 3 4 5

3. Board meetings are conducted in a manner that ensures open communication, meaningful participation, and timely resolution of issues.   1 2 3 4 5

4. Board members receive timely and accurate minutes, advance written agendas and meeting notices, and clear and concise background material to prepare in advance of meetings.   1 2 3 4 5

5. Board members evaluate Board performance on a periodic basis.   1 2 3 4 5

6. The Board reviews and adopts annual capital and operating budgets, which are regularly monitored throughout the year.   1 2 3 4 5

7. The Board monitors cash flow, profitability, net revenue and expenses, productivity, and other financially driven indicators to ensure the Company performs as projected.   1 2 3 4 5

8. The Board monitors Company performance with industry comparative data.   1 2 3 4 5

9. Board members stay abreast of issues and trends affecting the Company, and use this information to assess and guide the Company's performance not just year to year, but in the long term.   1 2 3 4 5

10. Board members comprehend and respect the difference between the Board's policy-making role and the CEO's management role.   1 2 3 4 5

11. The Board acts to help the CEO by setting clear and well-understood policy.   1 2 3 4 5

12. Board goals, expectations, and concerns are honestly communicated with the CEO.   1 2 3 4 5

13. The Board is actively engaged in succession planning for the executive officers of the Company.   1 2 3 4 5

Comments:

Appendix 8

◆

Sample Form for Board of Directors Self-Assessment

| SA-Strongly Agree | A-Agree | N-Neither Agree Nor Disagree | D-Disagree | SD-Strongly Disagree |

1. I devote an appropriate amount of time to the issues and the needs of the Company to be able to make informed decisions.　　SA A N D SD

2. I feel comfortable with my understanding of critical technical issues.　　SA A N D SD

3. I spend sufficient time with the materials and CEO to understand long-range planning.　　SA A N D SD

4. I initiate contact with the Chairman when appropriate.　　SA A N D SD

5. I understand the Company's industry and markets.　　SA A N D SD

6. I challenge the strategy and direction when necessary.　　SA A N D SD

7. I am able to remain objective, even in the face of the most difficult decisions.　　SA A N D SD

8. I often speak my mind during meetings, even if the views are different from other Directors.　　SA A N D SD

SA-Strongly Agree   A-Agree   N-Neither Agree Nor Disagree   D-Disagree   SD-Strongly Disagree

9. I have personal contact with senior management.   SA   A   N   D   SD

10. I am fully prepared for Board meetings.   SA   A   N   D   SD

11. I am fully prepared for Committee meetings.   SA   A   N   D   SD

12. When I am absent from Board meetings, I
gather enough information about the meet-
ing to stay sufficiently informed.   SA   A   N   D   SD

13. When I am absent from Committee meetings, I gather enough information about the
meeting to stay sufficiently informed.   SA   A   N   D   SD

14. When appropriate, I take the initiative to
obtain relevant corporate information.   SA   A   N   D   SD

15. I encourage contributions from other Board
or Committee members.   SA   A   N   D   SD

16. I offer creative and innovative ideas.   SA   A   N   D   SD

17. I make my individual expertise available
when called upon by management.   SA   A   N   D   SD

18. I derive satisfaction and a feeling of accomplishment through serving on the Board of
Directors.   SA   A   N   D   SD

19. I maintain discretion and confidentiality
with received information.   SA   A   N   D   SD

20. I feel comfortable with the amount of time
and level of commitment expected of me.   SA   A   N   D   SD

21. I have sufficient expertise to evaluate strategies, policies, market development and industry-specific idiosyncrasies from a higher
long-term oriented level.   SA   A   N   D   SD

22. I take tough, constructive stands at Board
or Committee meetings when necessary.   SA   A   N   D   SD

23. I am a valuable resource in fulfilling the accountabilities of the Board.   SA   A   N   D   SD

SA-Strongly Agree   A-Agree   N-Neither Agree Nor Disagree   D-Disagree   SD-Strongly Disagree

24. I am decisive, action-oriented, and get things done.   SA   A   N   D   SD

25. I ensure that the Board or Committee makes decisions.   SA   A   N   D   SD

26. I make effective contributions at Board or Committee meetings.   SA   A   N   D   SD

27. I have good conceptual and theoretical ability.   SA   A   N   D   SD

28. I am an effective troubleshooter.   SA   A   N   D   SD

29. I communicate persuasively.   SA   A   N   D   SD

30. I seek information and opinions from others.   SA   A   N   D   SD

31. I confront conflict and help manage it constructively and productively.   SA   A   N   D   SD

Appendix 9

◆

Board Governance Resource List

PERIODICALS AND NEWSLETTERS

Across the Board
The Conference Board
845 Third Avenue
New York, NY 10022
(212) 759-0900
bix@conference-board.org

AFL-CIO Executive Pay Watch
www.paywatch.org

Board Member
National Center for Nonprofit
  Boards
2000 L Street NW, Suite 510-L
Washington, DC 20036-4907
(202) 452-6262
www.ncnb.org

Boardroom INSIDER (Ralph
  Ward)
www.boardroominsider.com

The Corporate Board
4440 Hagadorn Road

Okemos, MI 48864
(517) 336-1700
www.corporateboard.com

Corporate Governance (Web site)
2461 Second Avenue
Sacramento, CA 95818
(916) 542-5338
www.corpgov.net

Corporate Governance Advisor
Aspen Law & Business
1185 Avenue of the Americas
New York, NY 10036
(212) 597-0200
www.aspenpub.com

*The Corporate Monitoring
  Newsletter*
10 Miller Place, #1701
San Francisco, CA 94108
www.corpmon.com

Corporate Secretary
American Society of Corporate
  Secretaries
521 Fifth Avenue, 32nd Floor
New York, NY 10175
(212) 681-2000
www.ascs.org

*The Crystal Report on Executive
  Compensation*
3519 Daybreak Court
Santa Rosa, CA 95404
(707) 591-0488
www.crystalreport.com

Director's Alert
www.directorsalert.com

Directorship
8 Sound Shore Drive
Greenwich, CT 06830
(203) 861-7000
www.directorship.com

Director's Monthly
National Association of
  Corporate Directors
1707 L Street NW, Suite 560
Washington, DC 20036
(202) 775-0509
www.nacdonline.org

Directors & Boards
1845 Walnut Street, Fifth Floor
Philadelphia, PA 19103
(800) 637-4464

Investor Relations Business
40 West 57th Street, 11th Floor
New York, NY 10010
(212) 333-9201
www.tfn.com

The ISS Friday Report
Institutional Shareholder
  Services
1455 Research Boulevard
Fourth Floor
Rockville, MD 20850
(301) 545-4555
www.iss.cda.com

Pensions & Investments
Crain Communications, Inc.
220 East 42nd Street, 9th Floor
New York, NY 10017
(212) 210-0117

LIST OF ORGANIZATIONS

American Society of Corporate
  Secretaries
521 Fifth Avenue, 32nd Floor
New York, NY 10175
(212) 681-2000
www.ascs.org

Business Roundtable
www.brt.org

California Public Employees
  Retirement System (CalPERS)
Lincoln Plaza

400 P Street
Sacramento, CA 95814
(916) 326-3000
www.calpers.org

Center for Corporate
  Governance (Tuck at
  Dartmouth)
100 Tuck Hall
Hanover, NH 03755
(603) 642-2733
www.mba.tuck.dartmouth.edu

The Center for Corporate Law
University of Cincinnati Law
  School
Cincinnati, OH 45221
www.law.uc.edu

The Conference Board
845 Third Avenue
New York, NY 10022
(212) 759-0900
www.conference_board.org

Corporate Governance
2461 Second Avenue
Sacramento, CA 95818
www.corpgov.net

The Corporate Library
www.corporatelibrary.com

Corporate Woman Directors
  International
1211 Connecticut Avenue NW,
  Suite 504
Washington, DC 20036
(202) 835-3713
nativassoc@aol.com

Council of Institutional Investors
1730 Rhode Island Avenue,
  Suite 512

Washington, DC 20036
(202) 822-0800
www.cii.central.com

Family Held Enterprise
77 Prospect Avenue, Box 4A
Hackensack, NJ 07601
201-488-9323
www.afhe.com

Hispanic Association on
  Corporate Responsibility
1730 Rhode Island Avenue NW,
  Suite 1008
Washington, DC 20036
(202) 835-9672
www.hacr.org

Institutional Shareholder
  Services
7200 Wisconsin Avenue, Suite
  1001
Bethesda, MD
(301) 215-9622
www.iss.cda.com

International Corporate
  Governance Network (ICGN)
crist@toto.csustan.edu

Investment Company Institute
1401 H Street NW
Washington, DC 20005
(202) 326-5800
www.ici.org

Investor Responsibility Research
  Center
1350 Connecticut Avenue NW,
  Suite 700
Washington, DC 20036
(202) 833-0700
www.irrc.org

Investor's Rights Association of
  America
340 Veterans Memorial Highway
Commack, NY 11725
(516) 864-1758
www.iraa.com

Kennesaw State College
  Corporate Governance Center
1000 Chastain Road
Kennesaw, GA 30144
(770) 423-6587
www.coles.kennesaw.edu

National Association of
  Corporate Directors
1707 L Street NW, Suite 560
Washington, DC 20036
(202) 775-0509
www.nacdonline.org

National Council of Individual
  Investors
1201 Martin Luther King Jr. Way
Oakland, CA 94612-1217
(510) 272-9461

National Investor Relations
  Institute
8045 Leesburg Pike, Suite 600
Vienna, VA 22182
www.niri.org

TIAA-CREF
730 Third Avenue
New York, NY 10017
(212) 490-9000
www.tiaa-cref.org

Appendix 10

Interviewees

Name	Title	Organization	Current Boards/Organizations	Past Boards/Organizations
Amberg, William F.	President	Management & Organizational Psychologists, Inc.		
Auch, Walter E.	Director		**Director,** Pimco Advisors, Nicholas/Applegate Inst. Funds, Brinson Partners Funds, Pilgrim Capital Funds, The Advisors Group, Banyan Strategic Realty Trust, Shearson Smith Barney, TRAK Funds, Shearson Smith Barney Concert Series Fund, The Semele Group, Legend Properties; Advisors Series Trust	**President,** Payne Webber; **Chairman,** Chicago Board Options Exchange; **Director,** Payne Webber Inc., Raymond James Financial Corp., Fort Dearborn Fund, Bohn Aluminum and Brass Company, Udylite Company, Essex Chemical Corp., Patlex Corporation, Colonial Hospital Supply Co., National Securities Research Corp., Express America Holdings, Aequitron Corp., Patton Corporation
Aucott, George W.	Former President & CEO	Motor Coach Industries International; Firestone	Universal Technology Institute, Diversified Inspections Inc; Planet Technology.com, New Millennial Homes, Inc.	Motor Coach Industries, Firestone Tire & Rubber Co, Dina, Cleveland Machine Controls, Bank One Akron Ohio
Bansak, Stephen A.	Senior Consultant	Concord International Partners	**Director,** Lighthouse Partners, Computerized Medical Systems, Inc., Global Health Care Partners, Troy Biosciences, Manschot Opportunity Fund	**Vice Chair,** Kidder, Peabody & Co. **Chairman,** Securities Industry Association's Corporate Finance and Rule 415 Committees; **Director,** Square Industries, Motay Electronics

Name	Title	Company		
Barnette, Curtis H.	Chairman & CEO	Bethlehem Steel Corporation	**Director,** International Iron and Steel Institute, Metropolitan Life Insurance Company, Owens Corning, Norfolk Southern Advisory Board; Policy Committee, Business Roundtable and the Business Council	**Chairman,** American Society of Corporate Secretaries; Legal Advisory Committee, NY Stock Exchange; Council, Antitrust Section, American Bar Association
Brock, William E., Sen.	Founder & Chairman	Intellectual Development Systems, Inc.	**Director,** Blackboard, Inc.; On Assignment, Up and Up; The Committee for Economic Development, Bretton Woods Committee, American Council for Capital Formation; **Trustee,** Center for Strategic and International Studies; United Payors/United Providers	**Chairman,** The Brock Group, National Endowment for Democracy, The Republican National Committee, The Republican Party, U.S. Secretary of Labor, U.S. Trade Representative, U.S. Senate—Tennessee
Brown, Bart A., Jr.	President & CEO	Main Street & Main	**Director,** First City Financial, Factory Card Outlet, Liberty House	**Chairman and CEO,** Circle K Corporation; **Trustee,** FoxMeyer Estates; **Director,** Spreckels Industries, Color Tile and Edison Brothers, Inc.
Bryant, Adam	Writer	Newsweek		**Writer,** New York Times
Bryson, John E.	Chairman & CEO	Edison International and Southern California Edison	**Director,** The Boeing Company, Times Mirror Company, W.M. Keck Foundation, Council on Foreign Relations, **Trustee,** Stanford University	**President,** Calif. Public Utilities Commission

Name	Title	Organization	Current Boards/Organizations	Past Boards/Organizations
Burke, Michael J.	Co-Managing Partner CEO	Keating, Muething & Klekamp, LLP; Consulting Company LLC	**Chairman,** LSI Industries, Inc., Superior Label Systems, Inc., Compensation Committee; **Director,** Keating, Muething & Klekamp, Bay Technologies; Intellitecs International, Inc., KDM Signs, Inc., LSI Industries, Inc., Service Management Systems, Inc., Superior Label Systems, Inc., United Audit Systems, Inc.; **Advisory,** Duramed Pharmaceuticals, Inc.	
Burleigh, William R.	Chairman, President & CEO	The E. W. Scripps Company	**Director,** Xtek, Inc., Ohio National Life Insurance Company	**Director and Vice Chair,** The Associated Press; **Chair,** American Press Institute, American Society of Newspaper Editors; Pulitzer Prize Juror
Carey, Dennis C.	Vice-Chairman Co-Managing Director	Spencer Stuart, U.S.; U.S. Board Services Practice	**Director,** The Director's Institute- The Wharton School, Directors and Boards Magazine, Closure Medical Corp.	
Christensen, Howard J.	President	Christensen & Associates	**Director,** Protection One	
Ciminelli, Paul F.	President	Ciminelli Development Company	**Director,** Buffalo Niagara Partnership	

Name	Title	Organization		
Crist, William D.	President Professor	CalPERS Board of Administration Economics, Calif. State University, Stanislaus	Council of Institutional Investors Executive Cmte; International Corporate Governance Network Board of Governance	**Chairman**, California State University-Dept. of Economics; **Co-Chairman**, Council of Institutional Investors
Curle, Robin Lea	CEO	Journee Software, Inc.	**Director**, Evolutionary Technologies International, Texas School of Engineering, Austin Software Council, Journee Software, Texas Property and Casualty Guarantee Insurance Board	**Executive Vice President and co-founder**, Evolutionary Technologies Int'l.
Dawson, Barbara J.	Partner	Snell & Wilmer, Phoenix	American Bar Assn. Section of Litigation	
Doheny, Daniel P.	Lead Partner in Charge of Audit Committee Institute	KPMG	Blue Ribbon Commission on Audit Committees; Conference Board's Global Governance Advisory Board, Center for Board Leadership; Accounting Advisory Board of Illinois	
Dorrance, Bennett	Managing Director	DMB Associates, Inc.	**Director**, Campbell Soup Company, Banc One	
Draizin, Stephen S.	Chairman	RAD Energy Corporation	**Chairman**, RAD Energy Corporation; **Director**, Pacific Aircraft	**Director**, Interway Corp., Superscope, Inc.

Name	Title	Organization	Current Boards/Organizations	Past Boards/Organizations
Driggs, Dr. Gary H.	Chairman	Camelback Hotel Corp.	**Chairman,** Camelback Hotel Corp., Covid, Inc.	**Director,** Newell Co., Black & Decker; **President,** Western Savings and Loan Assn.
Dunaway, Robert W.	Managing Director	Venture Cap Fund I, LP	**Director:** AllegroMedical.com, uGive.com, OpNIX, Inc., HumorWorld.com, Walrus Corporation, Geneva Nutritional Sciences, Inc., Netrageous.com, SecureServerNetworks, Inc.	
Duncan Jr., Charles W.	Director	**Director,** Newfield Exploration Company, Inc., The Welch Foundation, Methodist HealthCare System; **Chairman,** Methodist Care, Inc.; Trustee, Rice University and Brookings Institution	**Director,** The Coca-Cola Company, American Express Company, United Technologies Corporation, Texas State Board of Education; **Chairman,** Coca-Cola Europe, Rice University; **Co-Chairman,** Texas Business and Education Coalition	
Emerson, S. Thomas	Director	Donald H. Jones Center for Entrepreneurship Graduate School of Industrial Administration—Carnegie Mellon University	**Director,** Arizona Enterprise Network, Arizona Instrument Corporation, Essential Wisdom, LLC, NetPro Computing Corporation, Ventana Corporation, Institute of Electrical and Electronics Engineers, Foundation for Technology Financing	**Chairman and CEO,** Periphonics Corporation, Syntellect Inc., Xantel Corporation, Arizona Software Association, Arizona Technology Incubator; **President,** Arizona Business Leadership Assn.

Name	Title	Company	Roles
Foshee, Douglas L.	Chairman, President & CEO	Nuevo Energy Company	**CEO, President,** Torch Energy Advisors; **Director,** Texas Business Hall of Fame, Small Steps Nurturing Center
Franke, William A.	Chairman & CEO	America West Holdings Corporation	**Chairman,** Greater Phoenix Leadership; **Chairman,** America West Holdings Corporation; The Leisure Company; **Director,** Phelps Dodge Corporation, Central Newspapers, Inc., Beringer Wine Estates, Inc., Aerfi Group, Air Transport Association; **Managing Director,** Newbridge Latin America
Goldberg, Richard L.	Partner	Proskauer Rose LLP	Senior legal advisor to Boards of Directors
Hagberg, Carl T.	Chairman & CEO; Editor/Publisher	Carl T. Hagberg & Associates; The Shareholder Service Optimizer	**Director,** Minerva Fund, Inc., Manufacturers Hanover Trust Company of California; Independent Inspector of Election, over 300 shareholder meetings
Hartman, Robert D.	President	Universal Technical Institute	
Hawfield, William D.	President	Hillcrest Associates	**Founder & President,** Penquin Frozen Yogurt Franchise Company; **President,** The Hardin Group, Inc., Bowers and Ruddy Galleries, Div. of General Mills; **Vice President,** The Olga Company; **Advisory Board,** Guggenhiem Dental Supplies, American Etching and Manufacturing, Softub, Inc., Small World Toys, United Green Mark, Micro Publication Systems

Name	Title	Organization	Current Boards/Organizations	Past Boards/Organizations
Herberger, Jr., Roy A.	President	Thunderbird, The American Graduate School of International Management	**Director,** Inroads, Arizona; Inroads National; American Management Association International Council; **Chairman,** Pilgrim America Group, Inc.; Pinnacle West Capital Corporation; Bank of America, Arizona; MicroAge Infosystems; AMA International Council	**Director,** New Vernon Savings, American Federal Bank; **Trustee,** Lee Optical Pension & Profit Trust **Chairman,** Greater Phoenix Economic Council; **Advisory,** Mercury & Ben Milam Savings; Editorial Board, European Business Journal; Adv. Board, Society for Advanced Management Journal
Higgins, Thomas		Edison International		
Holliman III, John M.	General Partner	Valley Ventures	**Director,** Ellerbe Becker Company, Micro Photonix Integration Corp., OrthoLogic Corp., The Pilgrim Group, Sequencia Corporation	**Director,** AgriPro Biosciences, Inc., Antigua Group, Inc., Circle Machine Company, ComStream Corporation, DenAmerica Restaurant Corp., OP Club Corporation, Photometrics, Ltd., Safe Power Systems, Inc., Sports Tactics Int'l, Syntex Corporation, Topmetrix, VOXTEL, Western Security Life Insurance Company, Arizona Technology Venture Fund

Name	Title	Organization	Details	
Horton, Thomas R.	Chairman	National Association of Corporate Directors	**Director**, Center for Board Leadership, Commercial Bancorp; **Advisory**, Marquis Who's Who, Independence Standards Board, American Chamber of Commerce for Cuba	**Director**, American Precision Industries, Charlesbridge Publishing, Enesco Group, Inc., Med-Tech Corporation, Perrigo Corporation, Stanhome, Inc.; **Former Chair**, The American Management Assn.; Assn. Of Governing Boards of Universities & Colleges; The American Graduate School of International Management, American Management Association
Hunter, Shawn K.	President & COO	Phoenix Coyotes	**Director**, ProLink, Inc., Maricopa County Sports Commission	**Director**, Strategic Vision Task Force, Downtown Phoenix Partnership
Inman, Admiral Bobby R.	Adjunct Professor	LBJ School of Public Affairs and the Graduate School of Business of the University of Texas at Austin	**Director**, Fluor, Science Applications International, Southwestern Bell, Temple Inland, Xerox; **Trustee**, American Assembly, California Institute of Technology, Southwestern University	**Chairman**, Microelectronics and Computer Technology Corporation, Westmark Systems, Inc., Federal Reserve Bank of Dallas; **Director**, National Security Agency, Naval Intelligence.
Jackson, Ph.D., Don M.	Chairman and CEO	Sitek, Inc.	**Director**, M&I Thunderbird Bank, Flexpoint, Inc.	**Director**, IPEC, XYMOX Corp., ASM America, Superwave Technology, Formula IV Corporation
Johnson, Dr. Spencer	CEO	Spencer Johnson Company	**Author**, *One Minute Manager, Who Stole My Cheese?*	

Name	Title	Organization	Current Boards/Organizations	Past Boards/Organizations
Kile, Robert W.	Vice President & Partner	Rusher, Loscavio & LoPresto	**Co-Author,** *Strategic Board Recruitment: The Not-for-Profit Model;* **Board Officer,** Renaissance Entrepreneurship Center	
Kristie, James	Editor and Associate Publisher	Directors and Boards		
Lansberg, Ph.D., Ivan	Senior Partner	Lansberg Gersick & Associates, LLC	**Founder,** Family Firm Institute, Founding Editor, Family Business Review	
Lear, Robert W.	Former-Executive-in-Residence and Visiting Professor	Columbia University Graduate School of Business	**Partner,** Lear, Yavitz & Associates; Advisory Boards, David Deutsch & Co., NewsBank, Inc., RONIN Corporation, Strang Hayes Corporation, Transition Partners	**Chairman,** Advisory Board, Chief Executive Magazine; **Chairman,** The F&M Schaefer Corporation, Indian Head, Inc.; **Chairman,** Management Policy Council; **Director:** Cambrex, Inc., Champion International, Church & Dwight Company, Clevepak Corporation, Columbia Business School, Crane Co., Equitable Capital Partners, Interpace Corporation, Korea Fund, Krause Milling Co., Medusa Corporation, National Association of Corporate Directors, St. Regis Paper Corporation, Scudder Capital Growth, Turner Corporation, Waveny Care Center, Welsh, Carson, Anderson, Stowe Venture Capital, WICAT Systems

Name	Title	Company	Affiliations	Other
Lecker, Douglas L.	President and CEO	ProLink, Inc.		Software Innovator of Year
Lee, Terry G.	Chairman & CEO	Bell Sports Corporation, Bell Automotive Products, Russell Racing	**Director,** ProLink, Inc., Disson Furst & Partners; **CEO & Founder,** Thomas Weisel Partners; **Managing Director,** Hayden Capital Investments.	
Lutin, Gary	Owner	Lutin & Company	**Co-sponsor,** New York Society of Analysts case study on governance	
Mackay, Harvey B.	Chairman & CEO	Mackay Envelope Corporation	**Director,** Robert Redford's Sundance Institute, University of Minnesota Carlson School of Management; Columnist	**Author,** *Pushing the Envelope, Swim with the Sharks without Being Eaten Alive*
Marcus, Bernard	Chairman	The Home Depot, Inc.	**Director,** National Service Industries, New York Stock Exchange, Westfield Corporation, Inc., DBT Online, Inc.	**Chairman,** Handy Dan Improvement Centers, Inc.
Matthews, Phillip D.	Chairman	Wolverine World Wide, Inc.	**Lead Director,** Wolverine World Wide, Inc.; Washington Mutual, Panda Management Corp., Sizzler International, Case-Swayne, Applause, Dacor, Micro Source, National Association of Corporate Directors (LA); **Advisory:** Dresdner/Kleinwort Benson Equinox Fund, Oaktree Capital Management	**Chairman,** Reliable Company; **Director** Bell Sports, Inc., Dart Industries, Inc., H.F. Ahmanson & Co., Home Savings of America, AST Research, Inc., DEL Industries, CliniShare, The Mowry Company, Dr. Pepper-Seven Up Co. (St. Louis)

Name	Title	Organization	Current Boards/Organizations	Past Boards/Organizations
McConnell, Stephen A.	Principal	Solano Ventures	**Chairman,** G-L Industries; **Director,** Mobile Mini Inc.	**Chairman,** Mallco Lumber & Building Materials, Inc; CEO, N-W Group, Inc.
McGraw, Jr., James J.	Managing Director	KMK Consulting Company, LLC	**Director,** James J. McGraw Agency, Inc., Thinkronize, Inc.	
McGurn, Patrick S.	VP & Director—Corporate Programs	Institutional Shareholder Services		**Director,** Corporate Governance Service, Investor Responsibility Research Center
McLaughlin, Ann D.	Chairman	The Aspen Institute	**Director,** AMR Corporation, Fannie Mae, General Motors Corporation, Kellogg Company, Nordstrom, Donna Karan International, Inc; Board of Overseers, Wharton School, Univ. of Pennsylvania	**Chairman,** President's Commission on Aviation Security and Terrorism, U. S. Secretary of Labor; Undersec. Dept. of the Interior; **Director,** Harman International Industries, Inc., Host Marriott Corp, Potomic Electric Power Co., Union Camp Corp., Vulcan Materials Co. Rand Corp.
McLaughlin, David J.	President & CEO	Troy Biosciences Inc.	**Director,** Scientific Atlanta, Inc., Smart & Final, Inc., Troy Biosciences, Inc.	**Director,** Exide Electronics Group, Inc., Evolve Software, Inc., Watermark, Inc., HR Soft, Inc., Adams & Rinehart, Inc.

Millstein, Ira M.	Senior Partner	Weil, Gotshal & Manges LLP	**Chairman,** New York City Partnership Policy Center, Organization for Economic Cooperation and Development, Business Sector Advisory Group on Corporate Governance; **Vice Chairman,** Albert Einstein College of Medicine; Committee Special Advisor, The World Bank on Corporate Governance; **Co-Chairman,** Blue Ribbon Committee on Improving the Effectiveness of Corporate Audit Committees; **Advisory,** Yale School of Management; Professor, Competitive Enterprise and Strategy, Yale School of Management; Elected Fellow, American Academy of Arts and Sciences	**Chairman,** National Association of Corporate Directors' Blue Ribbon Commission on Director Professionalism, Advisors of Columbia University's Center for Law & Economic Studies, Institutional Investor Project, National Commission on Consumer Finance, Council of the Administrative Conference of the United States—Committee on Ratemaking and Economic Regulation, Governor's Task Force on Pension Fund Investment, Antitrust Law Sections American Bar Association and New York State Bar Association; **Fellow,** Harvard University's J.F.K. School of Gov't.
Minow, Nell	Editor/Founder	The Corporate Library	**Co-author,** *Corporate Governance, Watching the Watchers; Corporate Governance for the 21st Century*	**Principal,** Lens Investment Management; **President,** Institutional Shareholder Services

Name	Title	Organization	Current Boards/Organizations	Past Boards/Organizations
Monks, Robert A. G.	Principal	Lens Investment Management	**Co-Author,** *Power and Accountability, Corporate Governance;* **Author,** *Emperor's Nightingale*	**Director,** Esterline, Westmoreland, Jeffries & Company; John Hancock Capital Growth Management, Inc., Tyco Laboratories, Inc., Lambert Brussels Capital Corporation, Kennedy Group, The Boston Company, Tyco Laboratories, Inc., Lambert Brussels Capital Corporation, Kennedy Group; **Chairman,** The Boston Company, Mitsubishi International Corporation; **Director,** U.S. Synthetic Fuels Corporation
Narva, Richard L.	Co-founder and Principal Consultant	Genus Resources, Inc.	**Director,** NetMarquee, Inc., EKMS, Inc.	**President,** Morton Show Companies, Inc.; **Editor,** *The Family Business Lawyer*
Nyberg, Lars	Chairman and CEO	NCR Corporation	**Director,** The Sandvik Group (Sweden)	
Olson, Esq., John F.	Senior Partner	Gibson, Dunn & Crutcher, LLP	Executive Council, Securities Committee, Federal Bar Assn.; Legal Advisory Board, NASD; Legal Advisory Committee, NYSE; **Co-author,** *Director and Officer Liability: Indemnification and Insurance*	**Former Chairman,** Federal Regulations of Securities Committee, Business Law, American Bar Association

Name	Title	Company	Directorships / Positions
Olson, Kenneth			Avenir Pharmaceuticals, Bio-hydration Research, ChatSpace, Inc., Digirad Corp., One Stop Systems, Troxel, WD-40 Company
Ozer, Jay S.	Senior Partner	Arthur Andersen	
Perrin, Charles R.	Chairman & CEO	Avon Products, Inc.	**Chairman**, Avon Products, Inc.; **Director**, Campbell Soup Company, Catalyst, Perrin Family Foundation; **Chairman**, Duracell International, Inc.
Ridgway, Rozanne L.	Director		**Director**, 3M Corporation, RJR Nabisco, Union Carbide, Bell Atlantic, The Boeing Company, Sara Lee Corporation, Emerson Electric, National Geographic Society, Center for Naval Analysis, The Brookings Institution, George C. Marshall Foundation, Partners for Democratic Change, Catalyst, Institute for the Study of Diplomacy of Georgetown University; **Director**, Citicorps; **Chairman**, Baltic-American Enterprise Fund; **Co-Chairman**, Atlantic Council of the United States; Ambassador to Germany and Norway, Chairman of the Baltic-American Enterprise Fund; Foreign Service Officer, Asst. Sec. Of State for European and Canadian Affairs; Foreign Service Officer
Rock, Arthur	Principal Venture Capitalist	Arthur Rock and Company	**Director:** Intel; NASD Board of Governors; **Chairman**, Sci. Data Systems, Inc.; **Director**, Xerox Corp., Teledyne, Inc., Apple Computer, Inc., Argonaut Group, Inc., Echelon Corp, Air Touch Communications; Visiting Committee, Harvard Business School

Name	Title	Organization	Current Boards/Organizations	Past Boards/Organizations
Sanders, Elizabeth A.	President	Sanders Partnership	**Director,** Washington Mutual Savings Bank, Wellpoint Health Networks, Inc., Advantica Companies, Inc., Wolverine Worldwide, Inc., Wal-Mart Stores, Inc.	**Director,** The H.F. Ahmanson Company, Carl Karcher Enterprise, The Vons Companies, Sport Chalet, Inc., The Los Angeles Chamber of Commerce, The St. Joseph Health System, The National Bank of Southern California; **Trustee,** Gettysburg College
Schomer, Fred K.	Principal	Strategic Solutions Partners	**Director,** International Consolidated Investors Corporation	**Director,** Gerber Products, Gantos, Inc.
Schwartz, Alan "Duke"	Senior Vice President	Brown and Brown Insurance		
Seger, Martha Romayne	Chairman	Seger Financial	**Director,** Amerisure, Capital Holding, Fluor, Johnson Controls, Kroger, Tucson Electric Power, Xerox, National Chamber Foundation, Institute for Research on the Economics of Taxation, Catalyst	**Governor,** the Federal Reserve System, **Chairman,** Consumer and Community Affairs Committee; **Director,** Amoco, Michigan Blue Cross-Blue Shield, New England Life Insurance Company, Pontiac State Bank

Name	Title	Company	Directorships / Affiliations	
Shipley, Walter V.	Chairman	The Chase Manhattan Corporation, The Chase Manhattan Bank	**Chairman**, The Chase Manhattan Corporation and The Chase Manhattan Bank; **Director,** Bell Atlantic Corporation, Champion International Corporation, Exxon Corporation, Federal Reserve Bank of New York; **President,** Goodwill Industries of Greater New York Inc., Lincoln Center for the Performing Arts, Inc.	**Chairman and CEO**, Chemical Banking Corp.
Sonsini, Larry W.	Chairman, Executive Committee	Wilson, Sonsini, Goodrich & Rosati	**Director,** Novell, Inc, Lattice Semiconductor Corporation, PIXAR, Inc., SEC's Adv. Cmte. on Capital Formation and Regulatory Processes, Legal Advisory Cmte. to Board of Governors, NYSE; The American Law Institute; Stanford Law School Law & Technology Council	**Director,** Brocade, Inc.; Echelon Corporation, Gemplus (French Co.), Lattice Semiconductor, LSI Logic Corporation, NeTpower, Inc.; Novell, Inc., Packard Bell, Pixar, Inc.; Pure Atria Corporation, Silicon Valley Group, Inc.; VM Ware; NASD Legal Advisory Board; **Trustee,** Univ. of California, Berkeley
Tappan, David S.	Chairman, Retired	Fluor Corporation	**Director,** Genentech, Inc., Allianz Insurance Company, Beckman Instruments, Inc., U.S. Chamber of Commerce, The Center for International Private Enterprise, National Business Committee for the Arts; **Advisory,** Services Policy Advisory Committee to the U.S. Trade Representative, Trade and Development Program to the International Development Cooperation Agency, Stanford Research Institute	**Chairman,** Fluor Corporation, Morgan Bank International Council, Advanced Tissue Sciences, Inc.

Name	Title	Organization	Current Boards/Organizations	Past Boards/Organizations
Tooker, Gary L.	Former CEO; Chairman	Motorola, Inc.	**Director,** Motorola, Pacific Basin Economic Council U.S. Member Committee; Executive Committee, Council on Competitiveness, Eaton Corporation; Atlantic Richfield Company; Catalyst; Morehouse College; Arizona State university Foundation; ASU Advisory Council on Engineering; National Alliance of Business; **Chairman,** American Electronics Association; Semiconductor Industry Association; Policy Committee of the Business Roundtable	**Chairman,** American Electronics Assn. Semiconductor Industry Assn.
Weatherup, Craig E.	Chairman & CEO	The Pepsi Bottling Group, Inc.	**Director:** Federated Department Stores, Inc., Starbucks Coffee Company, Tuskegee University, Carnegie Hall, Nat'l Soft Drink Assn. Advisory Council, Arizona State University	**Chairman and CEO,** the Pepsi-Cola Company

Name	Title	Organization	Affiliations	
Weiss, Stephen J.	Partner	Holland & Knight LLP	American Law Institute; **Author,** *Navigating the D&O Maze; A Handbook for Purchasers of Directors and Officers' Liability Insurance;* D&O Insurance columnist, Directors & Boards	
Wellington, Sheila W.	President	Catalyst	**Director,** Business Council of New York State, Institute for Women's Policy Research; **Trustee,** Noveen Select Portfolios	
West, B. Kenneth	Senior Consultant for Corporate Governance	TIAA/CREF	**Director,** Motorola, The Pepper Companies, Inc.; **Co-Chairman,** $1 billion Campaign for Illinois; **Vice-Chairman,** National Park Foundation	**Chairman,** Harris Bankcorp Inc., University of Chicago, Civic Committee of Chicago, United Way/Crusade of Mercy/Chicago; **Director,** University of Illinois Foundation, Bank of Montreal, Chicago Stock Exchange Board of Governors, Economic Club of Chicago
Whisler, J. Steven	President & CEO	Phelps Dodge Corporation	**Director,** Phelps Dodge Corporation, Burlington Northern Santa Fe Corporation, Southern Peru Copper Corporation; **Member,** Business Roundtable	

Name	Title	Organization	Current Boards/Organizations	Past Boards/Organizations
Whiteman, John O.	Chairman and President	Empire Southwest, LLC	**Director,** Caterpillar Dealers' Financial Cooperative	**Director,** Security Pacific Bank–Arizona, Carter Machinery
Whiteman, Steven D.	Chairman and CEO	Viasoft, Inc.	**Director,** Viasoft, Inc., Actuate Software, NetPro, Unify Corporation	Ernst & Young Entrepreneur of the Year
Williams, Quinn	Senior Corporate and Securities Partner	Snell & Wilmer LLP	**Director,** Optimal Care, Arizona Technology Venture Fund, Arizona Innovation Network; **Chairman,** Greater Phoenix Economic Leadership	
Yastrow, Shelby	Of Counsel	Sonnenschein, Nath & Rosenthal	**Director,** Franchise Finance Corporation of America, Martin Engineering Company, Great Clips, Inc.	Former Executive Vice President and General Counsel, McDonalds Corporation; **Director,** American National Bank & Trust Company
Yearley, Douglas C.	Chairman of the Board	Phelps Dodge Corporation	Lockheed Martin Corporation, J. P. Morgan & Co., Inc. Morgan Guaranty Trust Company, Southern Peru Copper Corporation, USX Corporation; **Member,** The Business Council	**CEO,** Phelps Dodge Corporation

Yeutter, Clayton	Of Counsel	Hogan & Hartson	**Director,** Catepillar, Inc., ConAgra, Inc., Farmers Insurance Company, FMC Corporation, Oppenheimer Funds, Texas Instrument, Inc., Zurich Financial Services, Center for Trade Policy Studies-Cato Institute, National Advisory Council, Inter-American Development Bank, The Jamestown Foundation, Opportunity International, The Sound Science Advisory Board	**U.S. Trade Representative; Secretary of Agriculture; Republican National Chairman; CEO,** Chicago Mercantile Exchange; **Director,** B.A.T. Industries (London), Chicago-Tokyo Bank, Farm Foundation, Georgetown University School of Business Administration's Board of Visitors, IMC Global, Kislak, Inc., Lindsay Manufacturing Company, Meridian International Center, Mycogen Corporation, President's Export Council, The Vigoro Corporation, Winrock, Inc.; **Honorary Co-Chairman,** International Tax & Investment Center
Young, G. Douglas	Managing Director	Wilcap LLC	**Director,** Universal Technical Institute, Sun Orchard, Inc., Diversified Inspections Companies, Dynamic Rentals, Larson Company	**Director,** Neutron Industries, Inc., The Hamilton Group Limited, Sunbelt Holdings, Inc.

Index

succession, 85, 86, 180–184
Sulzberger, Arthur, 87
SunAmerica, 118
Sunbeam Co., 107
Sun Microsystems, 106
Sun Orchard, 19–20
SunTrust, 95
Swette, Brian, 49
Switzer, Walter, 111
Symbol, 75
Synovus Financial, 68

tactics, focusing on, 21
takeovers, 227
Tandem Computers, 121
Tappan, David, 48–49, 56–57, 113, 123, 148–
    149, 154, 159, 160, 177, 178, 184, 185, 187,
    204, 205, 210, 213, 214
team environment, 201
technology, briefing directors on, 149–150
technology companies, 36
Telxon, 75
tenure issue(s), 184–189
    age limits as, 186–188
    with merged boards, 188–189
    term limits as, 188
term limits, 34, 188
Texaco, 205
Texas Instruments, 183
"think tank," board as, 15–16
Thompson, John, 76
Thunderbird, 111
TIAA-CREF, 68, 98, 107, 122, 128, 164, 187,
    241–242
time requirements, 21
Time Warner, 122, 188–189
Tooker, Gary, 18, 28, 30, 37, 43, 51, 148, 181,
    187, 192, 243
Townsend, Don, 110–111
Townsend, Robert, 65–66, 154
trade journals, 143
transparency, 174–175, 215–216
Travelers Group, 105, 117
Trillium Asset Management Corp., 110
Trujillo, Solomon, 122
trust, 141, 250–251
Tuton, Ed, 15
TYCO, 68

Union Pacific Corp., 178
unions, 99–100, 109
United Airlines, 100, 115, 168
United Auto Workers, 162
United for a Fair Economy, 110
United Kingdom, 135
United Way, 233
Universal Technical Institute (UTI), 17, 21, 49,
    69, 161, 198–199, 210
Up and Up, 41
U.S. Surgical, 68
UTI, see Universal Technical Institute

value (economic)
    boards' providing of, 20
    governance and shareholder, 238–240
values, prioritizing of, 155–156
van Beuren, Archie, 89
venture capitalists, 15, 76–81
Viasoft, 202
Vogelstein, James, 177
Vogelstein, John, 107

W. R. Grace, 225–226
Walgreen's, 14
Waller, Joel, 97–98
Wal-Mart, 7, 40–41, 53, 131, 147, 150, 201–202
Walt Disney, 68, 74–75, 98, 122–123, 123
Walter, John, 122
Walton, Sam, 52–53
Wang, Charles B., 110
Waste Management Inc., 117–118, 172
Watermark, 68
Weatherup, Craig, 14, 18, 27, 33, 44–45, 132,
    143, 147, 196, 204, 206, 250
Weil, Sanford, 110
Welch, Jack, 12, 110, 117, 150
Welch, Julie, 135
Wellington, Sheila, 128
Wells Fargo, 99
Wendt, Henry, 7, 20
Wendy's International, 68
West, Kenneth, 68, 113, 151, 164–165, 170,
    187, 241–242
Whisler, Steven, 39–40, 208
Whitacre, Ed, 121
Whiteman, John, 22–23, 87–88, 144, 154, 157–
    158, 200
Whiteman, Steve, 199–200, 202
Whitman Corp., 16
Williams, James B., 95
Williams, Quinn, 232–233
Williams-Sonoma, 119
Winn-Dixie, 68
Winter, Rick, 160
Wisconsin, 120
Wolverine World Wide, Inc., 19, 193
women directors, 129–132, 276–277
WorldCom, 68
Wrigley, Julie, 46
Wriston, Walter, 123
Wynn, Steve, 119
Wyser-Pratte, Guy, 122

Yahoo, 31, 117
Yastrow, Shelby, 65, 78, 102, 145, 155, 165–167
Yearley, Doug, 28, 42, 71, 115, 149, 161, 163,
    168, 182–183, 199, 208–209, 211, 244, 250
Yellow Corporation, 114, 211
Yeutter, Clayton, 31, 65, 71, 176, 183, 211
Young, Doug, 13, 16, 158, 160

Zeien, Alfred, 121

CPSIA information can be obtained at www.ICGtesting.com
Printed in the USA
LVOW061006301111

257141LV00002B/161/P